D0983719

The Folklore
of Capitalism

THURMAN W. ARNOLD
with a new Preface

GREENWOOD PRESS, PUBLISHERS
WESTPORT, CONNECTICUT

Library of Congress Cataloging in Publication Data

Arnold, Thurman Wesley, 1891-1964.
    The folklore of capitalism.

    Reprint of the 1962 printing of the ed. published
by Yale University Press, New Haven.
    Includes index.
    1. United States--Economic conditions--1918-1945.
2. Capitalism. I. Title.
HC106.A684 1980   330.12'2   79-26573
ISBN 0-313-22199-5 lib. bdg.

© 1937 by Yale University Press

Issued as a Yale Paperbound 1959. Third printing with
new preface December 1962.

Reprinted with the permission of Yale University Press

Reprinted in 1980 by Greenwood Press, Inc.
51 Riverside Avenue, Westport, Conn. 06880

Printed in the United States of America

10 9 8 7 6 5 4 3 2 1

Preface—1962

THIS book was written to describe the frustrating effects, in times of revolutionary change, of ideals and symbols inherited from a different past. It therefore may be useful to describe what has happened to our folklore since 1937 when this book was published, a quarter of a century ago.

Since that time the greatest war in history has been fought. That war pulled us out of the stagnation of the depression. It forced us to utilize our industrial resources to the utmost and to expand them at a rate which would have been considered impossible twenty-five years ago. We came out of the war far richer in terms of real wealth, by which I mean productive capacity, than when we went in. We became the richest nation the world has ever known.

For a short time after that war we were a confident nation, sure of our destiny. We believed that we were at the beginning of a new age of world order based on fundamental principles acceptable to all civilized nations. The symbol of that belief was the United Nations, which represented world unity under a new kind of international law. The first step we took to dramatize the ideal of international law and order was the Nuremberg trials. The purpose of those trials was to establish a great legal precedent which would outlaw forever the kind of aggressive war Germany had forced on the Western world. And so the United States, England, and Russia set up a joint international tribunal to clothe the ideal of international order with a judicial opinion which would be a guide for the indefinite future. The Nuremberg verdict was designed to teach Germany a lesson it would never forget and to be a permanent warning to all future Hitlers that the new world would no longer put up with military aggression.

With the twin symbols—the United Nations, where international disputes were to be resolved, and the Nuremberg trials, establishing a new principle of international morality —we believed we had achieved an enduring foreign policy. The age-old dream of all utopians—that if we can get men to agree on a principle, institutions and social organizations will arise which will adhere to and carry out that principle— was the basis of short-lived optimism and confidence which followed the destruction of the German empire.

In saying this I do not mean to imply that the United Nations has not made a tremendous contribution to world order. It was the first formal recognition in our history that the industrial revolution of the twentieth century had created a world in which even a nation as large as the United States could no longer exist as an isolated economic or political unit. It would have been indeed a tragedy had the United States rejected the ideal of which the United Nations was a symbol. The significance of the United Nations was the fact that it marked the end of a century of isolationist thinking.

Nevertheless we expected too much of it. The apparent agreement between the Soviets and the Western democracies expressed in the Nuremberg trials, that international aggression was abolished as a matter of international law, coupled with a new organization designed to unite every nation in the world in a common humanitarian purpose, lulled us into a sense of false security. And so we cheerfully dismembered Germany into four zones, French, British, Russian, and American, so that all could be partners in eliminating the menace of another Hitler. To have established a corridor giving access to Berlin would have shown distrust of our Russian partner and disturbed that atmosphere of confidence and cooperation which was to remove the threat of future wars.

The disillusionment that followed the collapse of these shining symbols of peace and international morality gave rise to fears and anxieties about the stability of our own institutions at home which grew to a national neurosis. Somebody had to be blamed for our short period of amity with Russia. The idealistic attempt to establish in cooperation with Russia some sort of world order could only have been caused by the infiltration of local Communists into our own government. The idea spread over the entire nation that the American Communist Party, through devious and secret ways, had the potential power to overthrow the government of the United States. The real danger to our institutions was not Russian power abroad but Communist infiltration at home.

We became more afraid of ideas than realities. This fear increased in intensity as the Cold War proceeded. It wasn't enough to discharge suspected persons from government service. A public badge of infamy had to be pinned on them. We had to celebrate our achievements in ridding the country of its internal dangers by a public ceremony. And so President Truman established a hierarchy of quasi-judicial institutions clothing the hunt for subversives with the sanctity of judicial process. It was in this atmosphere that Senator McCarthy rose to power and was able to dictate to the President who should be discharged and who should be retained. Any idea which did not conform to the McCarthy pattern was sufficient to destroy the career of a liberal in government if by some accident his name got into the files of a congressional committee.

It soon became apparent that there weren't enough Communists to keep the costly and rapidly expanding bureaucracy of security officers, hearing boards, and congressional committees supplied with victims. Most of the material they had to work on was hearsay and secret reports by professional informers. To use such material as evidence was contrary to every American ideal of a fair trial. Indeed, an American tribunal in Germany had convicted German judges on the ground that the use of secret evidence was an international crime.

But this ideal of a fair trial had to give way in order to keep the vast bureaucracy in business. And so it was determined that accused individuals could be convicted on secret evidence given by faceless informers whose identity was unknown to the accused. Nor was the accused permitted to see and rebut the secret evidence given against him. This process tremendously enlarged the supply of game which the security system could track down and shoot. The Supreme Court of the United States gave its tacit approval to the use of this sort of evidence by affirming the conviction of Dorothy Bailey on secret evidence in a four-to-four decision. And from then on, for years, the most publicized policy of government was the rooting out of subversives in government and industry.

Our Cold War with Russia assumed all of the aspects of the religious wars of the Reformation. Both the Soviets and the United States engaged in worldwide propaganda appealing to the hearts and souls of men to adopt the only true religion. The preaching of each side was as violent as any delivered during the Reformation. The only difference was that in the Reformation hell was in the next world. In the religious war of the twentieth century the respective hells of communism and capitalistic imperialism were in this world, just around the corner. Millions were spent by the United States on the Voice of America, and counter-millions were spent by Russia in jamming its broadcasts. And so for years we believed that our national salvation depended on preaching the glories of capitalism abroad and the rooting out of subversives at home. This is the kind of phenomenon which always occurs when a religious war is being fought.

Today we have fixed our attention on Russian power instead of internal subversion. Yet the essentially religious character of the Cold War still continues. Neither Russia nor the United States is pursuing materialistic objectives. It is indeed a battle for the minds and hearts of men in which symbols are still more important than realities. For example, we have planted our flag in Berlin and are prepared to defend it even at the risk of an atomic war. Berlin is a symbol of the reunification of Germany. The ideological conflict could be resolved, at least with respect to that city, if the United States would recognize the legality of the East German government. Few intelligent men believe that as a practical matter reunification of Germany is even a remote possibility. Yet concessions by either side would be a moral victory for the other with far-reaching psychological consequences in Germany and Western Europe. When wars are fought over markets or for trade advantages they can be ended when they appear too costly. When they are fought for the minds and hearts of men, when it is a struggle between the Catholic and the Protestant churches, or between Communism and Capitalism, neither side can risk defeat on the issue of any symbol which dramatizes its faith. This is true even though defense of that symbol might possibly mean the extinction of half the human race. From a rational point of view this may seem like nonsense. From an anthropological point of view, however, we must recognize that such symbols as Berlin are the cement that holds Western society together, that holds the promise of unity, both political and economic, for Western nations. To abandon such a symbol might utterly defeat the brightest promise of the future. The risk must therefore be taken.

Out of this risk there is emerging a new ideal, and a new set of symbols. The European Common Market, which seemed completely utopian only a few years ago, has become a reality. An international court has been set up to adjudicate the trade practices of the citizens of independent sovereignties. An international code of antitrust laws after the American model has been enacted and is being enforced by the European international court. The United States and England are seeking to join that international economic union.

And here in the Western Hemisphere we have accepted the ideal of the economic unity of the United States and Latin America. That ideal has been embodied in an organization called the Alliance for Progress. The basic concept of that organization is expressed in a treaty by which the United States and Latin American nations committed themselves to an acceleration of economic growth, a more equitable distribution of the fruits of economic development, and recognized the need for tax, land, and institutional reform and new investment capital. In the language of the treaty of Punta del Este these nations and the United States agreed "to unite in a common effort to bring our people accelerated economic progress and broader social justice within the framework of personal dignity and political liberty."

These words could not have been written without a storm of outraged protest when *The Folklore of Capitalism* was published in 1937. No such treaty could possibly have been approved by the Senate of the United States at that time.

In those times Henry Wallace was being denounced as a man who wanted to give a bottle of milk to every Hottentot because of ideas which were insignificant in scope compared with the Alliance for Progress. And yet the Alliance for Progress, which goes further in assuming responsibility for the poverty and economic chaos of Latin American nations than anything Henry Wallace ever dreamed of, has become a political reality supported by liberals and conservatives alike.

Another tremendous change in our ideals and symbols that has taken place since this book was written is in our personification of great corporations as individuals. We no longer feel that government control of industry is something that will end in the destruction of individual liberty. My chapters on "The Personification of Corporation" and "The Ritual of Corporate Reorganization" are largely obsolete today. The amount of regulatory interference with business today which is represented by our vast government bureaus would have been unthinkable to a conservative in 1937. Now these tremendous bureaucratic hierarchies have lost their radical tinge. They have obtained an almost invulnerable place in the hierarchy of our institutions. Our courts, which before the great depression were accustomed to review decisions of administrative tribunals with meticulous care, now affirm them if there is the slightest supporting evidence.

The ideological doctrine which supports the immunity of our present administrative tribunals from judicial review is the theory that they are composed of experts in their particular narrow lines. Under the cloak of this doctrine many of the evils and oppressive bureaucratic practices which were protected by conservatives in 1937 have become a part of our administrative machinery. Yet so securely has our system of administrative tribunals become entrenched that there is no effective protest made today against bureaucratic aggression. This is indeed a revolutionary change since 1937 in our ideas of the proper function of government.

The chapter entitled "The Effect of the Antitrust Laws in Encouraging Large Combinations" needs comment in the light of what has happened since the book was published. That chapter was written after ten years of nonenforcement of the Sherman Act when the total appropriation for the Antitrust Division was less than $250,000. Today it is over $5 million. The decisions of the Supreme Court of the United States since 1937 have tremendously broadened the enforcement of antitrust policy. As Milton Handler said in a recent article (*Columbia Law Review,* Vol. 60, p. 930): "In few areas of the law is a mature jurisprudence reinforced by so powerful an arsenal of investigative powers and remedies."

That was not true when I wrote in Chapter IX of this book, page 212: "The actual result of the antitrust laws was to promote the growth of great industrial organizations by deflecting the attack on them into purely moral and ceremonial channels." This is no longer true today.

And even more astonishing from the point of view of one writing in 1937, when the ideal of the antitrust laws was recognized in no other country in the world except the United States, is the fact that the antitrust ideal has spread to Europe. The system of domestic and international cartels which in 1937 was legitimate in Europe is under heavy attack, though not completely abolished, in the European Common Market—a development no one would have dreamed of in 1937 before the Second World War.

In the field of monetary and fiscal policy, however, nineteenth-century economic symbols still cloud the realities of the twentieth-century industrial revolution and frustrate American economic progress. Just as during the depression we were unable to utilize our full productive capacity because of a lack of consumer purchasing power, so today we are still unable to utilize it for the same reason. Since 1953 our annual economic growth has not been enough to keep up with our tremendously increasing labor force. The top of every curve in the roller coaster of booms and depressions on which we have been riding since 1953 has shown greater unemployment than the top of the last curve. During this period of nearly ten years our economy has been stagnant and sluggish in growth. During the same period France, Germany, and Italy have been advancing, in terms of goods and services produced, more than twice as fast as we have. We are accumulating an increasing number of unemployed. During the same period France, Germany, and Italy have had an actual shortage of labor.

The actual cost in terms of goods and services resulting from our failure to utilize our full industrial capacity has been estimated by Leon Keyserling to amount to the stupendous sum of $387 billion from 1953 to the middle of 1962. This enormous wealth was available to us but we could not use it because there was not enough purchasing power in the United States economy to absorb the products which our industrial plant was able to produce.

And thus under the same economic symbols and rituals that we had during the great depression we are developing today the same symptoms that prolonged that depression. The only time we were free from the tyranny of these nineteenth-century economic images was during the Second World War. Then, for the first time since the depression began, we were able to use and to expand our production to the full limit of our industrial ability. As a result we came out of that war richer in our productive capacity than at any time before. But after the Second World War the old religion took over. Since 1953 we have been progressively slowing down and increasingly unable to sustain the economic growth necessary for full employment.

Today we write about ourselves as an affluent society. But in 1960 there were almost 10½ million families (households of two or more persons) with annual incomes of under $4,000 before taxes. This means that one family in every four was living in poverty in the United States in 1960. Out of this group of families with under $4,000 a year over 3,000,000 were living in actual deprivation with incomes of under

$2,000 a year, and as for the unattached individuals almost 4,000,000 had annual incomes of under $2,000. These figures are taken from Leon Keyserling's pamphlet *Poverty and Deprivation in the United States,* written for the Conference on Economic Progress. To sum up, Leon Keyserling concludes that there were living in poverty 34,000,000 people in families and 4,000,000 unattached persons. There were living in deprivation 37,000,000 people in families and 2,000,000 unattached persons. This makes a total of 77,000,000 people who are unable to attain what we like to think of as an American standard of living. They are unable to buy the products of our industrial economy. As a result the nation has lost in goods and services a staggering total of $387 billion in the last ten years.

Yet the *Wall Street Journal,* in a typical editorial (July 26, 1962) attacking government spending in a period when our industrial plant is 75 per cent idle, says with absolute religious conviction: "There is no visible lack of purchasing power today ..."

Under this set of beliefs we have been unable to realize the full productivity of our twentieth-century industrial economy except during the Second World War. If we could only achieve an economic philosophy which would permit the realization of our full capacity, as Leon Keyserling points out (*Poverty and Deprivation in the United States,* p. 78):

> We have the potentials, by 1965, to reduce the number of families living in poverty from almost 10½ million in 1960 to less than 2 million in 1965, and to about one-half million by 1970. We can reduce the number living in deprivation from almost 10 1/3 million to about 7 million, and then to 3½ million. This would mean that, allowing for population growth, the number of families living above the deprivation level would increase from

about 24½ million in 1960 to more than 40 million in 1965, and to more than 49 million in 1970.

We can reduce the number of unattached individuals living in poverty from almost 4 million in 1960 to less than 2½ million in 1965, and to about one-half million by 1970. The number living above the deprivation level can be increased from nearly 5 million in 1960 to almost 7 million in 1965, and to more than 10 million in 1970.

Our failure to realize these potentials has occurred during a period when Western Europe has no problem of unemployment and has been operating its industrial plant, in many ways superior to ours in efficiency, at full capacity. This is today a constant source of bewilderment to Europeans. Gunnar Myrdal, a famous Swedish economist, recently visited the United States. On his return to Stockholm he reviewed the economic conditions in America. He stated that the stagnant condition of the American economy was a menace to the prosperity of the Western world. He regarded it as inexcusable for so rich a country as ours to have so many slums, obsolete houses, inadequate schools, and inadequate social services. He attributed it to the illiteracy of our economic thinking. When asked to comment on Myrdal's observations all President Kennedy could say was the following (*New York Times,* July 24, 1962) :

> Well, I think it is regrettable that we have not been able to develop an economic formula which maintains the growth of our economy. If we were moving ahead at full blast today, of course, you would have full employment.

In July, when the President made his comment that a formula had not been found to maintain the growth of our

xiv   *The Folklore of Capitalism*

economy, the rosy January predictions of his economic advisors had collapsed. The Gross National Product, though it was the highest in our country's history, was billions of dollars short of the January prediction. There had been no change whatever in the problem of unemployment.

The reason why no acceptable formula has been developed to achieve full utilization of the tremendously increased capacity of the twentieth-century industrial revolution is that the majority of our respectable and conservative citizens are still obsessed with the economic picture of the nineteenth century which I have attempted to analyze in this book.

That folklore consisted of a series of very simple mental pictures. The government was pictured as the thrifty head of the family who balances his budget and saves money for the future. If he does not do so he goes bankrupt and his children suffer. The national debt which had been constantly increasing since the First World War was a mortgage on the property of every citizen, which sooner or later would have to be paid by the next generation. Prosperity and full employment could only be forthcoming by balancing the national budget and taking the burden of taxation from the backs of our taxpayers. The money and credit necessary to operate our economy and full employment would then be produced by private industry and our economy would begin to grow and expand, as it did in the nineteenth century. The idea that government credit or government debt could be used to create the purchasing power necessary to distribute the products of the twentieth-century industrial revolution was unsound, radical, crackpot, dangerous, and subversive. It was leading us straight to socialism. Such was the economic folklore of 1962.

When the President said that we had been unable to develop an economic formula which would maintain the growth of our economy he meant that we had no such formula which was consistent with our theology of balancing the fiscal budget. It was an admission that there was no way under the folklore of capitalism existing in 1962 in which we could maintain full employment and full utilization of our resources. We had to go on losing about $10 billion in goods and services every year, which wealth we might have had had our folklore allowed us to distribute it. The principle of balancing the fiscal budget was so sacred that any other course was economic sin and would inevitably lead to some sort of unspecified economic or social hell.

It was not true that no formula had been developed to maintain economic growth. It was only true that no *respectable* formula had been developed. For years a group of economists led by Leon Keyserling had advocated balancing the economic budget rather than the fiscal budget. By this they meant that on one side of the balance sheet the President should estimate the productive capacities of our national industrial plants. On the other side there should be listed the demands on that productive capacity for necessities such as schools, public works, water conservation, health, and so on through a long list. Congress could then formulate programs which would not put an inflationary burden upon our productive capacity but at the same time would utilize it to its fullest extent. France has such a plan. Germany though without a formal plan has for years thought in terms of production rather than money. In other words, balancing the economic budget consists in the establishment of economic goals and the implementation of those goals by practical methods.

But the trouble with this practical approach toward the problem of maintaining economic growth is that there is no automatic fiscal principle by which it can be carried out. Of course the practical ad hoc approach is the one we use in time of war. In the last war we were able to allocate production between the war effort and consumers' goods. We not only maintained our economic growth but expanded it tremendously. Indeed, it was only the enormous spending of the World War which pulled us out of the depression. We also have no difficulty in applying the concept of balancing the economic rather than the fiscal budget in our program for the Alliance for Progress among Latin American nations. Here economic goals are set. Economic planning is the key to the solution; the economic budget rather than the fiscal budget is the center of the program.

But the approach to the problem of economic growth which is possible in time of war, or is freely used in the Alliance for Progress, is as yet impossible in the domestic economy of the United States in time of peace. We are obsessed with the dream of an automatic economy which operates without planning, and the center of the whole thing is the balanced fiscal budget. Given a balanced fiscal budget the private economy is supposed, through credit mechanisms which it creates without government interference, to supply the purchasing power to operate the industrial plant of the twentieth century at full capacity. The fact that it has not been able to do so since 1929 is in conflict with this theory and, therefore, is ignored because it is inconsistent with our folklore.

The central idea of the economic folklore which frustrates our ability to use the capacity of the modern industrial revolution may be expressed as follows: Private enterprise with its tremendous variety of credit devices is able to supply the purchasing power which will not only utilize our full productive capacity but enable it to expand. It is the duty of the government to prevent that expansion from proceeding too rapidly. The government performs that duty by balancing the budget.

This was true prior to the First World War. But since the end of the First World War it has become increasingly apparent that private credit mechanisms are not by themselves sufficient to distribute the tremendously increased industrial capacity created by the twentieth-century scientific revolution.

The persistence of the idea that through the expansion of private credit alone the economy of the twentieth-century revolution can grow and be utilized to its fullest capacity is illustrated by a recital of our popular economic thinking during the boom of the twenties and through the depression. Prior to the First World War sound economic opinion estimated that a national debt of $500 million was all that our economy could safely absorb. But during the war our national debt grew from less than $1 billion to the incredible sum of $26,600,000,000 in 1919. We followed our accepted theory. The sole function of government was to balance the budget. The Republican Administration reduced the national debt in ten years by $9 billion, saving about $1 billion a year. And so, following our accepted theory that the sole function of government was to balance the budget and pay off the national debt the Republican Administration by 1929 had reduced the national debt from $16 billion to $9 billion.

Then came the crash of 1929 and the depression which followed. There was not enough purchasing power to begin to take up the productive capacity we had achieved. But our economic folklore prevented us from seeing this outstanding fact. Roosevelt ran for office on the tried and true principle of balancing the budget. It was not lack of purchasing power but rather lack of business confidence that was supposed to be the cause of prolonging the great depression.

Roosevelt was forced to abandon his devotion to the principle of a balanced fiscal budget in favor of measures which were absolutely required to keep people from starving. He was bitterly attacked on the ground that these measures were leading to inflation and would inevitably result in the destruction of the capitalistic system. The fear of inflation haunted the business community throughout the entire depression in spite of the fact that a realistic appraisal clearly showed that the only thing we had to fear was continued deflation and a sluggish, nonexpanding economy.

In 1937 Roosevelt did succeed in balancing his cash budget, that is, in taking out of the economy more money than the government was putting in. There followed the recession of 1938. But that recession was still not attributed to lack of purchasing power. Conservative economists and bankers pointed out that it was due to lack of business confidence as a result of Roosevelt's attack on the Supreme Court.

The war pulled us out of the depression. It gave us the greatest industrial plant the world has ever known. In spite of gloomy predictions to the contrary which were made by conservatives at the end of the Second World War the country enjoyed an unprecedented boom. Then in 1953 the conservative Republican Party took over, determined to combat inflation and to balance the national budget, and finally to stop inflation by stopping the money supply.

But it soon appeared that the program was impossible. The failure of the conservatives in power has been described by Edwin Dale, Jr., financial editor of the *New York Times,* in a brilliant book *Conservatives in Power: A Study in Frustration* (pp. 209–10):

> After five years of trying, the regime had produced (or found itself with), in fiscal 1959, the biggest budget deficit in peacetime history and the first really serious wave of "inflationary psychology" in modern times.
>
> The only answer seemed to be more conservative than ever. Squeeze the budget—Russian challenge and depressing slums and dirty streams to the contrary notwithstanding. Stretch out the national debt at every opportunity—at the risk of even more uncertainty in the

bond markets. Keep money tight and interest rates high
—even with nearly five million people out of work in
the winter of 1958-59. Keep trying to return functions to
the states to relieve federal finance—even with the State
of Michigan so tightly pinched for money that it had to
appeal to large corporate taxpayers to pay in advance.

And given their view of the world and the dollar, the
conservatives were right. The only cure for the disease
was a stronger dose of the familiar medicine.[1]

And so Eisenhower achieved through his budget-balancing
policies the greatest peacetime deficit in our history and the
greatest peacetime inflation.

The real difficulty is that we have failed to realize the tremendous productive capacity of the twentieth-century scientific revolution. That capacity is so great that the credit
mechanisms invented by the private sector of the economy
cannot fully employ it. Those credit mechanisms, which we
will call the private printing of money, have never before in
our history pumped as much money into the nation's purchasing power. The automobile companies print the money
for even the lowest income groups to buy cars. FHA prints the
money for private organizations to build houses. Never before
in our history has the down payment on houses been so little
or the mortgages so long that they outlast the houses themselves. Almost anyone can get an unlimited letter of credit
for travel by joining something like the Diners' Club. Department stores are printing the money their customers use
to buy goods through revolving credit accounts and whatnot.
No one has to pay cash for anything but food. In fact, anything which can be capitalized and on which a dollar income
may be attributed can be financed. And this financing,
though fantastically unsound according to nineteenth-cen-

[1] Copyright © 1960 by Edwin L. Dale, Jr. Reprinted by permission of
Doubleday & Co., Inc.

tury standards, is actually working. It is a new type of currency based on faith that the consumer will have a job and pay the installments on his debt. And by and large that faith has been justified.

But this new reservoir of credit, vast as it is, has only kept our industrial plant running since 1953 at about 75 per cent of its capacity and $10 billion a year in goods and services has been lost. We are as yet unable to think of our national wealth in terms of productive capacity. We are unable to utilize that productive capacity for pressing national needs such as schools, health, and education because it would unbalance the fiscal budget.

The Potomac River is a good illustration of this folklore. It is an open sewer. A vast recreation area badly needed has gone to waste. The more the sludge accumulates the greater will be the burden on posterity. We have the productive capacity to clean up this river and all the other rivers. But we cannot do so because it would be an intolerable burden on our taxpayers. According to our folklore there is only one economic situation which would justify cleaning up the Potomac, and that is if Washington, D.C., became a depressed area. In that case, perhaps, we might clean it up, not because the job itself was worthwhile doing but because the expenditures might prime the pump and get Washington on its economic feet again. But until Washington becomes a depressed area it is better to let the Potomac fill up with sludge so that it will remain a handy way of priming the pump in the future.

There seems no way, according to our present folklore of capitalism, to utilize our productive capacity to clean up the Potomac because it is a very necessary thing to do with respect to the health and recreation of our nation's capital.

In the nineteenth century our productive capacity was not enough for such public projects. To have engaged in them might have been inflationary. Today, when our productive capacity is so great that only 75 per cent of it can be absorbed by the purchasing power created by private credit, we still consider it inflationary to utilize that capacity. We cannot accept as a rational plan for ourselves the basic formula which even the conservatives have been willing to accept for Latin America.

And thus the old folklore of capitalism which I have attempted to describe in this book still frustrates our economic growth. The fact that Western European economies are not so frustrated is a continuing source of bewilderment to us. We are presently sending economists to Western Europe to find out why those countries have no unemployment and are moving ahead at more than double our speed. I suggest that nothing will come of such economic inquiries. Each inquiring economist will look at Western Europe through the spectacles of a preconceived theory. He will then disregard all the facts which do not fit in with that theory. Finally he will come back with the report that the lesson we must learn from the booming economies of Western Europe is to balance our fiscal budget at home. Many reports of this character are already being published in our conservative journals. To paraphrase Karl Marx, "Economic theology is the opiate of the middle classes."

Each year more and more goods can be produced with less and less labor. For the past ten years we have been able to use only about 75 per cent of what we can produce. As a practical matter it would not be difficult to avail ourselves of that unused production. As an ideological matter it is a present impossibility to carry on the public works and services which our economy could so easily afford. This is because private money and credit are not available for such things as conservation of our water supply, our health, our recreational facilities, and so on through a long list of public necessities. Things which cannot be bought and sold for dollars on the marketplace cannot be financed by private credit. Therefore, we must do without them even though this means a colossal waste of our real productive resources.

If it were just a matter of wasting resources perhaps we could live with it. The nineteenth century was an era of colossal waste. But the present industrial revolution is gradually destroying the purchasing power necessary to distribute its productive ability. This is in spite of fantastic credit schemes which provide private credit that a nineteenth-century banker would consider insane. And so the backlog of unemployment grows as our labor force increases. A new phrase has become part of our economic vocabulary, "structural unemployment." It means that an incredibly rich country can find no ideological way of providing its citizens with the standard of living which it is physically capable of giving them.

The problem is a psychological one, not to be solved by either preaching or learning. It involves a recognition that things without a dollar value on the marketplace are nevertheless national assets of incalculable value. A trained scientist, engineer, or physician is an asset. The university that trains him is as valuable to our economy as a General Motors plant. An unskilled laborer, or an unemployed person, is a liability. A public debt owed by a nation to its own citizens is not a mortgage which their children must pay off. The building of necessary public works is an asset both for the present and the future.

It is this central idea that gives the Russian economy such strength as it has. It is the rigid and inflexible philosophy that such assets cannot be built or maintained by private enterprise that is the principal weakness of Russia. Budgets of course have to be balanced. But the budget of the twentieth century is a balance between productive capacity and the effective demands which are made on that capacity. When those notions become part of our folklore of capitalism the only limit on American progress will be the extent to which modern science can expand productive capacity.

How will this change come about? I expect that the process of the adjustment of inherited economic images to the reality of the vast potential productive capacity of the twentieth century may turn out to be as painful as it was during the great depression when we finally became acclimated to social security, unemployment relief, guarantee of bank deposits, the TVA, control of security markets, and so on through a long list of changes for which Roosevelt was so bitterly denounced. Basic economic beliefs are religious in character. We are struggling today through a period more like the period of the Reformation than any other period in history. This book attempts to study the frustrating effects of religious economic beliefs in a period of revolutionary change.

Contents

personify their institutions, the point of view of the psychologist toward such personifications may offer a useful platform for studying social problems.

Contents

THE FOLKLORE OF CAPITALISM

CHAPTER I

The Systems of Government and the Thinking Man

IN which it is explained how the thinking man, without whom there would be no group free will in modern society, after learning the proper lessons of history chooses wisely between Capitalism, Communism, and Fascism—provided always he doesn't let emotion sway his reason or listen to the blandishments of demagogues.

DURING the 1936 campaign Stuart Chase wrote a book called *Rich Land, Poor Land,* in which he dramatized with brilliant persuasiveness the appalling waste of irreplaceable fertile soil. No one seemed to doubt that the statements were true or that the situation was serious. Did the political candidates make a major issue of what they were going to do to remedy this evil? They did not. The proposal of a practical plan might have been ruinous to either party.

The wastage of other resources had been apparent for a long time. It had been studied in a report of the National Resources Board, which hinted at plans of control. Did any political candidate dare talk about those plans before the public? Of course not. It was better to talk abstractions about "the American way." This, of course, did not apply to candidates who had no hope of being elected, like Norman Thomas. It did apply to those who were seriously seeking to form a government.

The wastage of human labor was so obvious that it needed no report to bring it to public attention. Yet plans for the utilization of this labor to stop the waste of resources were the most avoided of all political issues.

The reason for all this was that men did not want to be branded as Communists, or Fascists, or bureaucrats, or advocates of ruinous spending, or as opponents of the Constitution on the one hand and the capitalistic system on the other. Capitalism, Communism, and Fascism were the greatest political realities among people, none of whom could give an intelligible account of any of these "systems."

The Eternal Debate about Systems of Government

BUT why should the solution of these plans involve the calling of such names? The answer lies in the psychology which always attends the struggle of a new type of organization to obtain an accepted place in the folklore of the times, which today is called "law" and "economics."

In order to solve the pressing problems of waste of labor and national resources, new organizations were sorely needed; yet there was no logical place in the mythology of government to which they could be assigned. The social needs were felt by everyone, but the slogans which the new organizations used had a queer sound. Therefore, the spirit of the Constitution, the traditional symbols of economics, and the general picture of a "rule of law" as opposed to "bureaucratic control" were all arrayed against them.

This phenomenon always occurs whenever new types of social organization are struggling to arise to fill gaps left in an older order. A merchant class, slowly rising to power after the Middle Ages, had no place of prestige in the social hierarchy. Therefore, when the need for banking and credit began to be felt, only the despised Jewish money lenders could fill it. Society tolerated them but felt compelled to establish the fact that such techniques were unworthy by laws of the Church declaring them illegal and immoral. Today there is great pressure on the Government to take over the techniques of bankers, to form government corporations, to use government credit to promote the distribution of goods as bankers had used it and even directly to distribute the goods themselves. Such new activities, of course, meet the same kind of theological opposition as met the growth of private banking in the Middle Ages. They are immoral; they will cause the ruin of national character; they will break up the home; they will destroy freedom. There is no reason to be alarmed or irritated with such opposition. It is only necessary to understand why it is inevitable.

It may be asserted as a principle of human organization that when new types of social organization are required, respectable, well-thought-of, and conservative people are unable to take part in them. Their moral and economic prejudices, their desire for the approval of other members of the group, compel them to oppose any form of organization which does not fit into the picture of society as they have known it in the past. This principle is on the one hand the balance wheel of social organization and on the other hand its greatest element of rigidity.

A failure to understand this is responsible for all the nonsense which intelligent, scholarly persons always write about contemporary revolutions of any kind. This nonsense, however, occurs with such regularity that it should be regarded as one of the fundamental factors in social psychology rather than nonsense. Its pattern is always the same, though the words may be different. What was called heresy in the Middle Ages is called Communism today, but the essential ideology of the argumentative attack, then and now, is identical. The reactions to the French Revolution and to the modern German, Russian, or Italian revolutions differ only in that the vocabularies are different.

Law and morals and economics are always arrayed against
new groups which are struggling to obtain a place in an institutional hierarchy of prestige. The violence of the combat
depends on the extent of the departure from the older ways
of doing things. When John D. Rockefeller built an empire
in a world which was supposed to be composed of competing
individuals, he violated the mythology and folklore which
pictured what the great businessman was supposed to do. In
the same way, John L. Lewis, with his sit-down strike, violated the ideals of what respectable labor leaders should do.
Had Rockefeller and Lewis followed current scruples, they
would not have built their great organizations. The reason is,
of course, that such scruples were the products of a time
which did not recognize the necessity, or even the legality, of
such organizations as Rockefeller and Lewis were trying to
form.

The departure of John D. Rockefeller's organization from
established ideals was not great, and hence the moral revul-
sion was confined to the extreme liberals. It resulted only in
the "muckraking era." Today, however, the new organizations growing to fill gaps in a highly organized society violate current notions of the structure of government in a much
more dramatic way. Hence the spiritual conflict is much
more marked. The difference between the violations of current folklore in the rise of the Standard Oil and those in the
present growing participation of government in the distribution of goods is the difference between venial sin and outright heresy.

All arguments against heresy follow the same pattern. A
Devil must first be discovered who is trying to lead the
people astray. A Hell must be invented which illustrates
what happens to those who listen to the Devil. The conception of free will is essential. Then the age-old story is told.

Russia and Germany listened to the Devil. They are therefore in Hell.

In our rational and sophisticated age the Devil and the Hell become very complicated. The true faith is Capitalism. Its priests are lawyers and economists. The Devil consists of an abstract man called a demagogue. He is the kind of person who refuses to be moved by sound economists and lawyers and who is constantly misleading the people by making the worse appear the better reason.

Group Free Will and the Thinking Man

It is impossible to conduct public debate on political or economic questions today without assuming some sort of group free will. Without this assumption moral judgments about nations or institutions which refuse to follow the right economic principles would be impossible. People insist that such judgments be made and in order to make them two things are necessary: first, a set of principles to use as a standard and, second, the conception of group free will in order to assess blame against those who refuse to follow those principles. Therefore an abstract man is created who has the ability to understand sound principles and the free will to follow them. All public debate is supposed to be addressed to him.

This abstract man is usually called the "Thinking Man" because today rational thought is the way of economic and legal salvation. In earlier times when faith was thought to be better than reason, the men who feared God were at the receiving end of public exhortation. It was the doubters who created the breeding ground for heresy. Today, in an age of reason, the doubters are not considered dangerous. It is the unthinking man or the uneducated who are led astray by unsound principles such as Communism or Fascism, which are the modern equivalent of heresy.

This conception of a group of thinking men in society to whom rational appeals can be made, who are willing to accept right principles when they are logically explained, is much like the former ethical notion of individual free will which used to be applied in the treatment of maladjusted personalities. In the naïve psychology of the past "Free Will" was a little man in the top of one's head who caught bad impulses and suppressed them. He did this by asking the advice of another little man called "Reason." In order to listen to Reason, however, it was necessary for Free Will to dismiss from the conference a third little man called "Emotion," who had a tendency to obscure the clear advice of Reason.

Today no competent psychologist talks that way about the habits and conduct of the individual. However, these conceptions are still necessary for political, economic, and legal discussion. To understand the debate about Communism, Capitalism, and Fascism, it is necessary to analyze the "Thinking Man," who is essential to our notion of group free will. He is a most interesting fellow, because he is the person who is supposed to choose the system of government for America.

Let us briefly describe him. He is the fellow we might all become if the demagogues would only let us alone. He is the gentleman who accepts sound and rejects unsound principles. He does not sit upon the interpretation of the laws of the nation, because that requires the peculiar and artificial reasoning of the law. Here we must call on the sound jurist, who is in constant combat with unsound jurists. It is the duty, however, of the thinking man to distinguish between sound and unsound jurists and follow the former. In the field of sociology and economics, however, the thinking man sits on matters of principle in his own right. He chooses the reasoning of the Brookings Institution and throws out of the window the unsound theories of General Hugh Johnson. He

may be misled for a short while, but in the long run he is hard
to fool. He hates superficial reasoning and quack remedies.
He is imbued with the pioneer spirit of America. He knows
that we must balance the budget. His duty is to warn against
impending doom, so that if unsound theories are followed he
will be able to say that it was not his fault. He never sacrifices
principle for expediency. Our colleges are devoted to the
task of training him. It is through the study of things like
Latin and Greek that he develops the mental muscles which
enable him to understand complicated theories. He knows
the lessons of history and follows them. He distrusts politicians and sees through their wiles. It is to him that genuine
statesmen appeal. (Genuine statesmen, of course, do not
stoop to stir up the emotions of the mob.) Therefore, Mr.
Hearst, Mr. Landon, Mr. Roosevelt, the *Chicago Tribune,*
the *New Republic,* the *Saturday Evening Post,* Mr. Norman
Thomas, John W. Davis, and Earl Browder all address their
remarks to the thinking man. Of course, only the sound persons or publications named above *really* address their remarks to the thinking man. The unsound ones are stirring
up the emotions of the mob by misrepresentation and demagoguery and are just pretending to address the thinking man.
The thinking man is supposed to see through all of that and
make the proper selection from the above list.

Education makes more thinking men. A free press guides
them. Unlimited public discussion aids them in coming to
their unemotional and unbiased decisions.

Without the almost universal acceptance of this concept
of the "thinking man," the debate about the merits of *Capitalism* v. *Fascism* would be impossible. The whole rational
structure of this debate depends on group free will to choose
a "system of government" based on this abstract individual.
In the old debates on heresy the abstract man in the background was the "believer." Today, of course, we consider our-

selves too rational to rely too much on the believer. Beliefs and faiths are all right in a democracy only after we have first *thought them out* or hired someone to think them out for us. The Middle Ages, we think, were very wrong in relying so much on ceremony. Protestants often point out that this is a weakness of the Catholic Church. The capitalistic system is not supposed to be founded on faith but on reason. The thinking man analyzes it and then accepts it by observing the greater dangers which follow acceptance of other systems. The process is something like this. Germany was confronted with a choice between the right principles of government and the wrong. It chose the wrong ones, because people were misled by demagogues. Once the wrong ones were chosen, the persecution of the Jews automatically followed. This should have been clear to the thinking men of Germany, but either there were not enough of them in Germany or else the German thinking man was not particularly bright about government. The thinking men of America see this very clearly and warn people about the dangers which follow the acceptance of these foreign principles. On the other side, we find people in Germany and Russia talking in the same way about America and England. Russian propaganda in this country is based on the notion that thinking men can be educated in capitalistic countries.

The above is a description of a prevailing point of view. It is not a recommendation for reform, because it is a point of view which in daily life cannot be escaped. It is essential that the individual feel that he has free will and reason, as separate qualities, in order to conduct his affairs with dignity and force. It is equally necessary that he have that same feeling toward the institutions to which he is loyal. All the ceremonies of daily life are set in the confines of that stage. However, for purposes of diagnosis or dissection of social institutions, it is necessary to realize that what we call free will, and sin, and emotion, and reason, are attitudes which influence conduct and not separate little universes containing principles which actually control institutions. The world from the point of view of reason and free will may be compared to a highly idealized portrait of an individual which flatters him and makes him proud. It is useful to hang on the wall. It is entirely useless as a basis for diagnosis or prescription if the individual happens to be ill. The separate utility of these two points of view is seldom recognized in political or economic thinking. We are still convinced that appeals to the thinking man to choose his system of government are not ceremonies but actual methods of social control. We still use governmental creeds as a basis for diagnosis.

This almost universal point of view effectually prevents men from observing the complex series of events either in their own or in foreign countries. Having adopted a creed, they use the most convenient disagreeable incidents occurring in countries with different creeds to demonstrate the truth of their own creed. Therefore, the creeds of those nations where centralized governmental organization is operating with the most violence become the most potent political weapons against exercise of national power to solve national problems in America. It is for this reason that Sweden does not give us a good parallel for political debate in America. It is difficult to describe that country in simple abstract terms. Germany, Russia, and Italy are much more convenient for argumentative purposes because their misfortunes can be laid to the fact that their creeds contradict our own established principles.

The creeds of these countries, of course, do not describe or explain the events taking place there, any more than the *Book of Mormon* describes the actual development of the Mormon Church. They simply furnish the Devil and the Hell which are supposed to follow a departure from our own settled prin-

ciples. The lessons of history are used in the same way. Men
do not actually search history to avoid the mistakes of the
past. They seek convenient analogies to show the dangers in
failing to adopt the creed which they advocate. The legal or
economic prophet of today sincerely believes that he is using
a process of analysis and reason to help the thinking man in
a voluntary choice of a political or economic creed.

But how do men actually choose these creeds? The answer
is that they do not choose them. Men become bound by loyalties and enthusiasms to existing organizations. If they are
successful in obtaining prestige and security from these organizations, they come to regard them as the ultimate in
spiritual and moral perfection. This attitude is necessary for
the morale of these institutions. When a time comes that these
old organizations fail to function, new organizations struggle
to fill the need. The practical need for them must be plain or
they would not make any headway. Yet they can have no
slogans, traditions, or creeds, because they are so new. For
example, it was obviously necessary to form a governmental
organization to feed people during the depression. There was
no place in our creed for anything other than charity. Therefore, the feeding of those in need by the Government violated
that creed. Distribution of goods to unemployed who happened to possess no stocks or bonds had not as yet developed
a creed of its own. Hence the dole was supposed to lead to
the destruction of individual initiative, the ruin of national
character, and the downfall of Capitalism. Communism in
Russia became the favorite parable against the Government's
accepting the obligation to distribute available goods, because Russia was a country in which government had assumed that obligation and which also had lots of internal
difficulties. Had Russia been more prosperous, some other
country would have been used as a parable.

A beautiful example of this automatic religious opposition

to new forms of organization is found in the controversy between the Supreme Court and Roosevelt. The Court had been confusing and delaying every exercise of national power to solve national problems. It was paralyzing new administrative organizations of the Government by its attitude of hostility. In this way it gave great spiritual comfort to those who feared the exercise of national power to solve national problems. It enabled them to attack these new government activities from a mystical point of view and thus to avoid discussing the unpleasant facts which made these new activities necessary.

When the Government sought to free itself from the mystical domination of the Court, all practical discussion was drowned in predictions of moral catastrophe. Intelligent leaders of the American Bar reacted automatically to the spiritual conflict and indulged in the stereotyped pattern of debate which we have been describing without any realization that it was stereotyped.

In this atmosphere, for those who were seeking rational grounds to express their distrust of new forms of social organization, Communism and Fascism came to be political realities in this country. They were imported by newspapers like the Hearst chain and magazines like the *Saturday Evening Post* which constantly preached the dangers of changing our system of government. It was through such sources that these magic words got their greatest advertising and their widest currency. It was from our great institutions of learning that such prophets of disaster got their scholarly support. Parables were needed to dramatize for conservative American people their phobias against change. "Bureaucracy" and "regimentation" were entirely too vague without concrete examples. The parables of the wild Russian and the cruel German were admirably adapted for use as bogeymen. It was in this way that the notions of Communism and Fascism spread. In this way men in the United States became vitally interested in competing "systems" of government.

In Sweden, by way of contrast, new organizations to fill the same needs did not encounter such violent priestly opposition. Why it was that Swedes were able to accept the comforts of government-subsidized houses without worrying over the totalitarian state and the abolition of individualism is a complicated study in national psychology. One answer is that Sweden was sufficiently practical in its outlook to avoid this conflict. Therefore, the issues of Capitalism, Communism, and Fascism did not become important political realities in Sweden. Neither did they achieve such overshadowing importance in England. England, by electing a Socialist, discovered how little difference allegiance to a formal "system" of government made. They found him more conservative in action than the Tories.

The Conflict between Capitalism and Foreign Systems of Government

In this country, since it was particularly devoted to rational principle, the attempt of new organizations to rise in response to vital needs gave rise to a holy war between the great fundamental principles of good and evil. This was the "fault" of no one. It simply illustrated the inevitable working of a law of political dynamics. When a new organization attempts to rise in an atmosphere of religious devotion to a governmental mythology, it cannot succeed without the development of a set of principles and a mythology all its own. The emergence of this new set of principles and mythology cannot be accomplished without some sort of holy war, the violence of which depends on the habits and culture of the people.

As we have said before, the creeds of Communism and

Fascism were no more descriptive of what was happening in Russia or Germany than the current economic creeds were descriptive of what was happening here. Nor was their content important, because no one who used the creeds' words in public debate knew anything about their content. It was only important that these words could be used to surround new organizations in America with a vague atmosphere of disorder. Revolutions serve to emphasize very vague ideas and make them appear to have a specific content. Both the Russian and the German revolutions pictured the State in a new relation to other social organizations. These revolutions advanced that idea by focusing attention on the actual possibility of its practical realization. Yet at the same time they retarded the acceptance of enlarged state activity by creating new phobias of violence and suppression. This is important to remember because of the generally accepted notion that revolutions advance new ideas. What they actually do is to give morale and organization to radical individuals. This may or may not advance the new idea. Too often it creates a conflict in which even familiar progressive ideas appear to have a radical tinge.

Thus Communism and Fascism in this country gave impetus to radical organizations and at the same time made familiar humanitarian ideals look violent by coördinating them with events in violent and disorderly countries. The resulting conflict caused respectable people to oppose humanitarian ideals for fear of being identified with the radical organizations which advocated them under these strange names. The underlying philosophy of both Communism and Fascism was familiar enough in this country. It had been identified with a dissenting but nevertheless respectable group. Norman Thomas was not regarded as dangerous. He preached Christian ethics in government in a perfectly respectable way. At no time did he appear to offer the possibility of putting these ideals into practice. Therefore, he was never hated the way that Roosevelt was hated. He was never identified with an organization that seemed about to do anything practical. Here was the kind of Socialist that a decent Socialist was supposed to be—for whom romantic college professors could vote. He symbolized a conflicting ideal without creating a practical working institution which interfered with any of the ideals that Socialism contradicted. Thus conservatives liked to have him around, just as respectable married people of the Victorian age liked to read about Lancelot and Guinevere and admired Tennyson for writing the *Idylls of the King*. This is what a friend of mine meant when he said Norman Thomas made him "think."

The rise of actual institutions to accomplish a few of these ideas, however, threw them completely out of focus. It was as if Lancelot and Guinevere had suddenly appeared to conduct their affair next door to Mr. Tennyson (who would have been one of the very first to move out of the neighborhood). Conflicting ideals, respected in their place, become disquieting when they appear in the wrong rôle. If the function of the political or economic or legal creed as a ceremony is understood, this phenomenon will appear entirely normal. There are certain dramatic rules to be observed or the show is spoiled. No rage is equal to the rage of a contented right-thinking man when he is confronted in the market place by an idea which belongs in the pulpit; and this is as true of organizations as it is of individuals.

And thus the holy war between Capitalism, Communism, and Fascism is one of the greatest obstacles to practical treatment of the actual day-to-day needs of the American people. Even agricultural credit and soil conservation become tainted with Communism. All sorts of sensible suggestions are drowned in the din of battle. It is a fixed idea that any society has a free-will choice to make between these systems. Capitalism is a good system, in which the individual has freedom. Communism and Fascism destroy the freedom of the individual. The whole political campaign of 1936 consisted in ringing the changes on these naïve ideas. Every practical scheme for social betterment had to be tested for tendencies leading to one or the other of these systems. If it led to Communism or Fascism, it was thought better to humiliate the unemployed or to waste natural resources rather than take steps which would change the "capitalistic system."

To this way of thinking about government may be attributed the failure of such schemes as governmental housing and the control of agriculture. Waste and want were present on a large scale in a land of plenty. Yet people with no conceivable material interest at stake preferred that they continue because the practical steps to alleviate them led to another system of government. Coupled with this naïve belief that Germany and Russia had actually chosen the erroneous political theories that now threatened America was an astonishing ignorance as to just how the changes in Germany and Russia had come about and how the present governments in those countries operate. For a long time our editorial writers solemnly proved that these governments could not survive, because they were flouting every sound political principle. When their survival began to be recognized as an accomplished fact, these same editorial writers were equally convinced that America was about to become like Germany on the one hand, or Russia on the other, and to imitate both their culture and their institutions. It was thought that the safest insurance against such terrors consisted in stripping the Federal Government of all power of social control.

The Search for Universal Truth in a Political World

WE can better understand this way of thinking if we compare it to the splitting up of the Roman Church during the

Reformation into creeds and sects which mutually distrusted and feared each other. Each creed was thought by its followers to be the only way of salvation. Yet the supporters of each creed were in constant terror that their own sect might be seduced by the ideas of the others. There followed a constant series of petty persecutions and crusades, accompanied by an extraordinary literature of learned disputation, so similar to editorials of various kinds today as to leave no doubt of the character of the phenomena. None but the very learned men could readily explain the actual difference between the creeds, just as none but learned men can write economic theology today. It was enough for the ordinary men to devote their efforts to defending the faith. The essence of the faith was that we must undergo present inconvenience to save our souls for the future. That was hard, but worth-while. The present was transitory. Hell was the wage of violating the taboos of the medieval church. Inflation and dictatorship are the wages of governmental control of natural resources today.

The idea that a church could be judged by its effectiveness as an organization had not appeared above the horizon. It was supposed that the specific provisions of its creed made it a good or a bad church, because if the creed was right, temporary deficiencies would be bound to disappear. The public declarations of the church as to matters of belief were thought to be most important contributions to society. The real object of the church was neither charity nor any form of social work but the unremitting search for universal truth.

Today the attitude of the church has so changed that its function as a seeker for universal truth is more a part of its formal ritual than its vital ideal. For most people the standard by which churches are judged is their effectiveness as a social agency among the people with whom they work. This is evidenced by a complete change in attitude toward the functions of the missionary. Medical attention to under-privileged groups, or even to the heathen, is now thought of far more importance than the holding of services.

This has not yet happened to our political religion, which is the most vital religion of today in that it is the only one for which men are willing to persecute their fellows and to lead crusades.

Back of the ascendancy of creeds and the complete subordination of practical consideration is the notion that statesmen today, like the priests of the Reformation, must devote themselves, with the aid of scholars, to discovering principles of universal truth. This is an idea shared by Hitler, Hearst, newspaper columnists, and great scholars cloistered in universities. We cite as an example the well-known columnist Dorothy Thompson, commenting on a scholarly dissertation at the Harvard Tercentenary:

Prof. Gilson comes from Europe and he spoke with the feeling and apprehension of one who lives in the midst of a revolution which threatens to sweep away the very basis of the civilization in which we live. In his speech he made perfectly clear what that basis is. Its foundation is the belief that there is a spiritual order of reality, "whose absolute right it is to judge even the state, and eventually to free us from its oppression."

He said: "The conviction that there is nothing in the world above universal truth lies at the very root of our mental and social liberty." If it goes, he warned, there will be nothing to protect us against the worst kind of slavery to which mankind is now being submitted by totalitarian states—mental slavery.

In very different words, Prof. Gilson echoed the thoughts which were expressed some weeks ago in the epistle of the dissident Protestant clergy in Germany. Such ideas also lay behind the refusal of Oxford and Cambridge Universities to participate in the quincentennial celebration at the University of Heidelberg this year. They are the conceptions that truth, morality, social justice and beauty are necessary and universal in their own right.

They cannot be true alone for a certain social organization and economic system, or for a certain nation or for a certain race. Their validity must be universal. (*New York Herald Tribune,* September 5, 1936.)

Some of the eminent scholars thought that a supreme court of learning might be a help. This notion is illustrated by a report of the proceedings in the *New York Times.*

It is belief in the universality of truth, the conference was told, that gave the church its supreme and unquestioned moral authority for centuries during the Middle Ages.

This moral authority was sifted down to the masses of the people throughout the Western world from a fountainhead at the University of Paris, which gathered together all the leading intellects of the day, regardless of nationality, in a universal fellowship of truth-seekers.

It now behooves the present-day universities, particularly those in the United States, the scholars are convinced, to assume a role in this era similar to that played by the University of Paris.

It was this moral authority of the medieval church, it was pointed out further, that became a power so great that the temporal rulers did not dare disobey it.

The time has come for the learned men of the world, many of the present-day scholars believe, to recognize their supreme responsibility and to take the initiative in an effort to re-establish a universal moral authority, based on the tenets of universal truth as conceived by the collective wisdom of each generation.

A permanent body of organized intelligence, under the leadership of American universities, because of the world's respect for the unbiased and objective wisdom of its members, would exert such a profound influence upon the nations, the scholars believe, that the force of its moral authority would be similar to the moral authority of the medieval church.

.   .   .   .   .

The general questions submitted were:

1. Do you believe that a supreme court of organized knowledge for the intelligent guidance of humanity can be developed?

2. Can the organized scholarship of the world make itself felt as a power in the world?

3. How shall a beginning be made of achieving this desirable end?

The specific questions were:

1. What do you consider the principal points of potential importance to the world that might come from the Harvard Tercentenary Conference of Arts and Sciences?

2. Could the conference be described as a temporary supreme court of learning, a court for a week?

· · · · ·

7. Might the opinions emanating from such a group gain sufficient prestige so that States as well as individuals and economic systems would listen to them? (*New York Times,* September 14, 1936.)

It is very significant of the unconscious attitudes toward government that this particular symbol was chosen to represent the study of government. The Supreme Court, above all institutions, stood for the finality of rational principles. In the Middle Ages the University of Paris was actually a supreme court of social principles and judged both law and medicine. It was this University which, in its search for universal truth, placed its ban on quinine as a cure for fever. Today when the world's scholars sought an organization to represent the search for universal truth their minds instinctively seized on the symbol of a court, which for us represents the final authoritative solution of rational and scholarly debate.

This search for truth, instead of convenience, placed the emphasis on principles rather than on organizations everywhere but in business and politics. Nobody wanted a supreme court of business policy to tell Henry Ford and General Motors what to do to sell cars. No one suggested a supreme court of political strategy. Those things belonged to the temporal world of affairs, the day-to-day needs of the people—which matters the scholars gladly rendered unto Cæsar, as true priests have done from time immemorial. Unless they did this it is hard to see how the great game of scholarship could go on. One does not speak of a successful trial lawyer as a great scholar of the law—one does not speak of successful political strategy as statesmanship.

Of course, there were many among these scholars with exactly the same point of view as the writer's. Yet when the subject of organization was approached, they could do nothing but follow the attitudes of their time. Men—even learned men—cannot "think up" forms of successful organization. Had the writer been fortunate enough to have been numbered among these learned men, he, too, would have voted for a supreme court of learning.

It was in this atmosphere of a search for universal truths that "systems" of government achieved such paramount importance—that practical schemes were judged by their tendencies rather than their immediate effect on health and comfort. Learned men were not interested in bequeathing a physical plant to posterity. They were solely concerned with dictating the social organization of the future. In this they acted as learned men have always acted. Each age tries to dictate the social philosophy of posterity—and in the long run always fails.

CHAPTER II

The Psychology of Social Institutions

IN which is portrayed the hierarchy of divinities in American industrial society, whose leadership and inspiration affect our business, charitable, and educational organizations, both great and small.

THE preceding chapter is only an introduction to an analysis of the part that creeds play in social organization. Its purpose is to show that wherever men become absorbed in a medieval search for the magic formula of universal truth the creeds of government grow in importance and the practical activities of government are mismanaged. Holy wars are fought, orators and priests thrive, but technicians perish. Color and romance abound in such an era, as in all times of conflict, but practical distribution of available comfort and efficient organization is impossible.

When we attempt to analyze the actual operation of creeds in society, we discover the surprising fact that their content and their logic are the least important things about them. Socialists, thrown into power against a background of confusion, become more conservative than Tories. On the other hand, whoever obtains power in times of national humiliation and defeat is apt to express and intensify the persecution manias which that atmosphere develops in any people. This happened in Russia and Germany. It was not the result of the doctrines of Communism or Fascism. It would have occurred under any doctrine. Only those leaders who can respond to current aspirations and ideals can survive. Therefore, any governmental creed that is professed by actual leaders must change to fit the emotional needs of their people.

The theoretical systems of government are only argumentative tools by which priests and scholars condemn heresy or
else attack the established Church.

Back of every creed is a hierarchy of heroes or divinities
whose imaginary personalities give meaning to those words.
Without an emotional understanding of this hierarchy we
cannot even guess the meaning the words will finally take,
any more than those who wrote the due process clause in the
Constitution, intending to give protection to those unjustly
accused of crimes, could have guessed that it would be the
principal protection of public utilities against public service
regulation.

The study of the actual operation of the social creeds which
give logical form and unity to our so-called systems of government is confused by the fact that it is hard for us not to
think of them as guiding principles which we choose or reject. For example, a recent book, *In Defense of Capitalism,* by
James H. R. Cromwell and Hugo E. Czerwonky, carries this
statement on the jacket, which not only represents the attitude of the authors but also that of most conservative people
today:

The insecurity and degradation of the American working masses
is attributable, not to capitalism, but to ignorance concerning its
functioning. The fact is that capitalism is an ideal which never
has been achieved. Before discarding capitalism and economic
freedom for a system of regimentation and rationing, we contend
that the defects of our monetary organization should first be
remedied and capitalism thereby given a fair chance to show
what it can do.

In other words, from this point of view Capitalism is studied
apart from the living organizations which profess it as a
creed. If it is found to be good our troubles must come from
a sinful refusal to follow Capitalism logically. If it is found

to be bad our troubles are the result of not voluntarily abandoning it.

Such a point of view makes it impossible to observe how creeds actually operate in the world of temporal affairs. It leads only to pounding the table and preaching the evils of sin. This chapter will therefore be based on the assumption that social creeds, law, economics, and so on *have no meaning whatever* apart from the organization to which they are attached. To say that the organizations voluntarily choose them is as meaningless as to say that the Catholic Church voluntarily chose the Catholic religion in preference to Protestantism. To blame organizations for not living up to them is as meaningless as blaming feudal barons for not living up to the precepts of chivalry. Books like *In Defense of Capitalism,* from which we have just quoted, are an automatic response to an emotional conflict. They are not an explanation of the creed; they are part of it. In order to understand this we must discuss the psychology of social institutions which produces similar results regardless of the form into which the statement of the creed is cast.

Social Organizations, Large and Small, Like Crystals, Pattern Themselves after the Same Form

THE social organization of a nation is the unifying force which binds a people together. It is a complex thing based on habit and acceptance of certain common values. It creates an atmosphere in which thousands of smaller organizations with opposing interests succeed in getting along together. It does this by the force of public opinion which makes dissent, or even doubt, subject to various kinds of ostracism.

Smaller social organizations functioning within the general national structure resemble, in so far as their purpose permits, the larger organizations. They must do so to maintain a logical place within it. The smaller organizations in turn subdivide themselves in somewhat the same manner as the larger ones. A Rotary club or a national association of scholars follows the general national pattern of constitutional government. Indeed, a social organization may be compared to the organizations of physical energy described by scientists as "matter." The atom is a smaller solar system. In the same way one finds in all social organization, large and small, the same current taboos, political tricks, and *sub rosa* machines representing the conflicting ideals found in the national government. Smaller organizations in any culture follow the pattern of the larger ones. At the bottom (or at the top, depending upon which end of the telescope you are looking through) is the individual, who, in his own life, responds to the symbols and ideals of his government, the business organization which feeds him, and the social organizations which give him dignity. For example, at different periods of the same day the judge on the bench will successively take the rôles of a martinet, an easygoing man about town, a stern father, and a dreamy metaphysician, and probably belong to a series of organizations which offer him a platform upon which he may play each of these successive parts. He may even, in a spirit of adventure, play a criminal rôle for a time, visiting some low dive or searching release in some other disapproved activity supported by the so-called criminal elements. If he does not do this, he will play these parts vicariously by reading detective stories and attending melodramas in which the life of the criminal is pictured in more romantic aspects.

This being so, we shall attempt to analyze a few of the elements common to all social organizations, large and small, whatever their purpose. These elements obtain in more even balance in the larger national organizations compelled to represent all the aspects of human activity. Nevertheless, although the emphasis may be different, they are discovered even in such minor affairs as Rotary clubs, women's clubs, or Boy Scout troops. The elements which all social organizations share in common may tentatively be described as follows:

1. A creed or a set of commonly accepted rituals, verbal or ceremonial, which has the effect of making each individual feel an integral part of the group and which makes the group appear as a single unit. This is a unifying force and is as mysterious as the law of gravitation. It is ordinarily called a psychological factor because it is impossible to think of our language and our conduct except in terms of separate physical and mental universes, in spite of the fact that we are beginning to realize that these two universes are not separate.

2. A set of attitudes which makes the creed effective by giving the individual prestige, or at least security, when he subordinates what are ordinarily called "selfish interests" to those of the group.

3. A set of institutional habits by means of which men are automatically able to work together without any process of conscious choice as to whether they will coöperate or not. It is, of course, difficult to separate attitudes and institutional habits from creeds, and yet it is convenient to do so because in our way of thinking it is a custom to regard a habit as a different kind of process from action based on conscious thought.

4. The mythological or historical tradition which proves that an institutional creed has been ordained by more than human forces. This mythology may take every conceivable form, depending on the culture. It may emphasize humanitarian values or nonhumanitarian values, warlike or peacetime diversities. However, although the emphasis may differ in different cultures, all the common human values will be found represented in some form or other, whether the or-

ganization be a primitive tribe or the New York Stock Exchange.

Granted these essentials, we find successful organizations. Without them, organization can be maintained only by force, and force cannot continue long because it is too exhausting. A number of individuals cannot be found successively to represent the hard-boiled qualities necessary for such organizations.

The separation of the psychological mechanics of institutions into these four elements is, of course, artificial. Each is an outgrowth of the other; attitudes create the necessity for words to describe or celebrate them; words induce new and different attitudes. Mythologies which support creeds are distinguished from institutional habits by no sharp definition. Society functions like an anthill. If we were compelled to plan each day how to get food into New York City and garbage out of it, we would be lost and the people would starve. This separation of the psychological forces in society into various elements helps us to think because it follows the customary ways of thinking about society and at the same time permits us to observe institutions from without rather than from within.

Institutional Creeds

BECAUSE words and ceremonies are our only methods of communication, everywhere we find that the creed is regarded as the cornerstone of social institutions. "In the beginning was the Word" is an idea which has been repeated over and over wherever language is used. In this way of thinking we are as primitive as the people of the Old Testament.

Therefore, the folklore of every people runs in something like this form. A long time ago, with the aid of some sacred and infallible force, certain exceptionally gifted forebears formulated a lot of principles which contained the fundamentals of social organization. Nations which, like the United States, trace their beginnings to some single event think that their principles were discovered all at one time. This circumstance gives them a *written* constitution. Nations like England, which do not claim any sudden birth, always find their principles in a whole series of historical events, and hence their "constitution" is unwritten. The English constitution is unwritten, not because of an absence of writing in England, but because sentimental associations of the English did not concentrate on any single event or document.

In this country we like to think that we decided to write down all our governmental principles in one document called the Constitution. Actually, the Constitution consists of thousands of documents written at various times. Yet since our origin as an independent nation centered around one historic event, we emphasize what was written at that time and call it a written constitution. This folklore has caused many naïve books to be written on the advantages of a people getting together and deciding to write their constitution. Learned men who thought this was a better plan have often wondered why England did not decide to do it. The writer recalls a course in college in which one of the matters discussed was whether England had not made a mistake in not reducing her constitution to definite written form. In a similar way the myths of primitive governments may center either on a single event or on a series of events in which the actors are individuals of more than human capabilities.

In an age where Reason is God, constitutions or fundamental creeds are always supposed to be the result of rational thought on the part of our forebears. Thus Rousseau depicted a social contract by which men agreed to stop fighting because this seemed such an eminently reasonable hypothesis to a peace-loving man. In an age of mysticism the

tables are handed down from on high instead of being discovered by reason. In more primitive mysticism, which is unable to produce adequate literary lights, the constitution is
usually in the form of a sign or a poem. However formulated,
all these kinds of constitutions perform the same purpose.
They furnish the limits beyond which controversy must not
extend. Arguments may occur within the terms of the constitution, but to attack the constitution itself is heresy and
calls down penalties which vary with the culture of the
people from a mild ostracism to instant execution. In times
of security popular opinion will always stand for more skep-
ticism of fundamentals than in times of spiritual trouble, just
as discipline in the army always relaxes in a comfortable post.

Having acquired a constitution through the intervention
of exceptionally gifted men, the folklore of every nation then
assumes that the people accepted it as truth and proceeded to
live up to it. Dissenters are shown the light by the process of
education. Whatever gaps were left by the physical inability
of the forefathers to consider everything are filled by the
learned men of the time, with material which they manufacture, not out of whole cloth but out of the principles of the
original document. If this process is questioned it is always
answered that the forefathers wanted the constitution to be
a growing and not a static thing, and invariably some of them
are found who said just that. If, however, a gap is left un-
filled, it is always pointed out that a constitution cannot be
one thing today and another tomorrow, and invariably there
are found a number of great men who stated this with some
vehemence in the past. Each argument is used alternately by
the Supreme Court of the United States, but it should be kept
in mind that we are talking here not about the United States
Constitution but about every organizational creed. This type
of thinking is particularly evident in the theology of 1850,
when men spoke of the word above God. Not even God

could violate the inevitable logical principles deduced by true
reason, because to assume so would be to assume that God
was unreasonable, which would be heresy.

The language of the Constitution is immaterial since it
represents current myths and folklore rather than rules. Out
of it are spun the contradictory ideals of governmental
morality. For example, in 1937 we find the *American Bar
Association Journal* editorially recommending that the letter
of the Constitution be disregarded in a time of crisis. Referring to the President's Supreme Court proposal, the editor
says:

If the proposed act violates the spirit of the Constitution and
threatens the breakdown of an essential part of it, "constitutional
morality" certainly forbids it. To act under such circumstances
is simply to exercise a brute power. And the spirit is more important than the letter. As long as the spirit of the Constitution
is followed, there will be small trouble about the letter, and the
great instrument and guarantee of our liberties is safe. But when
the letter is followed in disregard of the spirit, catastrophe may
be near.

The beauty of this kind of argument is that it makes the
Constitution very elastic indeed, so that it can be used on
both sides of any moral question without the user being
bothered with what the Constitution actually says. It is essential to constitutionalism as a vital creed that it be capable of
being used in this way on both sides of any question, because
it must be the creed of all groups in order to function as a
unifying symbol. This way of thinking is essential to all governmental organizations. It is the method by which the organization can take pride in the superiority of its traditions.
Pride in his early struggles and a clinging to traditions which
have been handed to him by better men than he are deep
seated within the psychology of the individual.

The notion that men obtain a creed, either through the
exercise of pure reason or from some other superhuman
power, is so firmly fixed in popular and scholarly thinking
about government because it is the essence of all worship,
and of all religion. Nothing is so destructive of social habits
or of a mystical attitude which puts a divine character into
physical objects as the questioning of the existence of some
power or reason or mystic word, to which men can pray.
Nothing disturbs the attitude of religious worship so much
as a few practical observations. And yet that spiritual need is
something which cannot be denied to any group of men, not
even to scientists.

Illustrative of the search for the proper creed, we find the
universally held idea that the reason nations have trouble is
because of a sinful desertion of the right principles. Thus
Germany sinfully worshiped false gods, quit searching for
the proper principles, and got Hitler. The beauty of this argument, of course, is that Hitler himself is searching for
truth and right just as feverishly as his opponents. The question, therefore, boils down to which of the two is sound.

Since most civilized cultures are astonishingly alike, logical analysis usually uncovers the fact that the creeds are alike.
For example, as this is being written the greatest fear of
conservative people is that we are establishing a bureaucracy
like that of Germany. Hitler appears to be equally opposed to
bureaucracy, as appears from the following interview (*Washington Star*, September 14, 1936):

Germany will guard jealously the principle of private enterprise
in business, Chancellor Adolf Hitler asserted today.

The Nazi dictator denied that his plans for the future of the
nation included marshaling all industrial establishments under
governmental control and declared:

"I will never permit bureaucratization of German industry."

The Reichschancellor's views on the business future of his

country were outlined in an informal conversation at Nurnberg Castle after a source close to the Fuehrer had predicted a decree to make effective his four-year plan for economic independence might be made public this week.

"I am convinced there must be competition to bring the best to the top," Hitler declared. "I could take over all business, but what would I have then—nothing but a bureaucracy."

Nationalization of German industry, Hitler predicted, would result in "workers and executives losing interest" in their jobs and "it would not be long before they would become mere job-holders expecting automatic advancement by seniority instead of initiative."

"Great improvement in manufacturing processes springs from keen rivalry between competitors," the Reichsfuehrer said.

"But does not Socialist economy presuppose restriction of private enterprise?" one of his listeners asked.

"Of course," Hitler replied, "wherever private interests clash with the interests of the nation the good of the community must come before profits to the individual.

"But that still leaves abundant room for private enterprise," the Chancellor declared.

The Fuehrer earlier had emphasized before a session of the National Socialist Convention that Germany is armed and ready to defend "the miracle of its own resurrection."

It is considered quite a sophisticated observation in these curious times to say that both political parties are exactly alike. Few, however, understand that the reason for this is that where the center of attention is abstractions rather than practical objectives all parties are bound to be alike. The creed of each must represent all the current conflicting ideals and phobias. Only minority parties which do not expect to get into power can write creeds without internal contradictions. Opposing parties which hope to win will necessarily worship the same gods even while they are denouncing each other because they are talking to actual voters and not to some ideal society of the future. This is not something to complain about. It follows from the fact that every governmental creed must represent all the contradictory ideals of a people if it is to be accepted by them.

Institutional Attitudes and Habits

Since our chief concern in this volume is with ways of thinking about society, we will give little space to the social attitudes and habits which unify organizations. These two factors are easily understood in institutions where the creeds are admittedly ceremonial in character. Thus we understand the attitudes and habits which center around the Christmas celebration because the creed of Santa Claus is recognized to be pure drama. We therefore can talk about Santa Claus objectively without destroying his emotional value. With the recognition of the fact that church creeds are not searches for universal truth, we can understand better the function of churches in society. Preachers like Harry Emerson Fosdick preach realistically and effectively about the place that the Church can and should take in the community. Fosdick realizes that the creed is important only as a symbol of unity —and that the effectiveness of the Church must be judged by different standards from those of its theology.

In an institution where the creed is thought to represent truth and is supposed to describe what the organization does, as in government or law, the factors which we have described as habits and attitudes are generally ignored. Pathology gives way to mythology. When someone attempts to describe how such an institution works, he is called a "realist" or a "cynic" because he makes believers uncomfortable. Thus to describe how the law, or Capitalism, or the Supreme Court of the United States actually works is to appear to attack these symbols. The actual habits and attitudes which operate under the banner of the creed to make the institution effective have a slightly obscene appearance. Nice people do not want to discuss them, except for the purpose of getting rid of them.

We will not delay our exposition by attempting a definition of the distinction between what we have called attitudes and habits and what we have called creeds and mythologies. The writer as a lawyer has indulged too long in the vice of definition to have any illusions that it leads to understanding. If the words do not carry a picture of the kind of social phenomena referred to they are unfortunately chosen. However, they happen to be the best words which now come to mind.

The Mythology of Institutions

THE logical content of creeds never realistically describes the institutions to which the creeds are attached. Every phrase in the Constitution designed to protect the submerged individual has become an instrument for the protection of large organizations. There is not time to develop here this commonplace theme. To illustrate we use again the development of the due process clause because it has been referred to so frequently that it is familiar to everyone. Due process of law under the Fifth Amendment unquestionably referred to arbitrary criminal prosecution of individuals. The words are:

No person shall be held to answer for a capital, or otherwise infamous crime, unless on a presentment or indictment of a grand jury, except in cases arising in the land or naval forces, or in the militia, when in actual service in time of war or public danger; nor shall any person be subject for the same offense to be twice put in jeopardy of life or limb; nor shall be compelled in any criminal case to be witness against himself, nor be deprived of life, liberty, or property, without due process of law; nor shall private property be taken for public use, without just compensation.

Today this amendment is one of the reasons why railroads are protected from a Federal pension system. Public control of business becomes the same as taking away property. Great national organizations become individuals. Only a short time ago nobody saw anything strange or out of the way in the change. Scholars in law schools proved that it was not a change at all and were generally believed.

It is therefore not the content of the governmental creed which molds institutions, but the imaginary personalities which make up the national mythology. Every culture has its hierarchy of divinities, like the ancient Greeks. This hierarchy is never recognized as a mythology during the period when it is most potent. It is only the myths of other peoples or other times that we label as myths. The power of any currently accepted mythology lies in the fact that its heroes are thought to have a real existence. There is always a large number of them because each mood and aspiration must be represented. Every institution tries to represent all of these heroes at once. Thus the American industrial organization is a hard-boiled trader, a scholar, a patron of modern architecture, a thrifty housewife, a philanthropist, a statesman preaching sound principles of government, a patriot, and a sentimental protector of widows and orphans at the same time. Let me designate the heroes of a nation and I care not who writes its constitution.

In the days of chivalry national heroes were princes of the Church or warriors seeking high adventure for a holy motive. These imaginary personalities gave form and logic to governmental structure. King Richard went to the Crusades in an unconscious response to the demand that the Government of England imitate its myths, just as the ruling class of every time unconsciously imitates the little ideal pictures to which it owes its prestige.

In the United States the mythology used to be very simple. The predominant figure was the American Businessman. Warriors were respected, but they had a distinctly minor place. The National Government had to imitate the American Businessman. Whenever it failed, people became alarmed. A businessman balances his budget. Hence the unbalanced budget which was actually pulling us out of the depression was the source of greater alarm than administrative failures which were actually much more dangerous. The American Businessman bosses his employees. Hence the encouragement of the C.I.O. was thought to be the forerunner of a revolution, in spite of the fact that never had industrial unrest been followed with less actual disorder.

The creed of the American Businessman was celebrated in our institutions of learning. Since the American Scholar was a minor divinity, some of his characteristics had to be assumed by the great industrial organization. Therefore colleges were endowed to prove that the predominant divinity was supported by reason and scholarship. All the Christian virtues were also ascribed to him—for the selfishness of business was an enlightened selfishness which resulted in the long run in unselfish conduct if it were only let alone.

The American Businessman was independent of his fellows. No individual could rule him. Hence the "rule of law above men" was symbolized by the Constitution. This meant that the American Businessman was an individual who was free from the control of any other individual and owed allegiance only to the Constitution. However, he was the only individual entitled to this kind of freedom. His employees were subject to the arbitrary control of this divinity. Their only freedom consisted in the supposed opportunity of laborers to become American businessmen themselves.

It is this mythology, operating long after the American Businessman has disappeared as an independent individual, which gives the great industrial organization an established place in our temporal government. Every demand on these great industrial structures is referred to the conception of the American Businessman as a standard.

Thus pension systems for great corporations are all right provided businessmen inaugurate them. Economic coercion is permitted provided these heroes accomplish it. Boondoggling of every kind is subject to no criticism if businessmen finance it. Charity and welfare work, provided they are used to portray businessmen in their softer and more sentimental moods, are lovely things. When undertaken by the Government, they are necessary evils because such activity impairs the dignity and prestige of our great national ideal type. The businessman is the only divinity supposed to conduct such affairs. Therefore one never hears a community chest spoken of as a necessary evil as the dole is. Private charity even in times when it is an obvious failure is supposed to be more efficient than government relief.

In this mythology are found the psychological motives for the decisions of courts, for the timidity of humanitarian action, for the worship of states rights and for the proof by scholars that the only sound way of thinking about government is a fiscal way of thinking. Move Communism or any other kind of creed into this country, keep the present national hierarchy of tutelary divinities, and one would soon find that the dialecticians and priests were ingenious enough to make communistic principles march the same way as the old ones. So long as the American Businessman maintains his present place in this mythological hierarchy, no practical inconvenience is too great to be sacrificed to do him honor— every humanitarian impulse which goes counter to the popular conception of how the businessman should act is soft and effeminate.

Coupled with the national heroes in every institutional

mythology is the national Devil. Our Devil is governmental interference. Thus we firmly believe in the inherent malevolence of government which interferes with business. Here are people who are not to be trusted—they are the bureaucrats, the petty tyrants, the destroyers of a rule of law. Organizations always tend to assume the characters given to them by popular mythology. Hence the government is no career for an up-and-coming young man. Governmental institutions are not to be trusted to hire their employees. We must control their inherent malevolence by Civil Service rules. Civil Service is a great protection for mediocrity and thus tends to make the government fit the bureaucratic preconceptions. Thus the powerful influence of the national hierarchy of gods moves institutions into patterns from which they cannot escape until the attitudes change.

Germany is a country which loves to wear uniforms. It is said that it is difficult to keep even German railway conductors from wearing out their uniforms at home. The national hero is a soldier. Therefore, no economic principles ever designed have prevented Germany from assuming the atmosphere of at best a military academy with a scholarly faculty, and at worst an armed camp.

How far nations can be induced to revise their mythologies is a psychological problem not unlike the problem of how to change the admiration and dislikes of the individual. The politician does not attempt to change the mythology. He works with it unscrupulously to get results. The trouble with him is not that his technique is bad but that his ends are not broad or humanitarian. Yet in our present medieval atmosphere it is his techniques which are condemned. His ends, in so far as they are selfish, are supposed to work for the greatest benefit of all in a free economic system.

Probably the only way in which mythologies actually change is through the rise to power of a new class whose traditional heroes are of a different mold. Nothing seems clearer than that the attitudes of any given ruling class are so set that all the arguments in the world will not change them.

This can be observed in revolutions of all kinds, peaceful as well as violent. A ruling class ceases to perform the functions necessary to distribute goods according to the demands of a people. A new class appears to satisfy those demands. At first it is looked down on. Gradually it accumulates a mythology and a creed. Finally all searchers for universal truth, all scholars, all priests (except, of course, unsound radicals), all educational institutions of standing, are found supporting that class and everyone feels that the search for legal and economic truth has reached a successful termination. We can observe the rise of a race of traders and money lenders against the system of law and economics of chivalry and feudalism which today looks incredibly romantic, but which then looked like the very bedrock of reality. No one would have dreamed in the Middle Ages that the despised creed of the trader and the money lender—a creed of selfishness and worship of the then lowest material values—should rise to be a compendium of everything most respectable in temporal affairs.

Today we can observe the rise of a class of engineers, salesmen, minor executives, and social workers—all engaged in actually running the country's temporal affairs. Current mythology puts them in the rôle of servants, not rulers. Social workers are given a subordinate rôle. For purposes of governmental policy their humanitarian ideas are positively dangerous, because they put consideration of actual efficiency in the distribution of goods above reverence for the independence and dignity of the businessman. It is as if a usurer attempted to sit at the table in social equality with the medieval baron to whom he was lending money.

Nevertheless, it is this great class of employees, working for salaries, which distributes the goods of the world. Traders still are possessed of the symbols of power. The new class, however, has already shown signs of developing a creed of its own and a set of heroes. In our universities it is represented by a group of younger economists, political scientists, and lawyers. True, these men are often branded as unsound. Older universities look at their new economic thinking with suspicion, but its prestige grows with the prestige of the class of business and social technicians which it represents. Its mythology does not include the worship of the American Businessman. So far it is destructive only. On the positive side it is as yet undeveloped. However, one should remember that a fully developed creed and mythology are not found until the class which they support is securely in power. Adam Smith did not think up principles by which the merchant and manufacturer gained power. He supplied them with a philosophy after they had taken charge of the temporal government.

The creeds and mythologies of smaller institutions always follow the pattern of the larger ones. The writer found the transition from the life of a trial lawyer to that of a professor at the Yale School of Law a most interesting one. The academic life was different from practice in that the scholarly heroes were men who dug up little sections of truth for the love of it—a purely monastic ideal. Yet this mythology was tempered and molded by the great overshadowing divinity, the American Businessman. Yale was doing what it could to search for truth in the same organized efficient way in which the United States Steel Corporation made steel. There was therefore much about Yale in 1930 in common with the Rotary Club of Laramie, Wyoming, from which the writer hailed. "Service" was the watchword and the organized "project" was the crusade. In 1930 the Institute of Human

Relations at Yale occupied the center of the stage, dedicated
to proving that scholars could incorporate research and
thereby gain the advantages of mass production. Dinners
were held and speeches made in imitation of the annual dinner of a chamber of commerce. Had the large corporation
retained its magic, perhaps the Institute of Human Relations
might have maintained its prestige. However, scholarship,
incorporated like a manufacturing plant, lost caste with the
distrust of the great corporation during the depression.
Therefore, at the Tercentenary at Harvard in 1936, we find
scholars using the symbol of the Supreme Court of the
United States rather than incorporated scholarship, because
the Court at the time was a more important symbol of safety
and security than the American business corporation.

The Change of "Democracy" from a Creed
to a Political Fact

CURIOUSLY enough, in all this holy war against Communism
and Fascism to make the world safe for our prevailing
divinity, we find very little spiritual conflict about the principles of democracy. Democracy was accepted as a political
fact, not as something to be chosen or rejected. The democratic tradition had become recognized as a tradition and had
ceased to be regarded as a set of guiding principles. All over
the world, except perhaps in the Orient, there was a recognition that popular majorities were necessary for a successful
government regardless of what the creed happened to be. A
strange thing had happened to democracy as a creed. Few
believed any more that it was a peculiarly sacred or divine
thing. The "principles" of democracy were not worshiped
as they once were, as fundamental truths. Everyone recognized the limitations of the average man—and few thought
that these limitations disappeared in a group.
   Democracy ceased being a creed. It simply became a name

for a type of organization controlled by voters. From this point of view men made two great discoveries in the art of government:

1. They discovered that it is immaterial whether democracy is morally beautiful or not. They recognized as a fact that it was more important that an institution keep in touch with the mass of its members than that it follow rational principles. The word "democracy" therefore came to represent the notion that political techniques which had nothing to do with rational principles were a necessary part of social control. This was first discovered in connection with the distribution of goods by large organizations. Advertising men used slogans rather than descriptions of their products. Politicians soon found the advantages of such techniques over either appeals to pure reason or the grosser forms of vote buying. Polls began to be taken on public questions—experts began to develop in the ascertaining of public attitudes. Principles and political platforms became more and more of a ceremony and less a matter of belief to those who wrote them.

2. They discovered that all sorts of symbols are necessary for the preservation of the political fact of democracy, many of which violate its creeds. The fact that political platforms were inconsistent with political action troubled people less and less.

This sort of political realism about democracy was brought home to us by the success of the dictatorships in Russia and Germany. In these countries the revolutionary governments undertook deliberately to arouse the intense enthusiasm of their peoples and to keep it at a high pitch. The method used was not rational; it was the rhythm of uniforms, salutes, marching feet, and national games. The strength of Hitler lay in the fact that he put everyone to work and managed to develop national pride. His weakness lay in his persecutions. Such persecutions are not, I believe, *necessary* to the exercise of national power or the development of national morale. The reason why they are apt to occur in times of change is that respectable people in such times are too devoted to principles to solve immediate problems or to build up morale by the objective use of ceremony. They are too obsessed with the principles of government by the people to know how it works.

This principle that national morale is more important than logic and that the present is more important than the future is little understood in an age when people who should know how to rule are lost in a search for universal truth. They constantly strive to ferret out the true principles of democracy and follow them logically. They think that "democracy" is a "form" of government which nations educated up to it consciously follow and discard at their peril. They think that it is another of those "systems" of government.

The old creed of democracy as our fathers knew it was a useful slogan to bind together those who rose to fill the gaps left by an incompetent aristocracy. It was a useful slogan to stir national pride in a people who had no ruling class. Like all creeds it was in no way descriptive. It borrowed the old symbols of aristocracy since it had to represent all the current conflicting ideals. Thus the lack of an ecclesiastical hierarchy was filled by the slogan, "The voice of the people is the voice of God." The gap left by the absence of an aristocracy was bridged by the constant reference to the "nobility" of the common people and reference to the people as "king." The necessity to personify a ruler and invest him with divine power was filled in the personification of the people. Under these slogans a small ruling class developed in the United States.

The democratic creed of that ruling class, however, was full of so many hidden conflicts that it developed in America more *sub rosa* institutions than in any other Western nation.

The "people" in this democracy were supposed to choose sound economic principles in preference to unsound ones like a scholargarchy. They were to reject unsound legal principles like a theocracy. In fact, the people were permitted to play every conceivable rôle that had marched in the pageant of history since the Roman Empire. Only one thing they were not permitted to do in public, and that was to think realistically about their government.

Therefore, our real government was conducted by non-respectable politicians. Exceptions there were, such as Jefferson and Roosevelt, who combined political technique with aristocratic background. Such men incurred the bitter enmity of their friends as traitors to their class. Actual political leaders in the peculiar democracy we established were generally the type who theoretically should have been distrusted by the people, because they appealed to the emotions instead of reasoning analytically for the benefit of thinking men. Hence, when the people of New York City or Chicago sought real representation they were forced to choose organizations like Tammany Hall or the Thompson machine, since respectable people could not think politically. And choose them they did, in spite of the gloom of our editorial table-pounders at the refusal of the people to learn the lessons of history.

The only class which was permitted to think objectively about what it was doing without violating its own creed was big business. In this area both learned and popular philosophy proved that whatever mistakes business made canceled each other, that its greed was only a form of unselfishness, and that its corruption was only the work of an occasional emissary of Satan sent up from below to plague mankind.

Of course, the law and the economics which permitted this class to act practically allowed its members to be respectable and efficient at the same time. In this favorable atmosphere their natural organizing ability was not hampered by taboos. They developed a productive plant which was the marvel of the modern world. As a creed, democracy never even remotely resembled the actual democracy which existed in this country, but as a political fact it produced a spiritual government in Washington to represent its ideals and a temporal government in our industrial centers which gave scope for the productive energy of its people and which, at the same time, never lost their support, violated their taboos, or contradicted the mythology they had set up for themselves.

In our thinking about democracy we have dropped to a large extent the medieval atmosphere. We do not argue about it any more as we argue about a creed. We have ceased to write books describing how sacred it is. We realize that in its essence it means that an effective leader must maintain the morale as well as the discipline of his army. It has become for us a symbol which is not intellectually questioned and which at the same time may be practically used. Even respectable people today are acquiring skill in the use of political techniques. The effects are noticeable. A better class of political leaders is in charge of our political machines. Grosser and more unpleasant forms of political chicanery are not used to the same extent as in 1900. As men have gradually ceased to believe in the democratic slogans as truths, political techniques have become less the exclusive property of unscrupulous people.

Thus has democracy changed from a creed to a word describing a political fact—from a set of symbols which must be followed regardless of their practicality or convenience to a recognition that every institution must keep the faith and loyalty of its members, or perish. Today, when sophisticated men speak of democracy as the only workable method of government, they mean that a government which does not carry its people along with it emotionally, which depends on force, is insecure. They mean that it is better for a government to do foolish things which can have popular support than wise things which arouse people against it. They mean that if a man is not contented, material comforts will do him no good. They mean that the art of government consists in the technique of achieving willing popular acceptance; that what people *ought* to want is immaterial; that democratic government consists only in giving them what they *do* want; that progress in government can come only by improving the *wants* of the people through the technique of removing their prejudices; and, finally, that the removal of prejudice must come first or material and humanitarian progress, imposed by force, will fail. When we consider democracy as a political fact, we are no longer concerned with the question of whether it ought to be admired as a fine thing or condemned as a stupid thing.

Our thinking about symbols of money and credit seldom takes such a fact-minded point of view. Here we are caught in formulas which pretend to be universal truths. We believe in the capitalistic system, as we used to believe in democracy, not as a tool, but as a set of abstract principles to be followed. The systems of government over which we have our theological disputes are no longer monarchy, aristocracy, and democracy, but Capitalism, Communism, and Fascism. Capitalism is a good thing in the abstract. It has its following of learned men and philosophers. It is no more descriptive of social organization today than the theology of the monarchy was descriptive before the French Revolution. It is instead an arsenal of weapons to be used against new organizations, rising because of a compelling need, but hampered because they have as yet found no place in accepted institutional mythology. The terms Communism and Fascism are used to denounce these new organizations as breeders of heresy. The acceptance of the slogans of Capitalism as tools rather than as truths is still over the horizon.

CHAPTER III

The Folklore of 1937

IN which it is explained how the great sciences of law and economics and the little imaginary people who are supposed to be guided by these sciences affect the daily lives of those who make, distribute, and consume our goods.

THE folklore of 1937 was expressed principally by the literature of law and economics. Here were found elaborately framed the little pictures which men had of society as it ought to be. Of course, this literature was not called folklore. No one thought of sound principles of law or economics as a religion. They were considered as inescapable truths, as natural laws, as principles of justice, and as the only method of an ordered society. This is a characteristic of all vital folklore or religion.[1] The moment that folklore is recognized to be only folklore it ceases to have the effect of folklore. It descends to the place of poetry or fairy tales which affect us only in our romantic moments. For example, years ago Mr. Justice Cardozo pointed out that law was really literature. This is true. Yet if it were generally recognized to be true, the particular kind of literature known as law would not have the kind of influence it has today.

The effect of the peculiar folklore of 1937 was to encourage the type of organization known as industry or business and

[1] Polybius, writing about the Roman social order before the birth of Christ, observed:

"But it seems to me the most distinctive superiority of the Roman political and social order is to be found in the nature of their religious convictions; and I mean the very thing which other peoples look upon with reproach, as superstition. But it nevertheless maintains the cohesion of the Roman state." (*Polybius*, VI, 56.)

discourage the type known as government. Under the protection of this folklore the achievements of American business were remarkable. There was no questioning of myths which supported independent empires by those engaged in those enterprises. So-called private institutions like General Motors never lost their direction through philosophical debate. The pioneer efforts at industrial organization in this country had been wasteful beyond belief, but bold and confident.

With respect to political government, however, our superstitions had the opposite effect. They were not a cohesive force, but a destructive and disintegrating one. The pioneer efforts of the Government were timid, indecisive, and ineffective. When it became necessary for the Government to fill gaps in the national structure in which private business enterprise was an obvious failure, the myths and folklore of the time hampered practical organization at every turn. Men became more interested in planning the culture of the future —in saving posterity from the evils of dictatorship or bureaucracy, in preventing the American people from adopting Russian culture on the one hand, or German culture on the other—than in the day-to-day distribution of food, housing, and clothing to those who needed them. Mystical attacks on practical measures achieved an astonishing degree of success. Debaters and orators rose to the top in such an atmosphere and technicians twiddled their thumbs, unable to use their skills.

The operation of this legal and economic folklore which paralyzed organizations with the name "government" attached to them will make a fascinating study for the future historian. He will note a striking resemblance to the medieval myths which impeded medical knowledge for hundreds of years. He will observe men refusing benefits obviously to their practical advantage when tendered by the Government, because they violated current taboos. A few incidents will illustrate how men constantly sacrificed present advantage in order to avoid the future retribution supposed to result from the violation of these taboos.

In the spring of 1936 the writer heard a group of bankers, businessmen, lawyers, and professors, typical of the learned and conservative thinkers of the time, discussing a crisis in the affairs of the bankrupt New York, New Haven, and Hartford Railroad—once the backbone of New England, the support of its institutions and its worthy widows and orphans. They were expressing indignation that a bureaucratic Interstate Commerce Commission, operating from Washington, had decreed that passenger rates be cut almost in half. Every man there would directly benefit from the lower rate. None were stockholders. Yet all were convinced that the reduction in rate should be opposed by all conservative citizens and they were very unhappy about this new outrage committed by a government bent on destroying private business by interfering with the free judgment of its managers.

This sincere indignation and gloom had its roots not in selfishness nor the pursuit of the profit of the moment, but in pure idealism. These men, though they owned no stock, were willing to forego the advantage of lower fares to save the railroad from the consequences of economic sin. They took a long-range view and decided that in the nature of things the benefits of the lower rates would be only temporary, because they had been lowered in violation of the great principle that government should not interfere with business. Some sort of catastrophe was bound to result from such an action. The writer tried to get the picture of the impending catastrophe in clearer detail. Did the gentlemen think that, under the new rates, trains would stop running and maroon them in the City of Elms? It appeared that no one quite believed this. The collapse which they feared was more nebulous. Trains would keep on running, but with a sinister change in the character of the service. Under government influence, it would become as unpleasant as the income taxes were unpleasant. And in the background was an even more nebulous fear. The Government would, under such conditions, have to take over the railroad, thus ushering in bureaucracy and regimentation. Trains would run, but there would be no pleasure in riding on them any more.

There was also the thought that investors would suffer. This was difficult to put into concrete terms because investors already had suffered. The railroad was bankrupt. Most of the gentlemen present had once owned stock, but had sold it before it had reached its present low. Of course, they wanted the stock to go up again, along with everything else, provided, of course, that the Government did not put it up by "artificial" means, which would be inflation.

The point was raised as to whether the Interstate Commerce Commission was right in believing that the road would actually be more prosperous under the lower rates. This possibility was dismissed as absurd. Government commissions were always theoretical. This was a tenet of pure faith about which one did not even argue.

In addition to faith, there were figures. One gentleman present had the statistical data on *why* the railroad would suffer. In order to take care of the increased traffic, new trains would have to be added, new brakemen and conductors hired, more money put into permanent equipment. All such expenditures would, of course, reflect advantageously on the economic life of New Haven, remove persons from relief rolls, stimulate the heavy goods industries, and so on. This, however, was argued to be unsound. Since it was done in violation of sound principle it would damage business confidence, and actually result in less capital goods expenditures, in spite of the fact that it appeared to the superficial observer to be creating more. And besides, where was the money coming from? This worry was also somewhat astonishing, because it appeared that the railroad actually could obtain the necessary funds for the present needed improvements. However, the answer to that was that posterity would have to pay through the nose.

And so the discussion ended on a note of vague worry. No one was happy over the fact that he could travel cheaper. No one was pleased that employment would increase, or that the heavy industries would be stimulated by the reduction of rates. Out of pure mystical idealism, these men were opposing every selfish interest both of themselves and the community, because the scheme went counter to the folklore to which they were accustomed. And since it went counter to that folklore, the same fears resulted from every other current scheme which violated traditional attitudes, whether it was relief, housing, railroad rates, or the Securities Exchange Act. Anything which could be called governmental interference in business necessarily created bureaucracy, regimentation, inflation and put burdens on posterity.

All this discussion was backed by much learning and theory. Yet it was easy to see its emotional source. These men pictured the railroad corporation as a big man who had once been a personal friend of theirs. They were willing to undergo financial sacrifice in order to prevent injustice being done to that big man. The personality of the corporation was so real to them that it was impossible to analyze the concept into terms of selfish interest. Does one think of personal gain when a member of one's family is insulted? With that emotional beginning, the balance of the discussion flowed out of the learned myths of the time, and ended where all the economic arguments of the time ended, in a parade of future horrors. The thinking was as primitive and naïve as all such thinking must be when it is divorced from practical issues and involved in prevailing taboos. As to the merits of the rate reduction from a practical point of view, neither the writer, nor any member of the group, knew anything. Yet such was the faith of these men in the formula they recited, that they felt that knowledge of details was completely unnecessary in having a positive and unchangeable opinion.

The way of thinking illustrated by the above incident is a stereotype. Its pattern is the same to whatever problems it is applied. It starts by reducing a situation, infinitely complicated by human and political factors, to a simple parable which illustrates fundamental and immutable principles. It ends by proving that the sacrifice of present advantage is necessary in order to protect everything we hold most dear. All such discussions end with arguments based on freedom, the home, tyranny, bureaucracy, and so on. All lead into a verbal crusade to protect our system of government. In this way certainty of opinion is possible for people who know nothing whatever about the actual situation. They feel they do not have to know the details. They know the principles.

Take another example. In 1937 a new device known as the "sit-down" strike was most effectively used against the General Motors Corporation. Here was a fascinating struggle to develop labor unity and leadership in this country, headed by a great organizer, John L. Lewis. As in all combat situations, both sides believed intensely in the morality and sacredness of their cause. A realist observing the struggle without the moral preconceptions of either of the opposing organizations might make a guess as to the final outcome of the labor movement. He would realize, however, that it was only a political guess and that a guess based on a search for the proper fundamental principles of how strikes "should" be conducted by right-thinking conservative strikers would have no validity whatever.

But here again editorial table-pounders in our most respectable publications insisted that the real issue was whether, using the analogy of the sit-down strike, irresponsible men would not feel that they had the right to destroy our homes by conducting sit-down strikes in the parlors. Liberty, free-dom, the home, were again at stake as they had been in the case of the New Haven rate cut. Nothing could have been more absurd than the suggestion that this great industrial struggle was in reality concerned with the right of indi-viduals to undisturbed possession of their homes. Yet this was the position usually taken by most of the so-called "thinking" people who filed income-tax returns.

The great debate in 1937 over President Roosevelt's pro-posal to put more liberal judges on the Supreme Court of the United States offers another example of this way of thinking. There was, of course, every reason for those who opposed the extension of national power represented by Roosevelt's pro-gram, to cling to the Court as a last line of defense against a popular mandate. Here was a way of taking away from a great popular majority the fruits of their recent victory at the polls. Yet much of the opposition to the proposal came not from those who were opposed but from those in favor of the main outlines of the Roosevelt policies. They were actu-ally afraid of the exercise of an admitted constitutional power to reform the attitude of the judiciary. The argument cen-tered on the familiar symbols of regimentation, bureaucracy, freedom, and the home, which actually had as little to do with the issues involved as they had to do with the enforced reduction of rates on the New Haven Railroad.

We use as an illustration of this type of argument the issue of the *American Bar Association Journal* for April, 1937. In this issue eight distinguished and alarmed leaders of the bar and one editor made it abundantly clear that the proposal to increase the membership of that Court was fundamentally immoral. That being so, it followed that the wages of sin is death. Grave peril of a somewhat unspecific character lay in wait for us. The nation was about to lose its immortal soul and become at best a bureaucracy, and at worst a tyranny. The whole issue was keyed to a note of warning of impending doom.

For example, President Stinchfield, who contributed the first article, told us that if we adopted the plan "we shall have government from Washington covering a territory of 130 million people." The superficial observer might have thought that this was one of the objectives for which the Civil War was fought and therefore had its good points. But President Stinchfield went on to say: "We must inevitably become a government by bureaucracy. . . ." Such mysterious matters, of course, could not be proved, but President Stinchfield's faith in the malevolence of Congress was such that he didn't think proof necessary. He said: "I think we are in great danger at the moment."

Mr. Olney, who followed Mr. Stinchfield, was also gloomy and sad about the remote future, through whose mists his prophetic vision penetrated without any difficulty. He was particularly worried because he was afraid that labor unions would disappear if the President's proposal was passed. He said that the measure would put them "at the mercy of a President and Congress who choose to pass a law forbidding the persuasion of men to join a union." This was a very odd thing to worry about just after the triumph of John L. Lewis. However, Mr. Olney explained how foolish it was for labor to be cheerful about the future right to organize. He said: "It is no answer to this to say that such a thing could not happen in this country. It has happened elsewhere in countries no less civilized than ours. It has happened in Germany and Italy."

Elsewhere in the article Mr. Olney pointed out that Germany and Italy were not the only countries we may come to resemble. We might also become like the South American republics, of whose judiciary Mr. Olney seemed to have a low opinion. The trouble with Germany, Italy, and the South American republics was that in their blindness they bowed down to the wrong principles, like the heathen. This, Mr. Olney thought, was hard on Germany, but it was a lucky break for us, because as a result labor and the underprivileged groups in this country could now see the dangers of getting what they want.

Mr. Olney's analysis made the complex conditions in Europe and South America simple and easy to understand and showed just why we are on the verge of becoming like these countries.

The next article was by Louis A. Lecher, a distinguished member of the Milwaukee Bar. It was evident that he had been thinking along the same lines as Mr. Olney. However, he was more specific. The Potato Act was, he thought, not only an unwise agricultural measure, but also a subtly concealed attack on human liberty.

George Wharton Pepper contributed an article in which he said of the President's proposal: "Here the question is not whether A or B shall be elected to political office but whether A and B shall be deprived of their guaranties of civil and religious liberty."

He saw in the plan danger to labor and the Jews and the Catholics and the schools, and pointed out that professors like the writer were foes of education within its own household, because they did not realize that the defeat of the plan was essential to academic freedom. He observed that "unless labor leaders, Jews, Catholics, educators and editors come to their senses before it is too late they will find themselves in an America which is anything but a land of the free."

Mr. Donovan then spoke. He analyzed the groups that were in imminent danger from the plan. They were religious groups, racial groups, citizens of foreign descent, labor unions, and persons charged with crime. All of these people would, in Mr. Donovan's opinion, be in a bad way if more justices were added to the Court under the plan.

These symbolic arguments were almost identical with the arguments in the preceding presidential campaign, because they were the automatic response to the same kind of irritation. This same pattern of argument always greets the struggle of any new organization to find a logical place among traditional institutions.

Let us go back to the Middle Ages for our final example of this way of thinking. In the seventeenth century the University of Paris, supported by an ancient learned tradition, with faculties of law, medicine, and theology, occupied a position in medicine not unlike the position of the Supreme Court of the United States in government today. It was the duty of these carefully chosen scholars to make a unified whole out of the learning of the time. They spent their lives studying those fundamental principles, the violation of which brings ruin. Their logic was as unassailable as the economic and legal logic of today. They had the same distrust of immediate practical advantage, the same fear of mysterious and impending moral disaster lying in wait to destroy the national character of a people who deserted fundamental principles to gain present ends. The medieval physician could see no profit in saving a man's body if thereby he lost his soul. Nor did he think that any temporary physical relief could ever be worth the violation of the fundamental principles of medicine.

The remedy for fever established by the learning of the time was the art of bleeding to rid the body of those noxious vapors and humors in the blood which were the root of the illness. Of course, patients sickened and died in the process, but they were dying for a medical principle, so it was thoroughly worth-while. To depart from that principle would have the same effect on human health as the failure to shoot strikers occupying the plant of an industrial concern in a sit-down strike, or as the tampering with the Supreme Court of the United States has today on social well-being.

Magic had the same importance in the art of healing physical ills in the Middle Ages that it has today in the determination of governmental policy. Practical remedies, like sanitation, were not sufficiently mysterious to be respected. A people accustomed to living in filth had great faith in the curative properties of filth. There was more magic in disagreeable drugs than in pleasant ones, because disease was personified as an evil element that had to be attacked and driven away through some sort of combat in which pleasant remedies were a sign of weakness in the face of the enemy. The tactics in the war against disease bore a striking resemblance to the tactics in the modern war against social problems, in that the principles of medicine were much more sacred and important than the health of the patient.

Such were the attitudes of those learned in medicine in 1638 when the Jesuits in Peru discovered quinine. The cures which were accomplished by the use of this drug were marvelous, due in part to its own merit and in part to the fact that patients escaped the bleeding process. It was natural that such a radical departure from established precedent should be viewed with alarm. Therefore, it was not surprising that the University of Paris declared the use of quinine unconstitutional and banned the drug as dangerous.

The reasoning of the faculty was clear and persuasive. Since quinine did nothing to relieve the noxious vapors in the blood, immediate benefits must necessarily be an "artificial" cure or "panacea" which left the patient worse off than before in spite of his own temporary delusion that he felt better. The use of quinine was an attack on the whole fundamental theory of medicine, which had been carefully correlated with religion and theology. Certainly the temporary relief of a few sufferers could never be worth the overthrow of medical principles to the confusion of all the learning and experience of the past. They talked about it like this: "What is the emergency at present which should force the people to adopt the dictatorial rather than the democratic method for the solution of the very real constitutional problems which undoubtedly exist? There is none." (James Truslow Adams, "The Court Issue and Democracy," *New York Times Magazine,* February 21, 1937.)

However, it was more than a medical problem. It was a moral problem which affected the character, the freedom, and the homes of everyone. Fortunately, the unlearned people of the time, like those of today, were constantly forgetting the great moral issues of the future for the practical comfort of the moment. Hence the use of quinine eventually became common. The significant thing, however, was that it had to be introduced by a quack who concealed it in a curious compound of irrelevant substances.

In such an atmosphere there was at least a chance that a quack would be right; there was a certainty that a physician would be wrong. The Jesuits were considered by their enemies the most dangerous religious bureaucrats of the time, a fanatical group of zealots for whom the end always justified the means. They had made many people uncomfortable with their crusading. One could not adopt their remedies without adopting their principles any more than the United States today can develop national power without becoming like the Germans under Hitler. And so the dreaded specter of Jesuitism hung over the use of quinine, as Communism and Fascism hang over soil conservation and crop insurance today.

This way of thinking is as old as the desire of men to escape from the hard necessity of making practical judgments in the comfort and certainty of an appeal to priests. It controlled the thinking about the human body in the Middle Ages. It controls our thinking about the body politic today. Out of it have been spun our great legal and economic principles which have made our learning about government a search for universal truth rather than a set of observations about the techniques of human organization.

Medieval Attitudes in Law and Economics

THE years before and during the great depression in America, which were feudal in their economic organization, present a spectacle of a continuous search for a set of rational formulas designed to enable men to govern with a minimum of exercise of judgment, and with a minimum of personal power. The historian of the future will be amazed at a great people's simple belief that sound legal and economic principles, discovered by close students of these mysteries, were the only means to national salvation. He will be equally amazed at the naïve fears that opportunistic action or judgment based not upon learning but on political expediency, whatever its temporary benefits, would necessarily lead to disaster if it did not fit into some preconceived theory. The history of the time is the story of men who struggled gallantly and unsuccessfully to make government correspond to this theory about it. It is intelligible only if we start out with a bird's-eye view of what men thought were the principles which made the social structure survive.

We have already analyzed the conception of the "thinking man" which was essential to all political debate. Without him, public discussion of rational principles and systems of government would have been impossible. He was the great spirit which hovered over all governmental institutions.

This particular type of folklore had ceased to affect medicine in 1937. Medical principles were not supposed to be a matter which was to be thought out, in the way governmental principles were thought out. The difference between the attitudes of medical science and physical science was very subtle, particularly since the political scientist of 1937 always *claimed* to be doing the same thing as the physical scientist. That difference therefore cannot be defined; it can only be illustrated.

Thirty years ago medical men were still fighting for principle, just as political men are fighting for it today. There were the homeopathic and the allopathic schools of medicine. The thinking man was supposed to choose between these two schools in hiring his physician. There was much public debate on their merits. Disciples of each school were supposed to stand together as a matter of party loyalty. They were the missionaries of a medical creed.

Today the public is no longer asked to choose between conflicting medical principles (at least not to the same extent). Medicine has been taken over by men of skill rather than men of principle. The medical sects, such as chiropractic, which still argues fundamental principle in the way the political scientist argues it, are unimportant. There is little left in medicine for thinking men to debate. Physicians are chosen on a guess as to their expertness. Hospitals no longer take sides. Therefore the concept of the "thinking man" is no longer essential.

In advertising the "thinking man" has gone so completely that a modern advertising agency would be amazed at the suggestion that the best way to sell goods is by making a rational appeal.

In government the concept still reigns supreme. Men are still asked to diagnose the ills of social organization through the darkened lenses of "schools" of legal or economic theory. They still worry about choosing a "system" of government.

Fact-minded persons who do not believe in the "thinking man" and who do not expect to gain political objectives by making rational appeals to him are not considered respectable. They are called "politicians" and not "political scientists." The political scientists are the high priests of our governmental mythology. The politician is still in the position of the Jewish money lender of the Middle Ages.

In examining that curious folklore, still a powerful influence in 1937, the future historian will observe that during the first half of the twentieth century the principles of government were divided into two great branches, law and economics. Each had its specialists, who were supposed to work hand in hand in the joint enterprise of discovering the true principles of government. The law, on the one hand, preserved those great moral values of freedom and individualism by pointing out that the opportunistic action, which seemed best for the moment, often concealed dangerous moral traits. It was supposed to guard us against well-meaning individuals who, in their desire to alleviate human suffering and promote efficiency for the present, were leading us into future bureaucracy, regimentation, and dictatorship. Economics, on the other hand, supplied the principles which, if properly studied, would make incoherent legislative bodies act with unity and coherence, and which, if properly propagandized among the solid citizenry, would insure the selection of legislators who could distinguish between sound and unsound principles. Between the two sets of principles it was thought possible to avoid the personal element in government.

The future historian will also mark the paradox that there was little agreement on what were the sound theories in 1937, and at the same time almost unanimous agreement that good government followed only upon the selection of sound theories. No program for the alleviation of any press-

ing problem could win any sort of acceptance without having behind it some theory logically consistent with the more
general superstitions concerning the function of government.
Men believed that there were several defined systems of government—Capitalism, Communism, Fascism—which bright
men had thought up and lesser men accepted, all of them in
operation in various parts of the world. It was the duty of
the American people to make a free-will choice between
them. The great ideological battle in 1937 was whether Capitalism was worth preserving. Most people thought it should
be preserved. There were many intelligent humanitarian
people, however, who thought that it should be abandoned
and a new system inaugurated, usually called Socialism. This
new system on paper seemed preferable to Capitalism. Yet it
was constantly pointed out by its opponents that if one tried
to obtain Socialism, one got either Fascism or Communism,
with their attendant evils of regimentation, bureaucracy, dictatorship, and so on, and that individualism disappeared.

It was a complicated business, this preservation of the capitalistic system in 1937 against the other "isms" and alien
ideals. There was first the task of defining what Capitalism
really was. This was a constant process. It had to be done
every day and each new restatement led only to the necessity
of further definition. The preservation of Capitalism also required that practical plans be tested by expert economic theorists who looked at each practical measure through the spectacles of economic abstractions, in order not to be confused by
immediate objectives. Thus child labor had to be debated, not
on the basis of whether it was desirable for children to work,
but in the light of its effect on the American home in ten
years, if it were followed to its logical conclusion. Measures
for the conservation of oil, or regulation of agriculture, had
to be considered without relation to immediate benefits either
to oil or agriculture. Tendencies were regarded as far more

important than immediate effects, and the danger to posterity actually seemed more real than the danger to existing persons.

The capitalistic system in America had two sets of rules, one economic and the other legal, determining what the limits of governmental control should be. Economic theory had no separate institution to speak ex cathedra, other than the two political parties, each of which hired experts to study it and advise them. Whatever was produced by any political platform had to have its background of scholarly research. It was the duty of each party to consult only sound economists. Legal theory, on the other hand, was manufactured by the Supreme Court of the United States. There were two parties in the Supreme Court of the United States, each with its own legal theory. However, it was generally agreed that what the majority of judges thought was the real essence of the Constitution. It was not left to the people to decide between sound and unsound legal theory, and therefore the opinions of dissenting judges, unlike the opinions of dissenting economists, were not available in political debate, at least prior to Roosevelt's attack on the Court. This was because law concerned the spiritual welfare of the people and preserved their form of government, whereas economics concerned only their material welfare. In spiritual things it is essential that men do right according to some final authority. There was thought to be no such compelling reason to prevent them from ruining themselves economically.

The general idea of the Supreme Court's function is represented by the cartoon on the next page, in which the economic and social legislation of the day is thrown out of the august portals of the Supreme Court, stripped of the plausible humanitarian disguises which had deceived both the President and Congress. This gives a very accurate picture of what the great mass of conservative people thought the Court was doing for them. They did not trust themselves to

decide whether a humanitarian or practical scheme was really
government by edict, or would lead to government by edict.
They knew that such things seldom appeared on the surface, and that they required great learning to analyze. However, more intelligent people required a more complicated

Cartoon by Herbert Johnson in the *Saturday Evening Post.*
Reproduced by special permission.

THANKS FOR THE HORSE-AND-BUGGY RIDE

explanation, because they preferred long words to pictures.
Hence the years of the depression produced thousands of
learned dissertations, which came to every possible sort of
conclusion as to the constitutionality of various measures.
These articles did not make the law clear. They did, however, make it clear that there was such a thing as law, which
experts could discover through reason.

It was this faith in a higher law which made the Supreme

Court the greatest unifying symbol in American government. Here was the one body which could still the constant debate, and represent to the country the ideal of a government of fundamental principles. On this Court the whole ideal of a government of laws and not of the competing opinions of men appeared to depend. Here only was there a breathing spell from the continual din of arguments about governmental philosophy which were never settled.

The legislative branches of the Government were under constant suspicion, and their acts were presumed to be malevolent. The incompetency of Congress was an assumed fact everywhere. The great trouble with the legislative branches was that they were influenced by an unlearned, untheoretical, illogical, and often corrupt force called "politics." Politics was continually putting unworthy persons in power, as opposed to business, where, because of economic law, only worthy persons rose to the top. A body influenced by political considerations could not give any disinterested judgment as to the soundness of any economic theory. Hence Congress was constantly picking unsound theories, listening to unsound economists, and letting the practical convenience of the moment overweigh the needs of posterity. Politicians were the kind of people who would not care if a thing called bureaucracy was established as long as it gave them jobs.

The only trustworthy check against unsound economic theory was not the politician, but that great body of thinking men and women who composed the better class of the public. Yet even such people were easily confused in those days when the noise of competing theories was loudest. The only way of straightening them out was by constant preaching, which had the weakness of all preaching throughout the centuries, in that sin and heresy were always rising against it. Hence the age-old cry of the disappointed preacher to his erring flock was constantly heard in the land. As typical of this, a distinguished economist from Columbia University spoke the discouragement of his brethren in 1936 as follows:

NEED REALISTIC WARNINGS.—Professor Ralph West Robey, of Columbia University, appealed to professional economists to make more realistic warnings of economic disaster if present conditions continued. He had pointed out that, despite an 86 per cent increase in federal revenue since 1932, the nation was faced with the largest peace time deficit in its history. He added that the cost of government in the United States is now about one-third of the national income, and that if this deficit were provided for by taxation, the average per capita tax would be some 20 per cent higher than that in England.

But, he added, the public no longer listens to economists who foresee trouble ahead.

PUBLIC DEAF TO WARNINGS.—"The result has been," he said, "that the public has ceased to be frightened when it hears economists prophesying collapse and disaster. It has come to believe, if I may steal the phrase of a friend, that when an economist yells 'Wolf! Wolf!!' it probably means nothing more significant than that the administration has pulled another white rabbit out of the hat.

"Such a situation, it seems to me, is most distressing. I think it is distressing because I have the utmost confidence in economic reasoning and in economic principles." (*New Haven Register,* May 11, 1936.)

Economists generally felt in those dark days as Dr. Robey did. Here was careful scholarly work, leading to a set of theories which, if followed, would cure social disease as well as the imperfect nature of man permitted it to be cured. And here was an ungrateful public which would not listen to Dr. Robey's sound economics. It might seem strange, therefore, to the reader, examining this most interesting folklore from a detached point of view, that the sound economists did not demand a Supreme Court of Economics. Why should they entrust to popular judgment this scholarly task, when they

refused to entrust to popular judgment the somewhat easier
task of legal reasoning?

The answer to this question takes us into some of the un-
examined religious assumptions which the folklore of 1937
had in common with the Christian religion which was its
heritage. It went back to the paradox of the relationship of
sin and virtue, and the mystical nature of free will. God, according to an earlier theology, had his choice of making men
keep to the straight and narrow path by discipline, or by
persuasion. Weighing the advantages of these two different
methods, he preferred to make him free to sin in order to
make a more noble fellow out of him. Neither God nor the
economists of 1937 desired a nation of slaves. Therefore the
economists would have rejected as unthinkable the organization of a Supreme Court of Economics, on the ground that
even a benevolent dictatorship is bad because it abolishes
freedom. It had been evident for a long time that the only
possible method of making *laissez faire* economics, or indeed
any other planned system of economic principles work,
would be to force people to accept them. But it was far better
to trust to the feeble judgment of the common herd, and to
guide them through love of virtue and fear of hell, of Inflation, or Bureaucracy, or Regimentation, or whatever name
hell happened to have in the particular field of learning, at
the particular time. Of course, the results were discouraging
to the economists. They regretted man's tendency to follow
false economic reasoning, just as the preachers regretted
man's tendency to sin. Nevertheless, they felt that the only
refuge was in a deeper search for the Word and in more
fervent preaching.

This was the way that most intelligent, socially minded,
"thinking men" thought. Of course, those who actually ran
the Government were compelled to act on an entirely different set of assumptions. Politicians were interested in getting

votes, and such high-sounding theory had nothing whatever to do with the process. Everybody knew this, but it was regarded as a shameful thing that it should be so. Therefore, the efforts of reformers were directed toward abolishing this distressing phenomenon. They argued that if men who did not stoop to use political tricks would only go into politics, and if people only would elect them, then political tricks would disappear from government. The efforts along this line achieved about the same success as the age-old effort to abolish sensuality from love. Everyone realized this, but considered it no excuse for abandoning the effort.

Law and Obedience to Authority

THERE was only one area where the prevailing theory limited the operation of group free will. Men could choose between sound and unsound economic theories, but they must not be permitted to choose between sound and unsound constitutional theories. To prevent them from erring on this point, a scholargarchy was set up, with complete autocratic power. To a superficial observer, this might seem a denial of the beauty of group free will, but closer examination showed that it was not. For the function of the Supreme Court was not to prevent people from choosing what kind of constitution they desired, but to prevent them from changing their form of government *without knowing it*. Congress in its ignorance was constantly passing laws with purely practical objectives, which really changed the constitution without giving the people a chance to exercise their free will on that important subject. Therefore, some autocratic power had to be set up to apply the complicated scholarly techniques to such measures, not to prevent the people from exercising their free will on the Constitution, but to prevent them from doing it inadvertently.

Immersed in such theories, no student of government, economics, or law could look at the conduct of the institutions about which he was thinking without the same sort of nausea that an idealistic lover of bees and butterflies feels when she overturns a stone and sees some big black bugs crawling about in a loathsome manner. A similar attitude produced the same results in the study of government as it would have produced in biology. Facts about social organization of which men did not approve were not treated as facts, but as sins.

From this point of view it became the duty of everyone to denounce organized political factions as low things unworthy of the attention of courageous statesmen. Party platforms were the only reality—not the social and political pressures which force such platforms into a series of inconsistent compromises. The remedy was to ignore the pressures and make the platforms courageous and consistent. We were supposed to elect to office only those persons who did not care whether they were reëlected or not.

Of course, no political party could carry out these principles without political suicide, but this only meant that political parties were shot through with politics. Hence everyone demanded the kind of political party which thought more of posterity than getting votes for its leaders. Everyone realized, of course, that this was impossible, and the conflict created spiritual trouble, indecision, and a greater variety of literary and oratorical nonsense than the world has ever known heretofore.

To find peace, men denounced government by men, and sought relief by reciting principles. The fundamental assumption of the folklore about government during the great depression was that principles could be more trusted than organizations. Organizations were dangerous because of their tendency to err and stray. Principles, provided that they were sound, endured forever, and could alone make up for the constant tendency of social groups to backslide.

The Dawn of a Different Attitude toward Individual Maladjustments

ALL this folklore persisted in a time when the theory of free will, sin, and repentance was disappearing from the thinking about individuals' troubles. Psychiatrists and psychologists no longer explained individual conduct on the basis of a free-will choice between good and evil. Such a way of thinking had led in the past to curing the insane by preaching away the devil which had entered the patient. By 1937 people had lost interest in theoretical ethical principles for maladjusted individuals. The term "sinner" had gone from all sophisticated psychology. The concept of the devil had disappeared from the anatomy of the individual mind. Indeed, the idea that any man was a single integrated individual had disappeared, and it was recognized that each individual was a whole cast of characters, each appearing on the stage under the influence of different stimuli. In diagnosing an individual's maladies, the psychiatrist found out what his fantasies were and, without bothering whether they were true or false, attempted to cure him by recognizing these fantasies as part of the problem.

The psychiatrists, like physicians, were not concerned with the theoretical definition of the good mind, or the perfect human body. Even where they read of such definitions by their more theoretical brethren, they did not attempt to fit their particular patients into these molds. Ignoring the speculation of what the man would be in twenty years, or the effect of their treatment on posterity, they proceeded to make the insane person as comfortable and as little of a nuisance to himself and his fellow man as possible, from day to day. They

did not spend their time deploring insanity, or the existence
of psychopathic personalities. Their attitude toward their
patients was rather one of intense interest. And in this atmosphere curative techniques developed, and men actually
learned.

The Faith in Principles Rather than Organizations

In 1937 there was little of this point of view in legal or economic thinking. The point of view of the psychiatrist had
long been part of the stock in trade of that low class called
politicians. However, the attitude seldom was in evidence
when respectable people talked or thought about government. There were exceptions here and there in colleges, but
that influence had failed to reach the minds of respectable
editorial writers, forward-looking reformers, or molders of
public opinion. The conception of social institutions as having free will, and winning their salvation by a free-will selection of the right principles; the idea that politics, pressure
groups, lobbying, powerful political machines existed because people had sinful yearnings in that direction; the economic idea that depressions were the result of tinkering with
economic laws and preventing the automatic working of an
abstract law which would have functioned properly had it
not been for bad men who threw this law out of gear—these
were held as articles of faith by conservatives and radicals
alike.

This faith, held so implicitly, was sorely tried during the
years of the great depression. As in every time of great
travail, from the great plagues on to today, prayers went up
in all directions. These prayers, from businessmen, labor
leaders, and socialists, had one element in common. They all
showed distrust of any form of organized control. No one
would admit that man should govern man. No one would

observe the obvious fact that lay everywhere under their noses, that human organizations rise to power, not by following announced creeds, but by the development of loyalties and institutional habits. All these devoted people thought that the world could only attain that state of static perfection which alone was worth aiming at, by studying and developing the proper theories, and then following them, not by force, but by their own free will. Thus far the ideals of the Socialist party, the Liberty League, Dr. Townsend, and the budget balancers were all identical. The only difference between them was the proper application of the general principles on which all right-thinking men agreed.

The prayers of the house of bishops of industry were well illustrated by a typical speech of Mr. Sloan, at an annual dinner of the Association of Manufacturers in 1936. The speaker wanted American Industry, which he personified in a very beautiful way, to operate on an unselfish, or non-profit basis, and he wanted businessmen to assume the rôle of statesmen. The way to attain this was by making their minds pure and getting them to think about the right things. Within the General Motors Corporation, of which he was President, Mr. Sloan would never have substituted preaching for control. The lack of central control and the substitution of free will aided by preaching would have demoralized the concern within a year. However, it offered a marvelous intellectual escape for a man who felt the absolute necessity of business control, and at the same time could not fit actual control into his political religion. Portions of his speech which we have just analyzed are set forth, because they are so completely typical of the thinking of the day.

At the annual dinner last night, in accordance with the custom of the National Association of Manufacturers, the guests of honor were introduced separately as "men outstanding in the formulation of national industrial policy."

Mr. Sloan, introduced as "one in the forefront of this group," delivered the address of the occasion, entitled "Industry's responsibilities broaden." (*New York Times,* December 5, 1935.)

He said in part:

"Industry must further expand its horizon of thinking and action. *It must assume the rôle of an enlightened industrial statesmanship.*[2] To the extent that it accepts such broadened responsibilities, to that degree does it assure the maintenance of private enterprise, and with it the exercise of *free initiative,* as the sole creator, just as it must always be the most efficient creator of wealth.

"During the past few years it has become the vogue to discredit every instrumentality of accomplishment, be it the individual or the machine. It has been said that American industry is selfish. It would be far more just to say that it has been preoccupied—preoccupied in exploring the secrets of nature and creating a continuous flow of new products.

"But, as we look forward, and as we analyze the evolution that has occurred, I am convinced that industry's responsibilities can no longer be adequately discharged, however efficient and effective it may be, *with the mere physical production of goods and services.*

"First, let us ask whether our wealth-creating agencies, particularly that of industry, are to be based upon private enterprise or political management. I cannot see how any intelligent observer can have any possible faith in the capacity of political management to provide either stability or progress, if it should set out to operate the agencies of wealth creation, particularly industry. It is my firm conviction that any form of 'Government Regulation of Industry' is bound to result in an ever-increasing interference with the broad exercise of initiative—the very foundation of the American system. That is the natural evolution of bureaucracy. If that be so, might not the ultimate logical result

[2] Italics on this page, and all succeeding pages, unless otherwise indicated, are the author's.

be the necessity for the socialization of industry through the break down of the *profit system* induced by the accumulative effect of the ever-increasing political management? We do not need to go far afield to see definite evidences of that possibility." (*New York Times,* December 5, 1935.)

The medieval idea, that just because sin had always existed and probably always would exist, we were not justified in regarding it as commonplace or inevitable, was illustrated at the same meeting at which Mr. Sloan talked. In the platform of the organization it was pointed out that

"The American System . . . offers greater assurance than any other of equality of opportunity for all men, with rewards in accordance with the contribution of each." By speakers during the day, the "American System" was contrasted with the New Deal, which was variously denounced as "an alien importation" and as *"an Oriental philosophy."*

Government officials and legislators in general who had departed from the "American System" were denounced in the platform as having done so "in spite of their oath of office." (*New York Times,* December 6, 1935.)

Nevertheless, this American system would only work, in the opinion of the convention, if the invisible government of politics were kept out. The convention noted with horror the existence of men of influence in government who had not been elected, and commented on it by resolution:

A supplementary resolution later added to the denunciation a body otherwise unnamed called "the invisible government." The resolution read in part:

"It is a matter of grave concern that the germs of a dangerous invisible government have appeared in our national government. *It is a matter of common observation that our governmental powers, decisions and policies are being largely dictated by persons who have not been elected to official position and who are not re-*

sponsible to the people for their acts, decisions and policies. This is an unhealthy incubus in our national body politic which endangers the very life of our representative government and should be stamped out." (*New York Times,* December 6, 1935.)

In order to stamp out this invisible government by influential men not elected by the people, it was obviously necessary for influential men not elected by the people to enter into the business of influencing government. Thus another resolution was introduced to this effect, the report of which is as follows:

The "direct entrance" of industry into politics on this platform was declared to be a necessity by Charles H. Prentis Jr., president of the Armstrong Cork Company, who introduced it. Further, the declaration of entrance into politics the previous day by Clinton L. Bardo, president of the National Association of Manufacturers, was implemented yesterday by S. Wells Utley, who had been selected to make a broadcast convention address on the political tactics to be followed. (*New York Times,* December 6, 1935.)

There were very many, of course, who considered the Chamber of Commerce and the Manufacturers' Association hidebound groups of selfish people, pursuing their own interests under the guise of unselfishness. This attitude made the members of these organizations so speechless with indignation that they constantly reiterated that they had become too frightened and angry to assume the leadership which the crisis demanded. Criticism of this kind impeded recovery by scaring the natural-born leaders into such a state that they could only hide in cyclone cellars. Unfortunately, however, the critics were also engaged in a search for the holy grail, and therefore their deliberations resulted in the same kind of a hunt for two things: heresy and corruption. As a result of this, Socialists split into two wings, and the believers in true principles ousted the non-believers at a stormy convention in Cleveland. They wanted no patching up of a capitalistic religion. They wanted the true religion, if they had to go through chaos to get it.

We are using these speeches only to illustrate a common belief that social remedies could be found in the formulation of principles rather than in control and organization. In this respect radicals and conservatives were exactly alike.

Dr. Townsend belonged to the same church. He wanted goods distributed to the poor, but was convinced that the very worst way of doing this was to build a practical organization of human beings to do it. He, like his conservative foes, wanted an automatic scheme which would work for all time by encouraging free bargaining. His sole aim was to encourage private initiative by creating a proper credit system. His scheme was no more nor less utopian than the *laissez faire* economics of the conservative wing of the great medieval church to which he belonged. It would have worked if human beings had only been like the little abstract man in the back of his head. So also would *laissez faire,* if only human beings would leave things alone, and all act like good skilful traders who took their medicine when beaten, and did not try to overreach each other by unfair means. Thus we find Dr. Townsend endorsing a conservative general position in 1936 as follows:

Dr. Townsend, on the other hand, in addition to his fundamental plan of paying $200-a-month old age pensions from the proceeds of a transactions tax, remarked that "there are many fortunes which will have to be dissipated by the income tax and the inheritance tax route."

To FIGHT "DICTATORSHIP."—"We are presenting a common front against the dictatorship in Washington," said Dr. Townsend, showing a glint of gold teeth beneath his tiny mustache.

"Add to that Communism and Farleyism, and you have our

platform," added the Louisiana preacher, a red-faced gentleman who talks in a succession of tub-thumping phrases.

Dr. Townsend, who said that he considered the Supreme Court and the Constitution "a great safeguard," said that President Roosevelt "knew beyond doubt beforehand that his measures were unconstitutional," and that he had put them through in order to arouse resentment against the Supreme Court. Some one asked whether he believed the Supreme Court would find his proposals constitutional.

"They will if it is shown that they represent the will of the great majority of the people," replied Dr. Townsend in a grim tone. Later, however, he remarked that if it were possible to "capture the government" a constitutional amendment could easily be put through. (*New York Herald Tribune,* June 2, 1936.)

There is obviously nothing in these general principles to which the Liberty League could not have subscribed, in principle. There is a hint of breaking up large fortunes in both of them, in order to get back to the grand old days of free bargaining before large fortunes existed. In those days of the great depression everyone believed in the same God, and only fought about details of the service.

In such a situation there was only one safe speech which could be made, and that was to invoke all religions at once, and lump them under the phrase, "moral conscience and integrity." Such speeches, seeking the remedy through God, were therefore heard through the length and breadth of the land. Typical of them was the following from Governor Landon.

In the stress and confusion of recent years and in the din of conflicting counsel, we have lost our bearings and we have listened in vain for the commanding voice that might at once dispel our doubts and uncertainties and point us into safe courses.

We have waited and hesitated, the courage and resolution of

old has seemed to fail us, and our moral fiber has seemed to weaken.

There is peril in that situation.

Our economic welfare may be threatened for the moment, and our industrial progress may be retarded for a season without final or total disaster.

Far more serious is the possible collapse of character, a possible paralysis of individual initiative, and a deadened sense of personal obligation and responsibility. . . .

What is this intangible, yet very real thing we call the spirit of America? It may be found in the Bible. It is the slow groping of human thought toward the value of human personality and toward the one God in whose sight all men are equal. (*New York Times,* May 24, 1936.)

Of course, the God to lead us out of our economic bewilderment was not always the God of the Church. Lawyers found one in the Constitution. Huge organizations like the Liberty League and the Crusaders sought the truth from this document and the learned decisions elaborating it. They produced briefs, law-review articles, and sermons in publications devoted to the elucidation of the law. Like all great bodies of literature, the Constitution marched in all conceivable directions. An inflation of legal learning took place, the like of which the world has never seen. In the Middle Ages, men sought the "Word" just as diligently, but the available material resources did not permit so many thousands to seek it at the same time, and the printing presses were not so efficient then as now.

The Constitution, however, was only one symbol. Men feverishly attempted to make all written law march toward safety, security, and peace, through logical certainty. Millions were spent on restating all the law at once, and hundreds of learned men were employed by an organization called the "American Law Institute." Prominent lawyers gathered from all parts of the nation to hear the law, as it ought logically to be, read to them for their agreement and approbation.

The purely religious character of these exercises was shown in the complete lack of selfish interest in nearly all of those who participated in them. They sought nothing for themselves in this quest for simplified principle. No discouragement halted that search. Indeed, the obstacles were what made the search entrancing. The American Law Institute was ceremony of the very purest sort, dedicated to the ideal that this was a government of law and not of men. Some of the members of the Liberty League may have had a few selfish interests to further, but it is very doubtful if even these people thought about those interests directly, so absorbed were they in the search for ultimate truth, so preoccupied in contemplation of the future to the exclusion of the present. And in so far as the great membership of this institution was concerned, most of them were acting directly against the common sense interests which they would instantly have recognized if the phobias which motivated them had been brushed aside.

A poll of the Institute of Public Opinion showed that at least 30 per cent of even the unemployed men preferred the conservative to the liberal label. Persons on relief who had seen better days and were imbued with middle-class culture felt it only proper that they should be pauperized before aid was extended them. It was common to find persons who had gone bankrupt devoting the rest of their lives to working for their creditors. Some of these persons demanded new philosophies of government and became Socialists, or Communists, or whatnot. Few of them demanded with any articulate political force actual bread instead of religious principles. Only a few groups like the ex-soldiers, a few of the industrial leaders, and the politicians seemed to catch the beauty of the old proverb that "a bird in the hand is worth two in the bush." They achieved cash bonuses out of the tangled political situation, while most of their fellows were seeking symbols.

The deep hold which this highly religious folklore had upon the small business or professional man, a majority of our industrial leaders, and our press is evidenced by the fact that in 1936 the Constitution became for them a sort of abracadabra which would cure all disease. Copies of the Constitution, bound together with the Declaration of Independence and Lincoln's Gettysburg Address, were distributed in cigar stores; essays on the Constitution were written by high-school students; incomprehensible speeches on the Constitution were made from every public platform to reverent audiences which knew approximately as much about the history and dialectic of that document as the masses in the Middle Ages knew about the Bible—in those days when people were not permitted to read the Bible. The American Liberty League was dedicated to Constitution worship. Like the Bible, the Constitution became the altar whenever our best people met together for tearful solemn purposes, regardless of the kind of organization. Teachers in many states were compelled to swear to support the Constitution. No attempt was made to attach a particular meaning to this phrase, yet people thought that it had deep and mystical significance, and that the saying of the oath constituted a charm against evil spirits. The opponents of such oaths became equally excited, and equally theological about the great harm the ceremony might do. Nor was Constitution worship limited to upper strata. The Ku Klux Klan and similar disorderly organizations took the Constitution as their motto for the persecution of Jews and Catholics. In May, 1936, Michigan discovered a state-wide organization of misguided psychopathic personalities which had conducted a series of floggings simply because it was caught up by the solemnity of a ritual.

No one could belong who did not take a solemn oath that he was a supporter of the Constitution. The most interesting fact about this order was that it was recruited largely from the underprivileged and the unemployed.

Only radical parties refused to worship the Constitution, but the spirit of the age was such that they, too, put their faith in the written doctrines which they themselves had framed. Thus, the Socialist party, a group which could have no other conceivable purpose than to organize a protest vote, split wide apart in the crucial year of 1936 on purely theological doctrine.

When in 1937 the President proposed to put more liberal judges on the Court, liberals like Oswald Garrison Villard and John T. Flynn joined with the *New York Herald Tribune* to denounce this sacrilege. A group of men with completely irreconcilable views joined together in reciting the book of common prayer.

The essential characteristics of this type of thinking may be described as follows:

1. Everyone was so completely preoccupied with government as it ought to be that no action which was politically possible could escape condemnation in the terms of that ideal. Expediency was not a good public excuse for necessary imperfections.

2. Everyone was so much more concerned with the future life of social institutions than with the present that it seemed immaterial what happened to the legislation of the day directed only at temporary needs. Nothing could be considered really important unless it fitted into what was conceived to be the moral future of the nation. No one could quite explain what the moral future of the nation was, and therefore on such a question they were always willing to accept the word of any duly constituted authority whose remarks fitted their particular prejudices.

3. Everyone was more interested in the spiritual government than in the temporal. Temporal government consisted of busi..ess and politics. The theory was that these things ran themselves, the one being impelled by beneficent economic laws, which operated because of the inherent balance of human nature, and the other being an invention of the devil which ran automatically because of the weakness of human nature.

4. No one ever read the economic theory or the constitutional theory which kept the spiritual government in bounds. Nor was there any faith in any particular type of expert. The faith was in the pontifical nature of the utterances ex cathedra, and the belief in the centuries of learning supposed to lie back of them. Not everyone liked the particular set of such principles which happened to be uppermost. But they were convinced that further study and the elimination of politics from government would give them a set which they would like.

The attitude which we have just been describing colored all thinking and all public utterance wherever the activities of government were concerned. It completely confused the activities of government by subjecting them to unreal standards under which no human organization could operate. The election of 1936 brought out the fact that a very large number of people, roughly representing the more illiterate and inarticulate masses of people, had lost their faith in the more prominent and respected economic preachers and writers of the time, who for the most part were aligned against the New Deal. They repudiated the advice of the newspapers which they bought and read because they were more immediately affected by the economic pressures of the time which were depriving them of security. Nevertheless, after the election, people continued to talk in the old phrases as before. The political leadership which was demanded was also required to be cast in old formulas and these old formulas continued to confuse its direction. Although there were signs of a change in attitude everywhere, organized learning had not yet caught up.

This summary of the state of things leads, naturally enough, to a discussion of the place of scholarship and learning in the organization of society and in the distribution of its goods.

CHAPTER IV

The Place of Learning in the Distribution
of Goods

IN which it is shown how the scholar, seeking for universal truth
in the light of reason, guides the stumbling feet of a great modern democracy, and in which the never-ending battle of these
learned men against unsound theories and the selfish greed of
politicians is also discussed.

THE place of learning and scholarship in the distribution of goods is a fascinating subject. We are
talking, not about books containing technical information, but about the kind of learning which supports
the governmental folklore of people. This learning is supposed to disclose the fundamental plan of social organization and to lay down the principles which men must follow
to make it live up to its ideals.

Actually there has never been such a thing as a planned
organization of society, even in times when there is the most
social planning. Social plans are a symptom, not a cause.
Goods are distributed, not through plans, but through habit
and ceremony. Most of these ceremonies are not recognized
as such and are thought to be expressions of fundamental
truth. Their proper observance therefore is entrusted to the
wise men of the tribe. There are two methods of observing
these ceremonial truths found in every society. The first consists in parades of various sorts, the second in learned and
mystical literature. In our modern rational age we think of
the writing of books as more fundamentally sound than
parades. The literature thus produced is called "learning"
and "scholarship."

It is this kind of learning rather than the literature which attempts to convey technical knowledge that we are analyzing in this chapter. The difference between technical and philosophical learning, of course, cannot be sharply defined. An analogy therefore may be useful. The learning of medicine today is technical rather than philosophical. Therefore, every surgeon in his daily work must use books on the techniques of surgery. The literature of economics and law today is predominantly philosophical. Therefore, persons in actual control of either political or business government do not use that literature in their daily operations. Our great governmental and industrial organizers cannot by any stretch of the imagination be classified as legal or economic scholars.

They are not skilled in the literature of law and economics and do not read such literature. They prefer to hire other people to read it for them, taking great comfort in the fact that it is being produced in order to give stability to the governmental ideals on which their prestige is based.

This type of learning which points out what men should be ashamed of in modern society because it deviates from sound principles is one of the most important props of our folklore. Its influence in molding the forms and ceremonies of our institutions is tremendous. It is a factor in creating *sub rosa* institutions which keep under cover the activities of institutions which are practically necessary but must be kept hidden because they violate our creeds. It is the ceremony by which creeds survive in spite of their conflict with reality. It is never a practical guide for day-to-day conduct in government or business. Nevertheless, it is the lifeblood of our ideals and myths without which we would feel very uncomfortable indeed.[1]

---

[1] A single example will suffice. An eminent legal scholar recently reviewed a book written as a lawyer's guide in trying cases. He concluded as follows:

"Intended as a lawyer's book, it will in all probability be read only by

We are of course referring to the *total effect* of the learning of law and economics and not to particular lawyers or economists. That total effect is produced because of a demand for rounded explanations of institutions, for ideals and for principles which will extend the culture of the present into the future. This kind of learning is not in any sense a present guide for either business or government.

It is hard to convince lawyers or economists that this is true. Therefore, the place of learning in the distribution of goods, while a most important one, is not the one usually ascribed to it by scholars. Scholars like to think of the legal and economic principles which they formulate so laboriously as a practical guide. It is difficult to convince most of them that they are not practical advisers because when their guesses go wrong they can always ascribe the blame to factors such as human nature or politics, which lie outside their sciences. Therefore, the best way to understand the effect of modern legal and economic learning on institutional conduct today is to compare it to the effects of similar scholarly learning about medicine in the days when that science was still predominantly philosophical rather than technical.

lawyers and those who would be lawyers. And fervent prayers that the book be read by no others should be raised by those who want to believe, and want others to believe, that a law suit is a proceeding for the discovery of truth by rational processes. If only some lawyer could rise up and honestly denounce Mr. Goldstein as a defamer of his profession! If only Mr. Goldstein himself had written his book as an exposition of the evils inherent in our adversary system of litigation! If only a reviewer could assert that this book is a guide not to the palaces of justice but to the red-light districts of the law! But a decent respect for the truth compels the admission that Mr. Goldstein has told his story truly. He has told it calmly, without pretense of shame, and (God save us!) without the slightest suspicion of its shamefulness. He has shown by his own unperturbed frankness with what complaisance the profession, which would smile the superior smile of derision at the suggestion of a return of trial by battle of bodies, accepts trial by battle of wits. In all innocence, he has produced a document which is a devastating commentary upon an important aspect of our administration of justice." (E. M. Morgan, Professor of Law, Harvard Law School, 49 *Harvard Law Review* 1387, 1389, reviewing *Trial Technique* by Irving Goldstein.)

Scholarly medieval thought about medicine (like scholarly thought today about government) developed elaborate theories but no efficient techniques. Such surgical techniques as existed were the property of an unlearned class, the barber surgeons, who were not respectable. Respectable physicians could not tolerate the thought that the actual human body was not a philosophical and religious creation, not unlike a constitutional government, designed with omniscient forethought by a Providence which had a purpose in creating each detail. They wanted rounded and complete explanations for everything, and ignored or condemned observed facts in conflict with such explanations in the same way that thinking about social institutions today ignores the actual disorderly ways of group conduct which interfere with the picture of society obtained from rational theories. Things in conflict with rational theory were therefore set down as the work of the devil.

In this kind of atmosphere the more the men of the Middle Ages studied the body, the less they knew about it. They ignored practical needs; they sought comfortable intellectual certainties while epidemics rose and fell without any sort of human control. Today we are without moral preconceptions when we control physical epidemics; but we are still fettered with them when we consider social problems.

This contrast between two attitudes comes into clearer relief when modern treatment of venereal disease is examined, because these are the only physical epidemics still treated from a medieval point of view. There is no question but that the present ravages of these diseases could be tremendously reduced. Proof of that is found in the record of the United States Army in France. Yet such a solution means that we must recognize an obvious natural fact about human beings which interferes with both reason and morals. To the moral man of the twentieth century, there is a vast difference between smallpox and venereal disease, because smallpox is not the result of sin.

Nearly all of the literature of government is produced in that kind of moral atmosphere. Such an atmosphere produces doctrine which becomes much more important than practical needs. The emphasis is on the future rather than the present. This has profound effects on the day-to-day activities and personnel of our institutions. Some of these effects we will attempt to analyze.

The Contribution of Scholarly Learning about Government to the Rise of Quacks

A MOST significant effect of our scholarship and learning about government today is to remove from active participation in governing most of the kindly and tolerant people who might otherwise be a more important factor. Accordingly, important social changes often owe their impetus to quacks. In a contest between experts in governmental organization and political machines, the latter usually win.

The reason is that our students of governmental problems consider politics a low and unworthy pursuit. They think that sincerity and candor can be used in a political campaign. They feel a sort of spiritual trouble when confronted with the realities of a political situation, which makes them confused and ineffective. Unscrupulous persons who do not feel the same spiritual trouble when confronted with things as they are naturally become more proficient. The so-called demagogue has an advantage because he does not view the control of human institutions under the illusion that men in groups are composed of so-called thinking men, to whose knowledge of fundamental governmental principles he must appeal.

The student in government is therefore usually impractical, because all his acquired learning makes him so. He knows the right principles, and attempts to apply them by the preaching method. He knows no more about the techniques of organization than the medieval physician knew about the organization of the human body.

The influence of political quacks on social events in such an atmosphere is tremendous. They are the only persons who can espouse a growing social need before it is recognized by conservatives. Responsible labor leaders like John L. Lewis find serious handicaps in their way because they can obtain support neither from their intelligent conservative friends, nor from the radicals. For example, in the conflict to recognize collective bargaining, it was difficult indeed for any responsible conservative to treat the situation realistically. The burning issue was supposed to be whether sit-down strikes should be put down as an attack on government. Until this religious problem was solved, the real problem had to be ignored. The result was, of course, that a more irresponsible group became the most effective labor leaders and labor organizations were hard for even Lewis to control.

The same process may be observed before the passage of the Social Security Act. In a time when the practical problem of old-age relief was obscured by moral issues—when the moral character of the aged was more important than their physical wants—when distribution of goods to them, even though they were surplus goods, could not be justified under a profit economy, quacks could lead the most effective campaigns. In such an atmosphere it required a Dr. Townsend to compel the acceptance of old-age pensions in both political platforms of 1936. Sensible people had recognized the need for years, only to be drowned out by a flood of abstract economic argument. Dr. Townsend was successful because he linked the idea of old-age security to the prevailing popular economic conceptions. Men were afraid of central organization, and hence Dr. Townsend avoided Communism. Men wanted automatic schemes based on laws of supply and demand, hence Dr. Townsend gave them an automatic scheme. They thought of distribution and income in terms of money, and the Townsend Plan conformed to that. It was complicated, and one could write great books about it, thereby satisfying the need for learned authority. The Townsend Plan then became a movement which transcended in actual importance all the more sensible schemes of accomplishing the same object. In the thinking of economists Townsend was regarded as a dangerous phenomenon. He was attacked on logical grounds which are entirely irrelevant to the part he was playing in the social scene. Only in the thinking of *sub rosa* political machines was there a practical understanding of the nature of the movement and how it must be dealt with. Without his leadership the passage of the Social Security Act might have been delayed for years.

And this leads to the completion of the story of Peruvian bark, or quinine, which was started in the second chapter. After the University of Paris had banned the remedy, on the double ground that it led to Jesuitism and was only an artificial and temporary cure, a quack named Talbot conceived the brilliant idea of mixing Peruvian bark with other ingredients, such as honey, and putting it out as a secret panacea. He gave it a new name and sold it under a theory which did not conflict with the rational ideas of the time about the cure of fever. Naturally enough his cures were marvelous, because he was competing with the therapeutics of bleeding which had been so carefully reasoned out by the savants of the time. Finally he cured the Dauphin. He was offered a princely sum to disclose the secret, but he was too wise to accept. Instead he obtained a patent of nobility and a large annuity in return for his promise to disclose the contents of his remedy after his death. Ten years later he died and the

learned men of the time found that it was the despised Peruvian bark which had been the foundation of the career of this
distinguished medical statesman. It was only thus that medical remedies could triumph over the learned superstitions of
the seventeenth century. It is thus that political remedies
triumph over the learned superstitions of today. It is a cumbersome and painful process, but the honest observer must
record it and the practical politician must take it into account. Taboos do not mean that a nation ceases to progress.
They only mean that it advances in devious ways with most
of its cylinders missing.

This is beautifully illustrated in the testimony of Benjamin Marsh during the Senate Committee hearings on the
Black-Connery wages and hours bill. Mr. Marsh was criticiz-
ing the bill from a technical point of view. Nevertheless as a
realist he was in favor of it, even in the form submitted, as
"a shot in the arm." He said: *"I believe in taking the shot, because you have to do all the fool things* before you do the
sensible things. . . ."² (Author's italics.)

The Effect of Philosophical Learning on Political Compromise

THE search for rational and moral principles creates an atmosphere where compromise is difficult in times of change.
Most of the interesting and picturesque wars have been
fought not over practical interests but over pure metaphysics.
The greater the philosophical learning of the time, the more
difficult it is for a new organization to find a place in the logical structure of government. The reason is that once men
have articulated a creed their desire for consistency and their

² *Joint Hearings before the Committee on Education and Labor of the
United States Senate and the Committee on Labor,* House of Representatives,
75th Congress, 1st Session, on S. 2457 and H.R. 7200, June 7–15, 1937,
p. 552.

loyalty to authority are generally greater than any practical motivation.

To give a simple illustration, let us compare the Supreme Court of the United States with an administrative tribunal. The Court, since it represents finality in learning and research, cannot change without appearing to discard all its authoritarian pretensions. Where it takes an erroneous course, it is very difficult for it to change to another route. Compare this to an administrative tribunal, which is a lower form of institutional life. Such a tribunal has technical information but no great literature. Therefore, when we desire elasticity and compromise in any field we take jurisdiction away from courts and give it to administrative bodies. Yet even administrative bodies lose their elasticity as they develop learning and doctrine.

This process in the individual was illustrated by an experiment carried on by the late Professor Edward S. Robinson of Yale, during the latter part of the Hoover Administration when the depression had thrown governmental philosophy into confusion. He submitted to a group of several thousand persons, composed of members of the League of Women Voters, professors, readers of liberal magazines, and so on, a series of inconsistent statements of economic and political belief. The statements were so arranged that the inconsistencies were not apparent except upon close analysis. In general they represented two attitudes—one that the Government should take a large control over the distribution of goods and the other that it should allow the problems of society to be solved by the working of national economic laws.

Professor Robinson asked his subjects to mark the statements as follows: "True," "Probably True," "Undecided," "False," "Probably False."

After these answers had been handed in, the group listened in widely separated parts of the country to radio speeches of a learned character in which prominent men, using the benefits of statistical and scholarly research, discussed the public issues of the day. Weeks afterwards, when the speeches were finished, the group was given the same questions to mark again.

It was found on tabulating the results that scarcely anyone who listened to the speeches on both sides had changed any of his answers from "True" to "False" or even from "Probably True" to "Probably False." In other words, the discussion had scarcely any effect in altering the underlying reactions of the members of the group to the statements of policy. There were numerous changes but they were from "Probably True" to "True" or from "Probably False" to "False." What had happened in the minds of these listeners? They had been leaning in a given direction. They had heard a phrase which gave authority and learning to that direction and their uncertainty was changed to certainty. They had lost their tolerance and become uncompromising. They had found the truth which they thought they were seeking and were now ready to fight for it.

The effect of the scholarly elaboration of principles on compromise with practical necessity appears most clearly in revolutionary situations, where learned idealists seize power. The rise of uncompromising theorists is generally a direct result of the devoted belief of conservatives that there should be no compromise with principle. When men are excited, their devotion to logic and principle leads to violence. Security and order only come when practical politicians replace learned and idealistic men.

The seeds of the Russian Revolution were sown by learned theoretical idealists, who dreamed of a logical order accomplished by a preliminary period of disorder. These men, during the dark days of the Czar, were occupied in writing dull and complicated books. Their literary output consisted in large part of theological elaboration on Karl Marx. They used the ritual of scholarship to surround their revolt with the air of sound research and theory. In the first part of the revolution men who had not written learned treatises had difficulty in getting high positions in the new régime. In the course of time the learning which had occupied the revolutionists finally gave way to the dictatorship of a practical politician.

The Effect of Learning in Making Men Treat Ideal Conceptions of Society as Concrete Realities

SINCE the philosophical learning about government is the product of a demand for certainty and for a symmetrical and concrete explanation of social phenomena, it must leave out the complicated psychological factors which make organizations grow and develop in the same way as individuals. For this reason most of the learning is pure fantasy logically and mathematically developed. The process is to take an analogy which seems to march toward a preconceived conclusion and assume that it accurately pictures a social institution. Then "learning" about the situation pictured by the analogy is substituted for observation of the actual complicated events under discussion. We cite a column from one of the most learned economic pundits of the time, Walter Lippmann. He had an emotional bias against the exercise of national power to solve national problems. He converted that emotional leaning into certainty by pretending that the separate states were like physical or chemical laboratories, dealing with economic problems as a scientist deals with physical experiments. The notion that our checker squares of states were economic units or that they had the power to conduct experiments or that the experiments they conducted could be utilized by other states is of course pure daydreaming. And yet we find that daydream used as a factual argument in a way typical of the thinking of the day. Walter Lippmann wrote:

For the great virtue of the Federal system is that each state becomes, as the late Senator Dwight W. Morrow used to say, a laboratory in which the other forty-seven states can see how theories actually work when put into practice. No one state, however foolishly it legislates, can injure the nation as a whole, and the follies of one state are almost certain to teach wisdom to the others. A judicial interpretation of the Federal Constitution which denies to the states the power to experiment within wide limits makes the system as a whole far more rigid, far more uniform, than it can safely be made.

. . . . .

It will be particularly unfortunate if the states are to be prevented from trying out locally experiments in the fixing of prices and wages. For it must be recognized that there is a large body of popular opinion which favors such measures, and if that opinion is mistaken, as many of us believe, by far the best way to demonstrate the error is to let such measures be tested out practically here and there. This is the least costly and the surest way of reaching a decision.

No state can in fact regulate drastically many prices or wages. If it does, it will quickly feel the effects of competition from other states. Thus the freedom of the states to police local industries is almost certain to be exercised only where the abuses are so obvious that no one can or will defend them. The states can never carry regulation to the point where the government, as the arbiter of all wages and prices, has destroyed the reality of freedom of contract.

No such check would exist if the Federal government had the kind of power claimed for it under N.R.A. or the Guffey act. We should find ourselves quickly under the iron rule of national collectivism. But the separate states could not, even if they wished, revolutionize the American social order. They can attack only the gross abuses of free competition where they injure those who cannot effectively defend themselves. (*New York Herald Tribune,* June 2, 1936.)

The argument that state governments watch the legislation in other state governments as experiments are watched in the laboratory is, of course, the sheerest fantasy to anyone who knows how state legislation actually operates. The pure fantasy of the notion was ironically illustrated by the following news item which appeared on the previous day.

RAND CLOSES BIG PLANT AT MIDDLETOWN. STRIKE RESULTS IN ORDERS FOR DISCONTINUANCE OF FACTORY. MAYOR TO SEEK COMPROMISE. *Middletown, June 1.*—Less than 100 striking employes were around the Remington Rand factory here this morning as workmen took down the sign on the building and factory officials announced that the plant has been closed.

While workmen prepared the machinery in the factory for shipment, the strikers gathered in St. Aloysius Hall to discuss the situation. A week ago, they went out on a "sympathy" strike in protest to the discharge of 16 union employes at the Syracuse factory. Today, they faced the possibility of a $2,000,000 per year payroll leaving Middletown. (*New Haven Register,* June 1, 1936.)

The mobility of our great industrial organizations and their independence of state lines had been carefully studied by Carter Goodrich and others in a report, *Migration and Economic Opportunity.*[8] Yet the theory that states were experimental laboratories still persisted. Men argued seriously that states could control agricultural conditions, though they had not the power to exclude competitive agricultural products from other states. Administrative divisions which were in no sense economic units were supposed to be able to act like economic units.

When this was pointed out to men like Mr. Lippmann, the

[8] University of Pennsylvania Press, 1936.

answer usually was that great monopolies should be broken up. This slogan had wide popular appeal and was backed by an enormous literature of learning, both legal and economic. The obvious impossibility of this idea was explained away by the theory that it should be done step by step, just as the return of the horse to replace the automobile would have to be accomplished. The country was supposed to go back gradually, through the different makes, back to the old Model *T* Ford, until finally they had the little automobile which really was inferior to the horse. Then they would eagerly embrace the horse. Thus antitrust laws became popular moral gestures and their economic meaninglessness never quite penetrated the thick priestly incense which hung over the nation like a pillar of fire by night and a cloud of smoke by day.

The quaint moral conceptions of legal and economic learning by which the needs of the moment could be argued out of existence were expressed by "long run" arguments. Such arguments always appear in religious thinking. From this point of view the future is supposed to be the only reality, just as Heaven in the Middle Ages was the only reality. All else is regarded as temporary, shifting, and ephemeral. This way of thinking allows men to ignore what they see before them in their absorption with the more orderly blueprint of the future. Observe how the *New York Times* proves editorially that new techniques and machinery do not throw men out of employment because they do not do it "in the long run." Therefore, there is no real present problem.

PROGRESS AND JOBS.—In his speech in New York on April 26 the President criticized the contention of an unnamed economist that recovery could be achieved by lower prices brought about by lowered costs of production:

"Let us reduce that [he said] to plain English. You can cheapen the costs of industrial production by two methods. One is by the development of new machinery and new technique and by increasing employe efficiency. We do not discourage that. But do not dodge the fact that this means fewer men employed and more men unemployed. . . . Reduction of costs of manufacture does not mean more purchasing power and more goods consumed. It means just the opposite."

If this astonishing doctrine were true, then everything that we have hitherto called industrial and economic progress, every new invention, every move to increase productive efficiency, would be a cause for alarm. Fortunately, the whole history of industry proves that it is not true. If it were true, serious unemployment would have begun to set in with the Industrial Revolution in the eighteenth century, and would have piled up year by year with each new labor-saving device, regardless of the general ups-and-downs of the business cycle. Instead, we know that mechanical progress has created scores of jobs for every job displaced, and that it is the chief reason why American are incomparably higher than Chinese wages. The displacement of jobs by new machinery falls upon small special groups. It is our social duty to make provision for these groups. But much larger groups are benefited as consumers by the reductions in prices which more efficient production brings about; this leads to increased purchases of goods and hence to increased employment. (May 27, 1936.)

This is a beautiful example of the "long-run" argument. Because machinery does in the long run promote higher standards, it is assumed that anyone pointing out a present problem caused by technological improvements is making an attack on the permanent utility of such improvements.

In this way an industrial economist could prove that a hundred particular individuals who had been discharged because of the introduction of machinery had not really been discharged at all because of the *laissez faire* heaven which lay in the future.[4]

[4] For example, the Ford Motor Company distributed a pamphlet entitled *Machines and Jobs* by W. J. Cameron, December 1, 1935, at a time

It was the same way with housing. The vast housing projects in England were envied but not imitated. In 1936 former Senator Straus of New York had been appointed by
Mayor La Guardia to find out how England was solving the
housing problem. He discovered that the English had been
building houses by government subsidy, in spite of the fact
that their per capita national debt was much larger than ours.
A building boom had developed, and the subsidy was being
gradually withdrawn. The fact that it was being withdrawn
showed, of course, that it was wrong in the first place, because it was not a permanent cure. But there were other convincing reasons why the English practice should not be followed. We must not permit our Government to act until it
has developed a civil service like that of England. As the
New York Times put it:

when technological unemployment was a very serious problem. Mr. Cameron
proved it was not a problem at all by pointing to the distant future. He said:
   "No one could be indifferent to the charge that machinery diminishes
employment. But it was never easy to understand how anything so useful
to man could also be as harmful as was alleged. We hear the charge less
often nowadays because the conviction is growing that it is not true.

· · · · ·

   "It always surprises people to learn that most of the machinery in use
is not labor-saving machinery at all. Most of it is labor-creating or labor-
serving; it enables men to work at tasks that never would have been attempted otherwise.

· · · · ·

   "Regarding so-called 'technological unemployment,' there is no possible
way of rendering human beings obsolete. Rarely does a new industry entirely displace an old one."
   This was said when millions of people found themselves so obsolete
that there was no place for them. However, Mr. Cameron, like all medieval
priests, referred the unemployed to the beauties of the future world. The
method here is clear. It consists of regarding an observation of the obvious, that a new machine has put some actual men out of work, as an attack upon the machine itself. Then the argument proves that the machine
is a good thing. Since it is a "good thing," it cannot be possible that it has
thrown anyone out of work, because only "bad things" do that.

By these and other devices more than four million slum dwellers, according to Mr. Straus, have been rehoused in buildings erected with Government aid since 1919. If we are to achieve like results, he argues, we must "tread the same path." It may be wondered just how literally he intends that advice to be taken. Certainly it would be a fine thing if we could emulate British administrative technique, so steady, self-reliant, well informed and free from political manipulation. (October 21, 1935.)

Therefore, the best way to build houses is to attack Mr. Farley for his political manipulation of the civil service.

Mr. Hoover put the same idea in more general terms as follows:

Every spread of bureaucratic control that makes men more subjective or dependent on government weakens that independence and self-respect. National stamina suffers by encouraging parasitic leaners whether on doorsteps or governments. There is self-respect and dignity that marks free men.

Honor in public life begins with political parties. The people must depend upon political parties to carry out their will. When men are elected to high office on certain promises and those promises are cynically broken, how may we expect a citizen to feel the obligation of a promise and good faith? (*New York Times,* May 15, 1936.)

Here was the notion of making political parties better and better by imposing on them consistency to written documents, and inspiring them with vague terror of governmental action of any kind. This creed imposed impossible standards on the Government because it required that every practical action be undertaken by a debating society. It imposed impossible standards on political parties because it required absolute foreknowledge of the future in preparing their written documents. It made adherence to written documents the first law of government, above and beyond any practical considerations. Not everyone believed this, but such was the atmosphere of the times that no candidate for political office could safely have denied this nonsense in public.

Obviously, no one could win debates conducted in such an atmosphere, because each set of principles always seemed conclusive to its own adherents. As a result, compromise was made difficult because the debate was shifted from the uncertainties of affairs to the certainties of opposing schools of learning. Conflicting interests, unencumbered by doctrine, can always be settled by horse trading. But no man of intellectual integrity will compromise with a fundamental principle after he has thought it through.

The Effect of Philosophical Theory on the Treatment of Practical Problems

THE historian of the future, writing of the place of scholarly learning in the operation of social institutions during the great American depression, will observe that each theory sired a competing theory; each elaborate definition compelled other definitions. Law became a subject of bewildering complexity, in the mazes of which simple and practical problems were removed from the sphere of practical judgment of men. Economics took over higher mathematics. Each social science was a pyramid of abstract theory, imposed upside down on some simple myth believed by the man in the street.

The result of this devotion to theory was to obscure practical necessities and to prevent the alignment of groups according to their actual interests. It was impossible to form political parties to represent the interests of different economic groups because everyone believed in the same slogans and refused to talk about practical affairs. Therefore, party platforms in America were practically identical, except for minor detail. In the year 1936 it began to appear, in spite of the bitterness of the coming campaign, that they would again be identical. Sincere thinkers like John Dewey and ably written, intelligent papers like the *New Republic,* the *Nation,* and *Common Sense* were constantly demanding a third party. Yet, in spite of the apparent need for a party which represented different interests and different issues, none came into being and every attempt to form one failed.

The reason was obvious. Everyone belonged to the same church. Everyone believed in a written Constitution and a Supreme Court to save the nation's soul, and in the existence of sound economic principles discovered by impartial learned men in colleges to cure its body. And, above all, everyone believed in a government of principles and not of men. The idea that different classes of the country really had opposing interests, that they were *not* all working hand in hand toward the same goal—i.e., justice under the capitalistic system— never took any emotional hold on any extensive group. A separate labor movement was regarded as dangerous even by a large section of labor. This curious unanimity between the industrial East and the agricultural West, between the Republican North and the Democratic South, between labor and industry, and even between the rich and the unemployed began to be apparent when polls were first taken on current economic slogans, rather than on specific candidates.

For example, in 1936 the Institute of Public Opinion, a scholarly and impartial group, took a nationwide poll on the question of the necessity of balancing the national budget. This was in a time when it was obvious to any fact-minded person, not caught in the symbolism of the time, that in terms of the distribution of material goods there was no sense whatever in cutting down the distribution of comforts to the unemployed, or housing, or any form of activity leading to the utilization of the productive capacity which was at hand. We were rich, not poor, in those things which the economist called wealth. Budget balancing meant, in practical terms, that, for the present at least, many people would have less to eat, poorer houses, less electricity, and so on, in the face of an abundance. Yet even in such times an overwhelming majority of those who voted in the poll, rich and poor, agricultural and industrial, voted that the primary need of the Government was to balance its budget.

Of course, the budget was not balanced because the interests of the various groups who voted to balance it were diametrically opposed. Each demanded a different sort of governmental economy. The West would have opposed the tariff subsidy, the East would have denied a farm subsidy. Veterans were forming groups to see that relief to unemployed, particularly radicals, was cut down to the minimum, sincerely thinking that their own subsidy was simply a delayed payment of as sacred an obligation as the payment of interest on government bonds. And, naturally, no budget balancer was in favor of a balance obtained by repudiating sacred obligations.

The philosophical learning which made budget balancing a cure for all ills was inseparably intertwined with a larger learning surrounding the word "inflation." For most people inflation meant a repetition of what they had read had happened in Germany, which they believed was due to a wicked manipulation of the German mark intentionally engineered by people who were following the wrong principles. The problem actually concerned the production and distribution of goods. It was a problem in organization. Dr. Mordecai Ezekiel summed it up as follows:[5]

WE are in no danger of the astronomical kind of inflation which carried the values of the American continentals, the French as-

[5] Address made during a People's Lobby luncheon and broadcast over the Columbia Broadcasting System, Saturday, April 24, 1937.

signats, the old German marks, or Russian roubles, to zero. Rather, the only type of inflation that might threaten us is such a rapid rise in speculative values, as in 1928–1929, or in commodity values, as in 1918–1919, as might eventually plunge us again into a major depression like those of 1920 or 1929.

We may choose between several different alternatives to avert such a possibility.

The first method, and probably the most desirable one, is one that businessmen themselves can adopt. It is for them to put into action the program recommended to them by the Brookings Institution in its book, "Income and economic progress." That method is very simple: Use the reduced costs of production arising from technological improvements and full-capacity operation primarily to lower the selling price of the product, and to raise wages of labor; and only in small measure to raise profits. In that way the buying power of workers can be kept rising, more workers will be employed, and production and consumption will rise together. Also, that will avoid the vicious circle of rising wages, rising prices, and more rises in wages, leading to still further rises in prices, which many industries seem to be starting today.

In the essence, this program boils down to this: Increase pay rolls faster than you increase profits; and pay higher wages out of lowered costs, rather than passing them on as higher prices. Unfortunately, our leading corporations seem to be going in the opposite direction. From 1935 to 1936, industrial pay rolls increased only a little over 10 percent, while the profits of reporting corporations increased more than 50 percent. If businessmen continue to increase profits out of all proportion to pay rolls, disaster is sure to follow.

If one applied Dr. Ezekiel's observation to American industry, one would find immediately that the factors which affected different industries were completely different. In some there were signs of inflation; in others prices were actually being lowered in 1937. It is obvious that different industries required different treatment.

For example, in 1937 automobiles were produced in such quantities and at such prices that in spite of the increased cost of steel and labor even the unemployed could ride. Amusements such as moving pictures had become available to the very poor. Railroads were lowering rates and improving services. On the other hand, the price of housing was increasing by leaps and bounds. The differences between these two opposite tendencies—only one of which could be described as inflation—were due to the different types of organization. For example, the moving-picture industry had in effect conducted a great public-works campaign, building theaters on the proceeds of a sort of lottery tax on the investing public in every small town in the country. The automobile industry had been subsidized by the greatest expenditure for concrete roads ever known in the history of any country. The railroad systems had become almost a part of the Government. Their principal problem was not rates but pensions. The building industries, on the other hand, were so organized that no single organization could produce a complete standardized house in any quantity. The pressures all were toward raising prices. Agriculture presented a different problem; textiles another separate set of difficulties.

Had it not been for our elaborate economic and legal doctrine it would have been easy for the nation to fumble its way into a solution of these different problems by using different methods in each one. Some presented dangers of inflation; others did not. Some needed control; others did not. The learned theology of the time, however, convinced men that the same general principles of credit, noninterference with business, bureaucracy, the gold standard, the Constitution, and individualism operated without regard to particular organizations or personalities. The antitrust laws represented a social and moral philosophy which considered size the principal criterion, modified by something called "reasonableness." The laws of supply and demand were supposed to operate as soon as the antitrust laws were enforced. Freedom of contract, a great moral principle, was thought to be a set of practical directions. The sum total of the debate led to the following conclusion: If separate practical problems are treated as separate practical problems, the nation will perish.

The effect of this confused doctrine, which led either to no conclusion or to an absurd conclusion, was to reduce the thinking of intelligent people to a set of moral reactions.

This is nowhere better illustrated than in the ballots taken by the National Economic League on what were the paramount problems of the United States. This society represented a fair cross section of sound, conservative, educated opinion. Its membership was, so far as it was possible, composed of prominent people who thought they were abreast of the times. In 1937 they voted on the comparative importance of problems which confronted the United States as follows: Most pressing were (1) labor; (2) efficiency and economy in government; (3) taxation; (4) the Federal Constitution; (5) crime; and (6) public opinion and public sentiment. The problems which were voted to be of minor importance were *housing, tariff, agriculture, public utilities, social security, land, population, banking and credit, the cooperative movement,* and *equitable distribution of national income.*

The reader will note from this a complete immersion in theology. "Labor" in the abstract was the most important problem. It was not considered, however, to have any connection with housing, or land, or equitable distribution of national income, or population, which were minor affairs far down the list. Efficiency and economy in government was the second paramount problem. Public health, on the other hand, was near the bottom of the list, as if it were entirely irrelevant to efficiency and economy in government. The Federal

Constitution was the fourth most important problem. Public utilities and natural resources, the control of which was inseparably connected with the Federal Constitution, were treated as minor affairs having nothing to do with it. And finally and most ludicrous: while the problem of crime was one of our greatest difficulties, prison reform was down with such minor things as mortgage relief for farm and home owners, population, and speculation—as if it were a separate subject having nothing to do with crime.

The same way of thinking is illustrated in each yearly poll of this association. In 1934 efficiency and economy in government were at the top. Organized crime was third. Of wages, housing, and social security, which were then creating the labor problems which were to follow in 1937, the first two were at the bottom of the list, and the last was not on the list at all. In 1932 economy and efficiency in government were at the top. Restoration of confidence was near the top. Crime, under the heading of "administration of justice," was a close runner-up. Unemployment insurance and stabilization of price level were near the bottom.

Most amusing of all are 1930 and 1931. At a time when the nation was about to plunge into its worst depression and when solution of the prohibition problem was actually and in fact at hand, we find that administration of justice, prohibition, lawlessness and disrespect for law were the three most paramount problems selected by these learned men. Old-age pensions and insurance were not mentioned in 1930 and were near the bottom of the list in 1931.

These polls are so typical of representative thinking which was created by the impact of learned philosophical theory that we reproduce five of them on the pages which follow. The reader will note: (1) that abstractions always lead the list and practical problems get very few votes; (2) that there are no problems stated concretely; and (3) that the problem

[To be released for publication on or after Monday, March 17, 1930]

Paramount Problems of the United States for 1930

as selected by a preferential vote of the National Council of The National Economic League, taken in January 1930.

Number of Votes	Subjects	Comparative importance of subjects
2209	Administration of Justice	
2068	Prohibition	
1699	Lawlessness; Disrespect for Law	
1642	Crime	
1573	Law Enforcement	
1235	World Peace	
996	Agriculture, Farm Relief	
877	Taxation	
862	World Court	
811	Reduction and Limitation of Armaments	
810	Conservation of Natural Resources	
735	Efficient Democratic Government	
672	Foreign Relations	
654	Education	
644	Individual Liberty	
613	Law Revision, Federal and State	
611	League of Nations	
592	Unemployment	
570	Political Corruption	
567	Child Welfare	
554	Flood Control	
521	Consolidations and Mergers	
512	Tariff	
502	Eugenics, Defectives	
500	Desecration of Natural Beauty in the U. S.	
465	Moral and Ethical Standards	
455	Election Laws	
449	Economic Distribution	
440	Highways and Waterways	
435	Group Banking	
435	Penology, Prison Reform	
432	Co-operation vs. Competition	
424	Motor Traffic Regulation	
411	Freedom of Speech, of the Press	
400	Stabilization of Business	

THE NATIONAL ECONOMIC LEAGUE
6 Beacon Street, Boston, Mass.

EXECUTIVE COUNCIL:

JOHN HAYS HAMMOND   MINING ENGINEER
WILLIAM ALLEN WHITE   EDITOR THE EMPORIA GAZETTE
JAMES ROWLAND ANGELL   PRESIDENT YALE UNIVERSITY
A. LAWRENCE LOWELL   PRESIDENT HARVARD UNIVERSITY
ROGER W. BABSON   STATISTICIAN
FRANK O. LOWDEN   FORMER GOVERNOR OF ILLINOIS
DAVID STARR JORDAN   CHANCELLOR EMERITUS LELAND STANFORD, JR., UNIV.
EDWARD A. FILENE   MERCHANT
GEORGE W. WICKERSHAM   FORMER ATTORNEY-GENERAL OF THE UNITED STATES
NICHOLAS MURRAY BUTLER   PRESIDENT OF COLUMBIA UNIVERSITY

SECRETARY AND TREASURER
J. W BEATSON   6 BEACON STREET, BOSTON

The purpose of The National Economic League is to create, through its National Council, an informed and disinterested leadership for public opinion. The National Council is made up of men who are nominated as the best informed and most public spirited citizens of the country. They are elected separately from each state by preferential ballot.

In selecting subjects by means of the preferential ballot, the members vote by marking a cross before every subject which they consider important, indicating by added crosses the subjects which, in their opinion, are of greater and greatest importance. The votes on related subjects should not be combined, as this method of voting gives each subject its full vote and its proper place on the ballot.

Other subjects voted on receiving less than 400 preferential votes

393 Drug Traffic	302 Use of Leisure Time	215 Radicalism
391 State Rights	301 Latin-American Relations	165 Railroads
387 Citizenship	293 Religion	164 Lobbying
382 Centralization of Money and Power	279 Labor Problems	159 City Life Problems
375 Immigration	273 Finance, Banking, Currency, Credit	159 Federal License and Control of Corporations
362 Aviation	272 Thrift, Extravagance	141 Radio
360 Old Age Pensions and Insurance	269 Public Utilities	137 Merchant Marine
316 Public Health	261 National Defense	126 Governmental Principles and Policies
345 Installment Buying	257 Calendar Simplification	121 Civil Service
333 Marriage and Divorce	235 Public Safety	108 Land Policy
333 Investment Trusts	227 Industrialism and Agriculture	105 Interstate Commerce
310 Speculation in Stocks and Foodstuffs	226 Negro Problem	99 Housing
308 Foreign Trade Policy	222 Federal Reserve System	97 Public Charities
	222 Russia	70 United States Patent Laws
	222 Country Life Problems	

Document E-1   Issued March, 1930

(To be released for publication on or after Monday, March 2, 1931)

Paramount Problems of the United States for 1931

as selected by a preferential vote of the National Council of The National Economic League, taken in January 1931.

Number of Votes	Subjects	Comparative importance of subjects
1871	Prohibition	
1750	Administration of Justice	
1514	Lawlessness, Disrespect for Law	
1434	Unemployment, Economic Stabilization.	
1398	Law Enforcement	
1314	Crime.	
1106	World Court	
966	Taxation	
879	World Peace	
708	Efficient Democratic Government.	
694	Agriculture, Farm Relief. . . . . , ...	
647	Political Corruption	
624	Tariff	
555	Reconsideration of War Debts.	
529	Government in Business	
510	International Economic Relations.	
464	Foreign Trade Policy.	
462	Reduction and Limitation of Armaments	
460	Socialism, Communism	
456	League of Nations.	
442	Conservation of Natural Resources.	
419	Law Revision, Federal and State.	
392	Revision of Anti-Trust Laws	
391	Education	
387	Centralization of Money and Power.	
386	Child Welfare.	
382	Cooperation vs. Competition	
382	Moral and Ethical Standards.	
372	State Rights	
362	Individual Liberty	
353	Election Laws.	
350	Old Age Pensions and Insurance.	

Other subjects voted on receiving less than 350 preferential votes

338	Immigration	256	Thrift, Extravagance
333	Russia	244	Finance, Banking, Currency, Credit.
322	Motor Traffic Regulation	239	Group Banking
315	Consolidations and Mergers of Financial, Manufacturing and Mercantile Corporations.	218	National Defense
		216	Penology, Prison Reform
		213	Freedom of Speech, of the Press
310	Citizenship	200	Speculation in Stocks and Foodstuffs
306	Relations between Labor and Capital	198	Public Health
303	Social and Economic Readjustment	197	Marriage and Divorce
301	Public Utilities	170	Eugenics
280	Railroads	139	Industrialism and Agriculture
263	Stabilization of the Value of Money	117	Governmental Principles and Policies

The purpose of The National Economic League is to create, through its National Council, an informed and disinterested leadership for public opinion. The National Council is made up of men who are nominated as the best informed and most public spirited citizens of the country. They are elected separately from each state by preferential ballot.

In selecting subjects by means of the preferential ballot, the members vote by marking a cross before every subject which they consider important, indicating by added crosses the subjects which, in their opinion, are of greater and greatest importance. The votes on related subjects should not be combined, as this method of voting gives each subject its full vote and its proper place on the ballot.

Document P-9   Issued March, 1931

1932
Paramount Problems
of
The Present Economic Depression

as selected by a preferential vote of the National Council of The National Economic League.
1317 ballots were returned to April 15th.

Number of Votes	Subjects	Comparative importance of subjects
2238	Economy and Efficiency in Government. National, State, City	
1582	Taxation	
1528	Reparations and International Debts.........	
1460	Banks, Banking, Credit, Finance............	
1105	Reduction and Limitation of Armaments, Disarmament	
1075	Tariffs	
1071	Restoration of Confidence.................	
1026	Administration of Justice	
922	International Tariff Conference.............	
808	Unemployment, unemployment relief.........	
766	Economic Planning.......................	
765	Railroads, Transportation.................	
706	Over-speculation	
687	International Cooperation to promote prosperity and security.................	
665	Coordination of Production and Purchasing Power....	
643	Agriculture, Farm Relief...................	
592	Money, the gold standard, silver............	
581	Federal Reserve Policy	
576	Foreign Trade	
573	Equitable Distribution of Wealth or Income...	
531	Over-extension of Credit..................	
511	International Economic Conference..........	
491	Cooperation (vs. Competition) as a Social and Industrial Principle....................	
485	Efficient Distribution....................	
477	Germany's Situation......................	
453	Anti-Trust Laws	
445	International Monetary Conference	
401	Unemployment insurance..................	
398	Wages	
383	Installment Selling......................	
367	Land, administration, utilization, taxation.....	
364	Education	
328	Stabilization of Price Level	
299	Public Utilities, regulation, government ownership	
293	Over-centralization of Business............	
186	Socialism, Communism	
174	Capitalism	
153	Russia	
141	Unearned Increment	

The purpose of The National Economic League is to create, through its National Council, an informed and disinterested leadership for public opinion. The National Council is made up of men who are nominated as the best informed and most public spirited citizens of the country. They are elected separately from each state by preferential ballot.

In selecting subjects by means of the preferential ballot, the members vote by marking a cross before every subject which they consider important, indicating by added crosses the subjects which, in their opinion, are of greater and greatest importance. As this method of voting gives each subject its full vote and its proper place on the ballot, the votes on the related subjects should not be combined.

Paramount Problems of the United States

As selected by preferential vote of the National Council of The National Economic League, taken in May, 1934

Number of Votes	Subjects	Comparative importance of subjects
1172	**Efficiency and Economy in Government** ...... Federal (480) State (415) County (379) City (445) Town and Village (286)	
1014	**The Administration's Recovery Measures** ..... As a unified program.	
962	**Organized Crime** .... Breakdown of Law Enforcement	
941	**Taxation** .... Unification, Equalization, Reduction, Duplication, Sales Tax	
724	**Monetary Policy** .... Devaluation, Stabilization, Gold, Silver	
611	**Public Opinion and Public Sentiment** .... The need of adequate non-partisan activity under democratically chosen leadership to inform and unite public opinion and public sentiment, as the only power that can reach and enforce agreement for the establishment of a sound and stable economic and political order.	
608	**World Peace** .... Prevention of War, Elimination of Private Production and Sale of munitions and arms manufacture, etc. An effective peace pact.	
585	**Tariff**	
577	**Veterans' Benefits**	
570	**Labor**	
568	**Administration of Justice**	
551	**Agriculture**	
479	**Industry**	
473	**Unemployment**	
464	**Banking and Credit**	
441	**International Co-operation**	
440	**Federal Budget and Finances**	
407	**Inflated Debts**	
385	**Education**	
374	**Public Utilities**	
371	**Federal Securities Act**	
360	**The Consumer**	
347	**Capital**	
336	**Constitutional Aspect of the Recovery Program**	
322	**Transportation**	
279	**Stock and Commodity Exchange Regulation**	
272	**National Defense**	
267	**Mortgage Relief for Farm and Home Owners** ...	
263	**War Debts**	
244	**Equitable Distribution of National Income**	
238	**World Court**	
235	**Land**	
228	**Natural Resources**	
177	**Population Distribution**	
169	**League of Nations**	
164	**Pan American Relations**	
163	**Government Development Projects**	
138	**Housing**	
125	**Public Health**	
85	**Installment Buying**	

Paramount Problems of the United States for 1937

As selected by preferential vote of the National Council of The National Economic League.
(The vote was taken in February, 1937.)

Number of Votes	Subjects	Comparative importance of subjects
955	**Labor**.......	
	Industrial relations; control of labor unions; employment, wages, hours, organization	
914	**Efficiency and Economy in Government**.........	
	Federal (328) State (253) City (249) County (221) Town and Village (171)	
759	**Taxation**.......	
	Unification, equalization, reduction, duplication; sales tax, etc.	
660	**The Federal Constitution**..............	
	States' Rights; Supreme Court	
614	**Crime**.......	
	Breakdown of law enforcement; juvenile crime	
517	**Public Opinion and Public Sentiment**...........	
	The need of adequate non-partisan activity under democratically chosen leadership to inform and unite public opinion and public sentiment, as the only power that can reach and enforce agreement for the establishment of a sound and stable economic and political order.	
489	**Federal Budget and Finances**...............	
450	**Monetary Policy**........................	
449	**Democracy**.........................	
394	**Industry**.........................	
371	**Prevention of War**..................	
361	**Merit System in the Civil Service**...........	
330	**Capital**.........................	
311	**International Co-operation**..............	
300	**Unemployment**.....................	
282	**Administration of Justice**.............	
263	**Public Utilities**.....................	
259	**Natural Resources**..................	
245	**Agriculture**......................	
220	**Social Security**....................	
212	**Tariff**..........................	
194	**Education**.......................	
159	**Transportation**....................	
147	**Public Health**.....................	
136	**Liquor Control**....................	
135	**National Defense**..................	
132	**Child Labor**......................	
132	**Housing**.........................	
121	**Land**............................	
99	**Equitable Distribution of National Income**.......	
96	**The Cooperative Movement**.............	
94	**Banking and Credit**.................	
73	**Prison Reform**.....................	
62	**Mortgage Relief for Farm and Home Owners**.....	
52	**Population**.......................	
48	**Speculation**......................	

The purpose of The National Economic League is to create, through its National Council, an informed and disinterested leadership for public opinion. The National Council is made up of men who are nominated as the best informed and most public spirited citizens of the country. They are elected separately from each state by preferential ballot.

In selecting subjects by means of the preferential ballot, the members vote by marking a cross before every subject which they consider important, indicating by added crosses the subjects which, in their opinion, are of greater and greatest importance. As this method of voting gives each subject its full vote and its proper place on the ballot, the votes on the related subjects should not be combined,

selected as the most pressing is one which is already on its way to a solution through the emergence of a new organization which is rising to fill the need. Thus, when the organizations to break the prohibition impasse had become strong and effective, prohibition was thought to be our greatest danger. When government was filling the gaps in finance, relief, unemployment, and so on, governmental efficiency and economy were our most pressing difficulty. In 1930 and 1931, when government was refusing to meet the problems under its nose, there were thought to be no pressing problems of government administration. When labor organizations were beginning to represent labor effectively in 1937, and had conducted a series of strikes with less bloodshed and disorder than had occurred in any similar period of adjustment between labor and capital, labor was our greatest problem.

The learning and distinction of this group are illustrated by the names on its executive council, which appear in the exhibits.

The Effect of the Philosophical Learning of Government in Encouraging So-Called Private Organization

POLITICAL and legal thinkers of our time do not consider private business organization as "government." Great corporate organizations are looked at as rugged individuals. We shall analyze this interesting fiction later. It is sufficient here to point out that it is a pure fiction. For most people what the so-called "government" does is of minor importance. "Private" organizations dominate their credit at the bank, the prices which they pay for necessities like light, heat, water, and transportation, their promotion, and, finally, their security for the future. Nevertheless, political and legal learning does not think about business organization as "government" in any sense. Paternalism, bureaucracy, regimentation, arbitrary control, and so on, are not words which are ordinarily applied to our regimented industrial structure.

This curious attitude is the result of a philosophy that great organizations dressed in clothes of individuals achieve long-run unselfish and humanitarian results by pursuing their selfish interests. The only control needed is that of an umpire. The only formulas needed are standards by which the umpire can apply the rules of the game.

This philosophy gave enough freedom for opportunistic action to our temporal industrial government to make it one of the marvels of the world in productive efficiency prior to the depression. It was a creed designed to make any interference by political organization in industrial affairs a pure ceremony. Thus business achieved freedom to organize and to experiment. All of the formulas which hampered political government justified letting business government alone.

The entire priesthood of law and economics directed their detailed directions and inhibitions at political organization. The standards which they held up to private business were purely inspirational. "To be grandly vague," said Herbert Finer, "is the shortest route to power; for a meaningless noise is that which divides us the least."

Thus the ritual of business government was not encumbered with definition and learning. The late J. P. Morgan did not surround himself with professors when he organized the United States Steel. The theories of John D. Rockefeller did not interfere with his conduct as a businessman. Business during its great development was not concerned with waste or with thrift, or even with fair dealing. It had a philosophy which eliminated those standards as practical impediments.

The lack of learning and definition in business affairs is illustrated by the lack of order and logical symmetry in our schools of business organization. Most scholars found the study of such day-to-day activities uncongenial. They were

The Place of Learning in Distribution 109

responsive to no orderly logical classification. Therefore, schools of business administration had a very precarious status as scholarly enterprises. The study of advertising or arrangement of shop windows had far less academic prestige than the study of theoretical economics. The one was an unlearned and practical pursuit suited only to a trade school; the latter was real scholarship. The reason was that the superstitions and faiths which made business organizations cohesive were more like the early disciplines of the Roman State than like the elaborate learning which is essential to philosophical literature.

The basis of the business organization was discipline. It was expressed, not in terms of military glory, but in terms of hard work, instant obedience and loyal coöperation with superior officers. It was not a drafted army but a volunteer army. Just as military service was the only honorable career of an early Roman, so business service was the only honorable career of a wide-awake American, disdainful of the softer pursuits. The penalty for lack of obedience and loyalty was discharge from the business army.

Little did these businessmen worry about theoretical economics in the day-to-day conduct of their enterprises. Their religion of the beauties of competition was a symbol representing the early history of the tribe, performing the same function as the tradition of military glory in Rome. These men developed a real understanding of the public psychology necessary to conduct their own small principalities. They hired public relations counsel who used words and slogans for effect, rather than as part of the search for the holy grail. The techniques of advertising grew with amazing rapidity. They did not *follow* the legal or ethical religion but *used* it in moving people by rhetoric and by pictures. In this enterprise they called on the methods of a rapidly developing psychology—a psychology which did not deal in moral terms—which took man as it found him, not worrying about his tendencies or trying to abolish his sins, but trying to profit by them and to utilize them. Their underlying creed was "grandly vague" and inspirational enough not to interfere with their techniques.

Spiritual v. Temporal Government, and the Political Machine

THUS we developed two coördinate governing classes: the one, called "business," building cities, manufacturing and distributing goods, and holding complete and autocratic control over the livelihood of millions; the other, called "government," concerned with the preaching and exemplification of spiritual ideals, so caught in a mass of theory that when it wished to move in a practical world it had to do so by means of a *sub rosa* political machine. There was no question as to where the temporal power lay. Occasionally, the spiritual government could make a business baron come on his knees to Washington, but these were the rare occurrences. It was the general opinion in America before the depression that the government at Washington should render unto Cæsar the things which were Cæsar's, and confine its own activities to preaching. The attitude of the conservatives toward government in business was the same as toward a minister of the church who deserted his pulpit to buy a seat on the stock exchange.

There was something peculiarly medieval in the faiths which sustained the business government in America. In the first place, men, with that astonishing ability to shut out reality characteristic of group thinking, actually believed that it was not government at all. The American Telephone and Telegraph Company and the United States Steel Corporation were "individuals" who "owned" their industries.

Such intangible things as morale, a trained personnel, institutional habits, public acceptance and good will, indeed all the elements which distinguished a going concern, were thought of as private property, owned by an intangible individual, just as it was once thought that the King of France "owned" the State. The independent principalities of business were subject to the spiritual values dramatized by the National Government. But the rulers of those principalities thought of the National Government as something designed to preserve their "freedom." The fiction was carried so far that men thought of the employees as also "free" to work when and where they pleased. This curious faith could be expressed by the Supreme Court, in violation of all the observed facts, and achieve acceptance, even when contradicted in dissenting opinions by members of the Court itself.

In the light of the taboos and superstitions which surrounded the spiritual government, this separation into spiritual and temporal rulers—an unconscious hypocrisy—was the only practicable way of getting along. There had to be an area where men were free to move and to experiment, where men were free from learning and from theory, and where organizations could develop. No people has yet existed who could get along without putting its ideals and practices into different compartments. Indeed, no well-trained psychiatrist thinks that the individual patient can survive without some machinery for an escape from the world, or advocates it. Yet the thinkers about government had no objective grasp of the place which the corporate myth was playing in society. Even the social doctors believed in the fantasies of the great organization for which they prescribed, or else adopted the point of view of missionaries to the heathen and prescribed an alien set of fantasies without regard to the fact that they were planting them in uncongenial intellectual soil. And thus, since all cures based on this unreal conception of the social structure seemed worse than the disease, the notion of *laissez faire* was sure to be adopted sooner or later by all those who actually remained in power. However, the *laissez faire* of the theoretical economists was far different from the *laissez faire* of the business government. To the prince of business, *laissez faire* meant only that his principality should not be interfered with by an attempt to put the dreams which supported the spiritual government into actual practice. Therefore, the *laissez faire* economists constantly advocated free trade, while the *laissez faire* businessmen insisted on letting protective tariffs alone.

Nevertheless, in spite of this constant disagreement between the theories of the institutions and their practices, the temporal government worked out very well indeed, and developed efficient organizations.

Of course, industrial government never lived up to its creed. That fact created the atmosphere which produced our so-called liberals who studied the creed and preached about the sins of business in violating it. Such "attacks" on business organization did not hamper it because they did not propose organizational changes. Instead they strengthened the creed by showing that in it lay the way of salvation. When organizational changes began to appear after the depression, the liberals opposed change and lost their identity as a group. This is characteristic of liberal movements in times of change. They always disappear, because they are symptoms of belief in established forms. They stand on the same fundamental truths as conservatives and immediately join forces with conservatives when new organizations appear to violate those truths.

So long as liberals preached against business sin, they offered a safety valve through which the explosive energy of discontent could escape.

Actually, as any observer may note, the disagreement between the preacher and his congregation is one of the things which keeps the church alive, so long as the minister is willing to confine himself to preaching and exhortation. Men like to hear about their sins. They love to have theological doctrine expounded which they do not have the faintest intention of following. And since the economists and lawyers of the day believed that it was more important to leave the temporal government alone than to have even sound theories forced upon it, they operated like preachers in all churches since time immemorial. The barons of the Middle Ages didn't follow the Bible, but they felt that it was a great book just the same.

The Function of Learning To Reconcile Politics and Ideals

NATURALLY, there had to arise some machinery which would keep the spiritual and temporal government marching in step. Such machinery had to be placed behind the scenes, because the elaborate ritual which went on in front had nothing to do with the realities of the situation. This may be illustrated by looking back at the prohibition experiment. When men wanted to pretend that the nation was dry, a vast and complex organization of bootleggers became a necessity in order to meet the demand for liquor. There was a practical task before the social organization which had to be accomplished, i.e., the distribution of liquor. There was also an elaborate ceremony to be celebrated, i.e., that the nation was dry. It was the duty of the spiritual government to denounce the liquor-distributing organization as sinners and to put a few of them in jail, without however going to such extremes as to stop the actual business of supplying alcohol.

For this duty, the myths of the time were completely adequate. The conceptions of freedom, individualism, and so on, became sacred things which justified the purely ceremonial enforcement of prohibition which the demands of the time required. When it again became recognized that the distribution of liquor was legitimate, the machinery for that purpose became much less complicated. Ritual, learning, literature, disappeared. Bartenders, a comparatively decent and law-abiding class, were substituted for bootleggers. The business was done better and more efficiently.

Today there is a desperate spiritual need to impose impossible standards on governmental organizations, and to pretend that it is principles which govern, and not men. Hence the political machine arises as the only kind of organization which can obtain the necessary freedom from those principles to do the practical tasks of government. It is the task of governmental theory to prove that we are governed by political machines only because right-thinking men have not abolished them. This will happen through an awakened public conscience caused by preaching.

Everyone knows that political machines cannot be abolished so long as the conflict between ideals and practical needs in government exists. Yet the attempt to abolish them is part of the ritual which makes them survive by showing we are true to our ideals in spite of our frailties. Situations like this are quite understandable when discovered in maladjusted personalities whose fixed ideas interfere with their practical necessities. However, they seem more difficult to grasp when they occur in government. Yet these results are obvious and inevitable. The United States Steel Corporation would develop a *sub rosa* political machine the moment a set of ideals was imposed on it which interfered with the distribution of steel. In minor conflicts of ideals, our great corporations do develop such machinery (as in the case of strike breaking), and both stockholders and executives regard them with the same mingled horror and regretful acceptance with which statesmen regard Tammany Hall.

It is, therefore, natural that the country whose theories of government are the most unrealistic in the world should develop the greatest and most powerful *sub rosa* political machinery. It is not civil service that makes England less subject to *sub rosa* influences, but the fact that the English do not have the same inhibitions about the open exercise of power by their government. For example, the United States Government maintains an army the equal in discipline and efficiency of any in the world. The reason is that once the American people are willing to admit the necessity for a governmental enterprise, their genius for organization is as great as any in the world.

The Inflation of Legal and Economic Learning

WHEN men are confronted with a contradiction between their myths and reality, they have only two recourses. The first is ceremony, drums, and oratory. The second is reason and dialectic. The conflict must be made to disappear under a thick blanket of incense of some sort or other. And it is only natural that a people with a mystical reverence for reason should demand books.

When men make plans for the conduct of an actual institution whose workings they understand, and whose objectives they believe legitimate, they feel the need for no great philosophical outpouring. But when men plan crusades based on an institution they do not understand, a vast dialectic literature pours forth to aid a faith which is in conflict with the facts that they observe. Thus, the depression witnessed the greatest flood of legal and economic literature the world has ever known.

The difficulty in the depression was that men were making plans for a paper government which had no real existence. In such a situation the search for explanations and theories

became the more intense the more men felt that something
was wrong. In law, books streamed off the presses at a constantly accelerating rate. Twenty-five thousand printed decisions a year, over a hundred law reviews, added to the confusion. Commercial digests and treatises coördinating all
these books kept appearing. It became impossible in a law
school for students to write even about simple things without
an amount of labor that was appalling.

The situation was similar to that of the Church when minis-
ters were multiplying treatises and sermons went to "sixthly"
and "seventhly." This created a great counter-literature written by people called realists, which in turn called forth a new
set of defenders of the faith. Legal doctrine grew so huge it
became difficult to argue a case without presenting a longer
brief than the case could bear.

Economic literature suffered the same inflation. The books
were of two general classes. The first pointed out that from
the point of view of a census of resources and labor there was
no earthly reason for so many slums, such inadequate medical care, so much waste of mineral or agricultural resources,
so few clothes, and so little food. They demanded that the
nation get together and utilize its plant efficiently. The second class pointed out the danger of efficient national organization by reciting the parable of the wild Russian and the
cruel German. All these volumes developed theories and
counter-theories. None of them developed organizations.
The net result was that economic theory became so complicated that it was almost useless for the only practical purpose to which it could be put; that is, for authoritarian
argument.

The burdens on the politicians coping with this inflation
of legal and economic learning led to an influx of professors
into Washington. Proposals had to be dressed up so that they
fitted into a rounded economic and legal system. The first

impulse of practical politicians was to hire learned men to help them. Thus we find Roosevelt in the early days of the depression employing a brain trust. Like all groups of learned men since the council of Nicæa, this brain trust split in all directions on doctrinal points. There was a succession of resignations by bright and very articulate men whose pride of opinion had been violated by political action. The brain trust fell into disrepute and became a political liability rather than an asset.

Yet the emotional need for authoritarian learning was still there. The Republican party felt a gnawing vacancy which could be filled only by establishing a counter-brain trust. And thus we had two sets of professors disputing over which were the sound fellows and which the quacks, following the general lines of theological dispute since the invention of the art of writing. How much of this stuff to put into a political platform was a burning question. It could not go in at all unless reduced to meaningless generalities, but it was important that some of it appear. Wise candidates dodged the issue as long as they could, but no one could dodge it completely. The text that finally appeared was reduced to its ultimate in terms of harmlessness so that it was actually impossible to tell the difference between the platforms of the various opposing groups in terms of the practical action to which they might lead.

In 1936 the inflation of legal and economic thought in America had achieved a volume never before experienced. The thinking men of the country were all busy thinking and the more they thought, the more mixed up they became. No one could fit the social organization which he saw before him into the organization of his dreams. And then on top of all this inevitable development, theorists wrote books complaining that political platforms were meaningless *because of the stupidity and insincerity of politicians.*

CHAPTER V

The Use of the Language of Private Property To Describe an Industrial Army

In which the inconvenience and discomfort of using an ancient language in public discourse are pointed out.

THE confusion in political thinking which we have just described arose out of the gradual decay of an old legal and economic religion. The difficulty with the religion was that it had become an obstacle to the organizing ability of the American people. It was producing phobias instead of inspiration. Economic principles had become an arsenal of weapons used against new organizations instead of for them. Governmental morality had become an excuse for government not to meet obvious social demands.

In a period when rational philosophies of government were necessary for our comfort, everyone was demanding a new creed; yet every new creed advanced violated the old ideals which were still sacred. This is usual in times of social change. It is one of the inevitable symptoms of progress from one form of social organization to another. The literature of the time is typical of any similar age which is experiencing a conflict between its ideals and its needs.

The most obvious conflict of 1937 was that in which the creeds accepted by respectable people described social organizations in the language of personally owned private property, when as a matter of fact the things which were described were neither private, nor property, nor personally owned. The complete failure of the language of law and economics as a means of communication of sensible ideas created the endless debate about principle and the exhortations to heed the lessons of history which we have been observing in courts, in colleges, and in the editorial pages of newspapers. Before analyzing the failure of our economic and legal language as a means of communication of practical ideas it is first necessary, at the risk of repetition, to discover why old gods always thrash around so violently before they die, and why most respectable people become so uncomfortable in the process.

The Discomfort of a Changing Mythology

THE reason for this confusion which attends the growth of new organizations in society lies deep in the psychology which concerns the effects of words and ceremonies on the habits of men in groups. Men always idealize these habits and the structure they give to society. The idealizing is done by magic words which at first are reasonably descriptive of the institutions they represent. At least they represent the dreams which men have of those institutions. When the institutions themselves disappear, the words still remain and make men think that the institutions are still with them. They talk of the new organizations which have come to take the place of the old in the terms of these old words. The old words no longer fit. Directions given in that language no longer have the practical results which are expected. Realists arise to point this out and men who love and reverence these old words (that is, the entire God-fearing, respectable element of the community) are shocked. Since the words are heavily charged with a moral content, those who do not respect them are immoral. The respectable moral element of society will have nothing to do with such immorality. They feel compelled to turn the power over to nonrespectable people in order to reserve the right to make faces at them. Yet they recognize that those immoral people are doing something which has to be done. This fact can only be explained under the curious age-old concept of sin. No religion ever got along without this concept. It is useful because everyone can continue to work to abolish it, knowing full well their objective will never be reached. Thus, in these times of confusion, everyone believes that human character is disintegrating. This happens whenever the rising generation thinks differently from the old.

By this process the formulas become more important than facts. They cease to be tools and become objectives in themselves. Legal and economic literature (or whatever other ceremony is current in such times) becomes more important than life. And in the confusion which results from this conflict respectable men become angry, sad, romantic, cynical, disillusioned, last-ditch defenders of a faith. They do not become cheerful, practical technicians dealing with the facts before them.

In such times men get to talking about the decline and fall of civilization and worrying about Greece and Rome. A vast literature of explanation and exhortation pours forth. This is a symptom that the class which produces that literature is becoming uneasy and impotent and needs a great deal of printed matter in order to prove to itself that it still represents the only sound type of organization. The blame for that uneasiness is all ascribed to the immorality of a society which has perversely and sinfully become unlike the little ideal pictures which represent what a proper society should be like. At such times men predict Fascism, Communism, and all sorts of similar catastrophes. They prove this by putting it on the printed page, because they have more faith in the printed page than in the spoken word.

The result of this uneasiness may be a war, or may be only a lot of oratory, poetry, and romantic economics. What happens depends on whether the kindly, tolerant, respectable elements of society are able to emerge from this mood of impotence before less kindly and tolerant people seize the reins of power. The mood does little harm if it is only a temporary escape from reality, like being in love, or mourning for the dead. Indeed, it would be a drab human race which did not shed a tear over departed institutions. Romantic lovers and inconsolable widows are both very lovely dramatizations of important ideals and the writer would not abolish them if he could. Nevertheless, it is an incontestable fact that they are hard people to put up with outside of books and when there is a job to be done.

The Mythology of Private Property in an Age of Organization

WHY has the literature of law and economics become today more like a funeral service than the pep talk for salesmen which it should be to promote organization? The reason is that it is using the little pictures of private property and profit motive to describe a society which is much more like an army than the group of horse traders which it is supposed to be. Against the background of such a society the terms do not make sense. Men believe that a society is disintegrating when it can no longer be pictured in familiar terms. Unhappy is a people that has run out of words to describe what is going on.

It is obvious today that private property has disappeared. The writer, for example, owns some furniture which he can use without the assistance of any large organization, though not to the extent his parents could, because he is unable to repair it as his father was. For transportation he has an automobile, but he does not know what is going on under the hood and could not run it without a great organization to assist him. His father owned a western ranch and raised his own horses. These horses burned hay, but the hay did not come from a filling station, which in turn required a still larger organization to supply it. Yet today furniture and automobiles are the nearest we come to private property generally owned by any large group of our population.

The other things the writer "owns" are all claims to rank or privilege in an organizational hierarchy. He is a professor at the Yale Law School and hopes that Yale will feed and lodge him. He has a piece of paper from an insurance company which he hopes will induce that organization to take care of his wife if he dies. He has other pieces of paper from other organizations operating buildings and railroads and manufacturing plants which give him precarious privileges in those industrial governments. Wealth today consists in nothing any one individual can use. The standards of wealth are simply current expectations of how the individual stands with the rulers of industrial baronies coupled with a guess as to the strength of those principalities.

I have a friend who "went broke" during the depression. Everyone said he was "poor." In material things he had a large house and servants and a number of automobiles. However, these did not count because a number of financial organizations were thought to be on the verge of taking them away from him by virtue of pieces of paper which enabled them to storm his castle walls. Therefore, though my friend's standards of living were beyond my own hopes in this world, nevertheless I was the more "prosperous" because men had more faith in Yale than in the organizations to which he was attached.

Today my friend is no longer broke. The organizations in which a fiscal heraldry gives him rank above the common herd are now thought to be strong enough to repel attacks. He "lost" his money and "gained" it back again. In doing so he had to enter into new allegiances with other feudal barons, but he picked the right ones. He is now rich. His standard of living during this process changed very little. He lived in the same house with the same servants all along. His feeling of security, however, went from the top to the bottom and up to the top again. The guesses of his neighbors as to what was going to happen to him went through a similar cycle. He is happy again because he now has a secure place and privileges in a number of great industrial empires.

There are, of course, people in this country who still own independent private property, but they are far down in the social scale. Such people live in states like Vermont. They have scarcely any cash income but are able to produce enough to eat and to heat their homes. Home owners in smaller cities may have certain independent ownership of houses, but since they can neither heat nor light their homes, nor move from their homes to their place of work without calling on organizations, their independence is pretty much of a fiction. Owners of business blocks in smaller communities are also somewhat independent and deal with individuals as tenants instead of great industrial governments. They are disappearing. Great moving-picture organizations and chain stores are getting control of business property in smaller towns and substituting claims on organizations for this remnant of private ownership. In large cities the process is complete. The erection of great office buildings has become a method by which an industrial government levies taxes on persons seeking old-age security by investment. The building of these magnificent structures prior to the depression was not dictated by the kind of motives which would make a profit-seeking *individual* build a building.

Take for example a great real-estate concern, responsible for the financing of all sorts of business and residential structures. Actual building had become a mere incident to the circulation of little pieces of paper, which in effect were a tax on the investing public by organizations who regarded

the collection of that tax as more important than the buildings themselves. Thus S. W. Straus and Company spent most
of its energy supporting the slogan that they had never
lost money for an investor.[1] The long-time utility of the
buildings for purposes other than selling securities was given
little thought. The bonds were sold to men who had never
seen the buildings and who cared little about them. They
bought because they thought Straus would protect them in
their old age.[2] Straus built to extend its position and power.

In the debacle which followed it appeared that the power
of the Straus organization was not dependent on whether

[1] We quote from the findings in the case of *People* v. *S. W. Straus &
Co.*, 285 *N. Y. Supp.* 648 (1936), which are also incorporated in the Report on Protective Committees of the Securities and Exchange Commission
(1936), Part III, "Committees for the Holders of Real Estate Bonds," p. 66:
   "After the defendants' [Straus's] many years of intensive advertisement
to the effect that they issued real estate bond mortgages which were first
liens in every respect, it can be readily understood that a heterogeneous public might well be misled into believing that it was actually purchasing first
mortgage bonds when in fact the security received was one of a junior lien."

[2] *Ibid.* "As a result of this intensive advertisement there was created in
the public mind the impression and the belief that such bonds were the
direct obligations of the defendant, S. W. Straus & Co., Inc. The examination before the attorney-general of one Frank C. Schlitt, a salesman in the
employ of one of the defendants, is illuminating on this point. 'Q. As a
matter of fact, Mr. Schlitt, you realize that the greatest selling point you
had was the fact that it was a Straus bond? A. Yes. Q. You told people it
was a Straus bond? A. Yes. Q. You didn't tell them that it was simply
underwritten and that Straus had nothing to do with the payment of the
bond—you simply told them it was a Straus bond? A. Straus bond. . . .
Q. You knew that thousands of people were buying these bonds in the
belief that they were a direct obligation of Straus? A. That they were
guaranteed by Straus. Q. And you did nothing to disabuse the minds of
these people to the contrary? A. Only when a customer would ask if they
were guaranteed.' "

   The Securities and Exchange Commission states in the same report
(p. 72): "Real estate underwriters consistently concealed from investors material facts in connection with the earnings of properties securing issues
which they distributed. But emphasis on the proved safety of their underwritings recurred constantly in their sales literature."

the buildings themselves were profitable. It made profits on foreclosing and liquidating the properties by further manipulation of the paper symbols created when the buildings were erected.[3] The reason was that ownership of the buildings was a pure fiction. The only important factor was the position of power which an organization had obtained and the fact that no other organization of equal power existed to take over the control.[4]

The Straus financing was not an isolated instance. In every field of industrial activity great organizations had

[3] *Idem*, p. 168. "An examination of the property management fees received by S. W. Straus & Co. of California indicates clearly the importance of this business to the Straus organization. With the depression the underwriting business of this company vanished. For a period it confined its activities mainly to the purchasing and selling of securities. But in its attempt to maintain its sales organization it steadily lost money. By 1932, with the advent of numerous defaults in California issues sold by Straus, the trustees (Straus officials) had taken possession and were operating or supervising the management of many properties through the company. The management and supervision fees received by the company transformed the previous deficit into a profit." (The various types of patronage which were available to the underwriting houses on default are described in detail in this report.)

[4] The entire five volumes of the Report of the Securities and Exchange Commission on Protective Committees are full of the various ways in which control over financial reorganizations was kept by the organizations which had originally underwritten the securities. We quote a typical bit of testimony from Part III, of the report on p. 96:

"Q. So when a bondholder finds himself in the predicament as the holder of a defaulted bond, what choice has he?

A. Practically none.

Q. He can go in, or stay out?

A. And if he stays out, they bring on foreclosure, bid as little as possible, and he gets a small distributive share.

Q. And if he goes in?

A. He takes just what the committee wants.

Q. And in many cases he cannot get out once he is in?

A. Exactly.

Q. And there is no supervision over this committee that you know of under the law?

A. No."

built themselves into similar positions of power. They had done so under a mythology of private property which prevented those who were exploited from observing what was going on. The public saw the whole series of events as a series of horse trades by independent individuals. This mythology had become so completely misleading that men could not diagnose what was wrong when these corporate principalities failed to function, or why they injured so many people. The remedies proposed on the assumption that the corporations were individuals working for profit came out wrong because the corporations were not individuals. It was as if men assumed that an automobile was a horse and tried to run it on hay.

The class of people who could use these financial symbols realistically and unscrupulously rose to power, regardless of their efficiency as producers. They operated within a folklore which regarded the trading instinct as the salvation of the country. Traders are necessarily ruthless men. The ethics of trading is a series of ethical contradictions. Therefore, when everyone else had dropped the reins of power, this small group was in a position to seize them. Thus the Van Sweringens, who had acquired their trading skill in real estate, obtained control of great railroad enterprises. Small blocks of stock representing an infinitesimal part of the so-called partnership gave them power over an empire. The power thus gained was without any responsibility because these blocks of stock were thought of as private property. Men skilled in the tricks which could be played with these cards could always dominate experts in transportation when the control of a railroad was at stake.

If one reads the careful investigation made by the Securities and Exchange Commission into the activities of protective committees in reorganization, one finds that those in control were almost always financiers and not technicians. A trading class was elevated to power who knew nothing of the techniques of the organizations which they led. Actual goods and services were dispensed by a great army of salaried technicians who were given neither power nor security. Economics and law assumed that everyone was acquiring private property under the impulsion of the "profit motive." "You can't get efficiency in operation without a profit motive," said the profound students of social organization.

When such organizations got into trouble, the remedies proposed were formulated on the assumption that they were to be applied to individuals who were exercising independent control of tangible things which they owned. Had there been a realization that these organizations were not dealing with private property, it would have been obvious that the remedy lay in giving the control to men with a different sense of responsibility. The romantic legal and economic ritual of the time, however, was built up around the ideal that a trader without responsibility to the groups involved made the best general in an industrial army. In the situation which resulted only those could rise to power and rank who were more interested in the manipulation of financial symbols than in transportation, or housing, or the actual production and distribution of any sort of goods. Position and rank obtained in this fiscal world had carried no social obligation because they were subject to the rules which governed the accumulation of private property.

The Difficulty of Describing Industrial Organization in the Learned Terminology of the Time

THE objective observer who attempted to describe what organizations were actually doing found it almost impossible to communicate his idea because there was no accepted terminology which could be used to describe the activities of an industrial or financial organization. Learning about such organizations was divided into separate compartments, each with its own experts. If the observer was a lawyer, he was supposed to stop on the threshold of economics and let someone else do his thinking from that point on. If he was an economist, he was supposed to stop on the threshold of the law. If he was a layman, he was supposed to make only a few limited practical observations and then consult lawyers and economists as to the meaning of what he saw. No one could describe an organization as a complete whole and maintain any pretensions to authority.

In describing Tammany Hall and predicting whether it would be successful in maintaining its power in New York City, everyone recognized that the predictions must be based upon estimates of the quality of leadership and the morale of the organization. No one based his conclusion upon current quotations of the "assets" of Tammany Hall. No one "capitalized" the disciplines, habits, morale, or spheres of influence of that organization and called them private property. Men dealing with Tammany Hall did so practically and realistically. The reason why this was possible was that Tammany lay outside the field of law or economics. There were no learned books written which could be consulted to find by formula whether Tammany Hall was a better organization for a man desiring influence and security in political position than the Vare machine. There were no brokers' analyses or current quotations on political machines.

It was impossible, however, to describe the industrial organizations of the nation as political machines were described. The queer country of scholarship in law and economics, which was supposed to be the home of financial principles and legal rights which controlled these organizations, could not be used as a whole by any individual. It was mapped out in little irregular patches of domain, staked out and appropriated by different groups with names derived from Latin and Greek sources. It was all right for the neighbors to get together for a housewarming, or for a coöperative effort in which the resources of their respective principalities are joined for the common good. But when one man crossed to his neighbor's domain to make maps and sketches of the fortifications, as if he contemplated changing the boundaries, he was greeted with suspicion and alarm. Scholarship had its own capitalistic system and thousands of earnest and industrious men were dependent on the inability of men to think about organized society in practical and political terms which cut across scholarly boundaries. They did not want their separate properties taken away without due process. They had spent endless effort building books and articles on those properties. The separation of powers between lawyers, economists, and psychologists was a most important concept in the federation of independent intellectual sovereignties known as a university.

Even inside these independent sovereignties learned enterprise was far from communistic. The law had its own little fields within its larger field. Deans of law schools, when a "property man" resigned, sought to replace him with another "property man," and would not hear of hiring a "conflicts man" to take his place. Economics and psychology, and all the rest of the scholarly states, were divided along the same lines, and the rolling stone which rolled over these lines was permitted to gather a minimum of moss.

Of course, these scholars knew that the tumbling stream of events was not divided this way and so great defenses were erected to keep these events from bothering their pious meditations. Actual events were supposed to take place in a temporal world. The scholar lived in the spiritual world of principle and formula. Political scholars were advised not to mingle in politics, trial lawyers were avoided in law schools, and advertising men were looked at with suspicion in faculties devoted to the study of the psychology of men in groups. When a real scholar wanted to visit the temporal world of events, he protected himself from its vanities by a pair of dark glasses called "the statistical method." These obscured his vision so much that he could not see enough at any one time to contaminate him.

Today, in spite of the fact that law and economics are aspects of social psychology, a psychologist can enter the field of law and coöperate with jurists *only* provided that he take the word of sufficiently respectable legal scholars as to what the law is. If he makes his own observations, he is treated with the same scorn that an anthropologist describing savage customs would be treated with by the priests of the tribe he was observing.

This reaction on the part of both economists and lawyers is natural and inevitable. It is part of the process by which newly observed facts become assimilated into an old religion. It may be compared to the impact of Darwin on the Church of England. It may also be compared to the reaction of the ethical philosopher at the beginning of the century toward psychoanalytical descriptions of "love" and "honesty." The churchman and the philosopher felt their ethical world crumbling, just as legal scholars today feel their jurisprudential world crumbling under the impact of an objective analysis.

This frame of mind made the predictions of both lawyers and economists very bad indeed. In the first place, persons of such responsibility were not supposed to guess at all, but to seek certainty in a changing world. Guesses about the future power of any human organization or about the future activities of any culture must take as fundamental factors an estimate of the morale and habits and disciplines of groups and also the quality of their leadership. The peculiar folklore of lawyers and economists considered these factors the business of someone else. They were thought of not as part of law or economics but as confusing elements which marred the clean outline of those sciences. Therefore, such factors were put into separate compartments of learning such as psychology or sociology where they did not interfere with more orderly learning.

In the second place, respectable people felt a moral responsibility to prescribe the social bookkeeping of the next generation. This compelled them to take sides. "Is Mussolini worth the price Italy had to pay for him?" was a favorite topic. Something or other was supposed to be solved if this question was answered yes or no. There was a hint of immorality about objective observation which did not take sides. It was like being neutral at Armageddon. This prevented such observation from obtaining a respectable place in institutions of learning.

Finally, an ideal called "intellectual integrity" sterilized the efforts of many observers in the social sciences. Such people saw that creeds were never descriptive and that they suppressed the unpleasant facts about institutions in order to give them prestige. "Intellectual integrity" compelled these observers to become "realists" and to denounce the creeds as "bunk" and to "expose" them. There was a vague expectation on the part of some of the "realists" that this would start men to "thinking" and make them "intellectually honest" about their institution. Realists were ordinarily disillusioned about the entire human race because they saw through its ideals. Disillusioned people seeking comfort in a creed of "intellectual honesty" are poor diagnosticians.

The power to make accurate guesses about a political situation is of the essence of an understanding of government. Yet these are the very kind of guesses which educated men seem incapable of making. The more learned they are, the more books they read, the less accurate their guesses are. Politicians of the professional type are better at such diagnosis than men who have "thought the subject through" after the conventional manner. Hence politicians are the prevailing influence in our government.

The world of business organization was no better understood by the learned than the world of politics. From the point of view of the learned, Henry Ford's ideas were naïve. He constantly got mixed up about the lessons of history. This did not prevent him from being one of the most skilful organizers of the age. He has had as much effect on our daily lives and habits as any man in his generation. Suppose he had acquired a corps of economists, lawyers, and social scientists to advise him from the inception of his enterprise. In that case someone else would have been in his place today.

Let us go back to see what the thinkers thought about the automobile. Woodrow Wilson, the political philosopher, was gloomy about it. He said it would have an unfortunate effect on American democracy. Before the automobile we had had nothing which was an absolute mark of aristocracy. Now a distinction would be made between the rich and poor which would cause particular envy, because only the rich could afford an automobile. The poor man, driving a horse, would be covered with dust as the rich man passed by.

Later, when the automobile industry was most vigorous, economists proved that there were too many cars. Instalment buying was going to decrease purchasing power and a collapse was imminent. The automobile was a luxury anyhow and economic theory of the time had much to say of the evil economic effects of spending for luxuries. The fact that a great organization was growing up which was keeping people busy was noted. But the strength and permanence of organizations, once they have acquired disciplines, habits, and morale, were not considered factors in making a guess as to their future. Economists did not study personalities, habits, and disciplines. It was assumed that laws of supply and demand were more important.

In thinking about an army in time of war, men made better guesses because they took these considerations into account. Also, in thinking about a political machine, observers were more accurate because there was no law of supply and demand to bother them there. There was no demand at all from the properly constituted economic abstract man for a political machine. Such illegitimate organizations only bothered him. Therefore, economic science had no place for them except as an excuse to show why economic law did not work better. For this reason men's judgment about the strength and permanence of any given political machine could be based on observation, not principle. Their judgment of the future of the automobile industry was clouded by abstract principles.

Had Ford followed current beliefs at any time, he would never have built his plant. He was, however, thinking in terms of organization. He did not understand the complicated fiscal world of the economist and hence it did not hamper him.

A technique of thinking consciously in terms of organization did not exist among the learned. The times were uncongenial to its development as a dignified intellectual pursuit. Religions require rounded systems of principles and the hope of certainty. Priests hate to think in the present. They want to build an intellectual edifice which will endure through the centuries. The realistic observer or diagnostician on the other hand knows that he cannot see into the future and that any of his guesses may be wrong. It was not respectable for learned men to be wrong. If a scholar made an error, it proved that there must be something loose in the machinery of his logical principles. Therefore, scholars could not safely deal with the present. They were called propagandists if they did. They preferred to talk in terms of eternity. Every prediction had to have a fire escape to prove that the learned men would have been right had not some unsound persons appeared who mixed up the situation in a way that would not have occurred if people were more educated.

The result was that Education became the cure for everything. Voters had to be educated, businessmen had to be trained, people had to be taught to respect the Constitution, and so on. The word "education" was simply a substitution for preaching in a more mystical age. The phenomenon is one which always has occurred and always will.

Therefore, while the guess of a technician has a fair chance of being wrong, the guess of a student of governmental or economic theory is almost sure to be wrong. This is not easy to prove, particularly to a theorist, because he can always show that he was right all along, since the words in which he puts his predictions are so vague and slippery. Yet a review of expert guesses made before the depression seems to indicate the truth of the assertion. Fred C. Kelly has written a most penetrating book called *How To Lose Your Money Prudently*.[5] His answer is to give it to the most respected financial experts to invest for you. His proof of this point is complete and devastating. The book is not an attack on the integrity of financial experts. It is a discussion of the psychological forces which lead men who have a profound theological grasp on the theories of finance into a succession of inevitable errors.

In larger affairs the diagnoses of the majority of those trained in legal and economic science were even worse. It was Walter Duranty, a newspaper correspondent, who made

[5] Philadelphia, Roland Swain Co., 1933.

the most accurate analysis of Russia because he looked at it as a growing organization. Learned men at the time were proving that the Bolshevists could not succeed because they were departing from sound principles. In the same way they proved that Mussolini and Hitler were doomed to failure. During the 1936 campaign, and later while Roosevelt's attack on the Supreme Court was going on, they proved that Fascism was about to sweep over this country because of the same forces which had made it so powerful in Germany and Italy. The most careful and scholarly lawyers, leaving out of consideration the limitations of the Supreme Court as an organization, proved conclusively that the Wagner Labor Act would be declared unconstitutional. There had been some doubt about the Agricultural Adjustment Act. A decision against the Labor Act was forecast with absolute certainty.

Of course, particular economists and lawyers were not always blind to these organizational factors. However, they could not base their public diagnosis on them without losing caste as dignified members of their professions and appearing like mere newspaper writers beyond the pale of learning and authority.

CHAPTER VI

A Platform for an Observer of Government

IN which it is suggested that since men are compelled to personify their institutions, the point of view of the psychologist toward such personifications may offer a useful platform for studying social problems.

THE reason why old myths create such a problem in times when old institutions are not functioning effectively is that they induce men to act in direct contradiction to observed facts. Such conduct is of course one of the great cohesive forces of society, for when institutions are functioning effectively it is the power of superstition rather than the power of reason that holds them together. However, when the institutions have become impotent to meet social needs, these same superstitions have the effect of throwing respectable, moderate, and kindly people out of power because they cannot free themselves of the old myths long enough to be effective leaders.

This is illustrated in the defeat of business leadership in the campaign for President in 1936. Here we had a powerful class of supposedly efficient industrial organizers, supported by most of the educated people in America, who were fighting for a principle. Their superstitions made them unable to create the new organizations which the times demanded. They also compelled them to fight, instead of seeking to gain control of the new organizations which were arising. Their conduct in the campaign violated every canon of common sense. Long before the election it was obvious to anyone with the least political sense that Landon would be defeated. Nevertheless, the Republican party raised and spent ten million dollars in ways which businessmen should have known to be idiotic. These men of common sense (when not emotionally excited and engaged in crusades) had apparently induced themselves to believe that America was in danger and that they had a chance to save her. The trouble with these individuals was their religious obsession during these trying times when practical common sense was necessary to preserve the unity and political machinery of the Republican party.

The editors of the conservative press apparently convinced themselves that principles as sound as they thought theirs were *must* be victorious. They therefore could give no accurate picture of what was going on.

The present status of fact-minded observations on governmental affairs can be pictured by comparing it with the diagnosis of a physician. Such diagnoses may be, and often are, wrong; everybody knows that they are only the guesses of experts. A consultation of physicians, however, does not descend to the level of oratory about principle. It gets its authority from the standards by which men judge the expertness of physicians. The best physician under these standards is not the one who can make the most powerful public speech, giving the reason for supporting his diagnosis. Ability to expound reasons in public, which is the ability of an actor, has nothing to do with correct diagnosis or prediction. In fact, it usually obscures that ability.

In order to lift fact-minded diagnosis of governmental problems into a respectable position so that the public generally will have at least the same ability to select the best experts as they now have to select the best physicians, it must be made respectable.

We suggest therefore that the platform of the observer be the following:

1. Institutions are like personalities playing a dramatic part in society. They are to be judged by their utility in the distribu-

tion of physical comforts and in the development of an atmosphere of spiritual peace.

2. When institutions fail to function, reforms must be attempted with something like the same point of view with which a trained psychiatrist reforms an individual. That point of view must recognize that an institution has something which may be called a subconscious mind. This means only that its verbal conduct must be calculated to inspire morale and not to describe what it does.

3. Law and economics are the formal language of institutions on parade.

We suggest this creed, not because it is an absolutely true description, but because it gives us a point of view which permits the expert to direct the play of affairs from behind the scenes without the feeling that he is engaged in an unworthy procedure or that he is a mere politician. It recognizes that drama and ceremony are as important as food and shelter and overemphasizes neither.

Of course, the writer does not know what an "institutional subconscious mind" is. The phrase is neither true nor untrue. Nevertheless, in the development of psychological techniques the word "subconscious" has become very handy to describe a different source of behavior from the ones which people have to take into account in the conduct of ordinary affairs of life. Its utility lies in the fact that it permits us to rid ourselves temporarily of moral rational judgment. It is therefore convenient in describing individual conduct to use the term "subconscious mind" to describe the impulses which are not expressed in formulated religions and creeds.

Of course, institutions are not like individuals. Nevertheless, they are organizations in which men become bound together by habits and disciplines and ideals so that they cooperate in very mysterious ways. Getting food in New York City is not a planned operation. All sorts of taboos, beliefs, illusions, struggles for prestige, loves, hates, lusts, and fears furnish the motive power which moves this tremendously complicated organization. Economics describes it as a struggle for money and credit among traders. This is obviously not true. The law describes it as a group of men following logical precepts. This also is not true. The device of the institutional subconscious mind permits us to describe the theories of law and economics as part of all these habits and coordinated social conduct, but not as controlling them. Such description requires a different kind of creed before it can be recognized as a legitimate occupation for serious men. This new observational creed necessarily must share the characteristics of all which made the old creeds acceptable before it can be used by the respectable and the learned.

Let us briefly review those characteristics:

1. The creed must be based on a very simple and understandable ideal capable of personification so that the public may have confidence in it.

For example, a popular personification of the physician is found in the term "Man in White." This gives him a recognized place among our institutions and frees him from the necessities of public debate on general medical principles. The words have emotional associations with efficiency, humanitarianism, service, and whatnot. All physicians are "Men in White" today—experts and not orators. Compare this ideal of "Men in White," which permits us to select the best physicians, with a current ideal of how the labor problem should be solved. The National Economic League, in a bulletin of July 15, 1937, devoted to "order and justice in employer and employee relations," thought that the problem must be approached from a highly abstract angle before anything practical was even suggested. We quote:

NOTE—Some of our members have suggested that The National Economic League attempt to secure agreement as to the basic principles underlying the solution of the labor problem.

Are not these principles the same as those governing our political order? It will undoubtedly be agreed that a stable political order must be based upon justice and democracy, and that efficient methods of keeping these principles alive and working are equally important.

In studying the labor problem is it not necessary to keep in mind, as of first importance, the question of justice, not only to labor but to all the other factors entering into production and distribution, including the consumer? Is it not essential, too, that democratic principles and efficient methods be adopted by employers and employees in the consideration of questions affecting the interest of the workers and in respect to the organization of labor?

Does this statement seem to you to be of value as a background for consideration of the problem?

Vote of	*Vote of*
The National Council	*The Special Committee*
Yes: 444 No: 11	Yes: 13 No: 0
(98%) (2%)	(100%)

In other words the idea expressed by this recent bulletin of The National Economic League is that in order to solve labor problems you must first get back and talk about the fundamental principles of democracy. Suppose that cancer research, in a time when no one knew anything about cancer, started its experiments by laying down the fundamental principles which govern the disease as a preliminary step to discovering what it was.

Other essentials of any creed, even the creed of an observer, are:

2. The creed must be inspirational and therefore cannot be an accurate description.

3. The creed must not be so fantastically idealistic that it creates impossible standards. Impossible standards inevitably create a conflict which leads in the end to the fulfilment of practical needs by nonrespectable people.
4. The creed must not be realistic in the sense that it is an "exposure" of human frailty; it must be sweetened by what the realist is apt to call hokum. There is no room for disillusionment in an effective social platform.

The Creed of a Political Observer Has Utility and Truth Only in Diagnosis, not in Action

ONE of the most difficult adjustments for modern intellectuals is the realization that different points of view have equal validity provided they are used in different settings. When one appears on the public stage to take part in some important ceremony, he should not question the assumptions on which that ceremony is based. Public debate of all kinds today, whether before a court or in a campaign, assumes the existence of group free will and a thinking man who will be persuaded. If that assumption is questioned on the stage, the advocate will be a failure. The reformer who questions it will spend the rest of his life condemning the human race because its institutions are not what they pretend to be. Public management on the other hand is based on the assumption that men in groups are not rational. That assumption has given impetus to the various political techniques of industrial organization in which we excel. If public management is carried on under the assumptions of public debate only failure will follow.

The point of view which we are attempting to sketch here is one which allows a place to the folklore necessary for social organization, which does not mislead us with respect to its function in society. It is the point of view of modern psychiatry without its classifications. This attitude has not attained the dignity of a formulated philosophy. It is one which the realistic politician has taken all along. The task of the philosopher is to make it respectable so that respectable people can use it.

Objective v. Rational Diagnosis

I WILL illustrate the increased ability to diagnose and predict which this platform gives by describing the kind of diagnosis and prediction which resulted from the pioneer work of the late Professor Edward S. Robinson of Yale, a psychologist who chose to observe law and economics. Professor Robinson was gradually acquiring a technique which enabled him to diagnose social conflicts and predict the results with startling accuracy.

Late in 1932 I attended a conference in New York assembled by a gentleman of some prominence in the banking world, who foresaw in November the impending collapse of our banking system, which finally took place the next March. It was a small group of bankers, economists, and lawyers. The meeting was conducted in an atmosphere of intense gloom because everyone was convinced of two things: (1) That a collapse of the banking structure was imminent, and (2) that some drastic preventive measures were needed. On the question of the particular measures needed no two men of the group agreed. Everyone saw dangers in everyone's else plans. The meeting ended in complete disagreement (as all meetings ended in those troubled times, no matter who attended them). Everyone, however, agreed with the statement of a prominent lawyer, who said: "My mind fails to function when I think of the extent of the catastrophe that will follow when the Chase National Bank closes its doors."

I returned to New Haven much depressed and saw Professor Robinson, who remained quite unaccountably cheerful about the whole situation. I said: "But you don't seem to realize that there is a crash coming." He replied: "Did any of these experts specify in any concrete terms what human beings would do when the crash occurred?" I admitted that they had not done so. He asked: "Do you think that when the banks all close people will climb trees and throw coconuts at each other?" I admitted that this was a little unlikely but that a bank crash of this magnitude certainly sounded like rioting and perhaps like revolution. Professor Robinson replied: "I will venture a prediction as to exactly what will happen. When the banks close, everyone will feel relieved. It will be a sort of national holiday. There will be general excitement and a feeling of great interest. Travel will not stop; hotels will not close; everyone will have a lot of fun, although they will not admit that it's fun at the time."

Months afterwards I happened to be in New York on the day that all the banks did close. I was amazed at the accuracy of Professor Robinson's diagnosis. I had very little cash but was able to give checks at hotels for food and lodging without any difficulty. Everyone was excited and interested. They had something to think about and talk about. It was a great emotional release. Space doesn't permit me to go into the reasons Professor Robinson gave for this guess. It was, however, among all the predictions which I heard about the impending crash, the only one that was accurate.

I will give another illustration. Nearly a year before the election Professor Robinson was commenting upon the press campaign against President Roosevelt, which was just getting under way. He said: "These anti-Roosevelt editors are all wrong. They completely misunderstand the effect of what they are saying and doing. Newspapers are a powerful influence in this country. They will continue to be a powerful influence. However, the people who write the editorials and columns do not understand very well the nature of that influence in our peculiar intellectual atmosphere. They are now calling Roosevelt every possible name. Starting out with violent language, the language will necessarily become more and more violent. They cannot help themselves when they make it impossible to describe a really good picture because the words 'colossal' and 'stupendous' have been used so frequently to describe inferior pictures that they have no meaning when applied to good ones. As the campaign goes on, attacks from newspapers will become more and more meaningless. Men caught in this type of psychology simply cannot stop. It isn't anybody's fault; it's just something that is going to happen.

"Now the effect of all this is going to be to make Roosevelt a popular hero. Take an illustration from dramatic techniques. The ordinary melodrama exposes the villain in the last act. The hero denounces him; the heroine points the finger of scorn at him and everyone goes away thoroughly disgusted with his conduct. But this exposure *must* take place at the end of the play. If it took place at the beginning of the play and kept up throughout the production, you would find that the villain was assuming heroic proportions and that the hero was becoming somewhat namby-pamby. The same thing will happen in this campaign because editors do not realize that a political campaign is a dramatic production. Their technical propagandists think it is something like advertising for tooth paste, in which a slogan becomes impressed on the public mind by constant reiteration until everyone buys the tooth paste. In fact, it is entirely different. The denunciation of Roosevelt is laying the ground for a triumphal march for him at the end of the play. This doesn't mean that the press is losing its influence. It only means that the influence of the press on public opinion is not very well understood by the people who own the newspapers. Newspaper men are beginning to learn how an advertising campaign sells soap. They do not yet understand how to bring a political drama to a climax. That is a difficult technique, like producing a play. It may fail even in skilled hands. However, it is bound to fail in the hands of people who think that dramas can be successful with high-pressure salesmen on the stage instead of actors. The press campaign is going to get results, but not the results the editors expect."

The accuracy of this prediction as to the results of the newspaper campaign was verified in a most startling way. Yet even after the campaign newspapers do not understand this phenomenon. As this is being written men are talking about the "waning influence of the press," while the press is engaging in the same kind of attack against Roosevelt, a year and a half before the congressional elections. The trick of being tolerant between elections and starting a mass attack when the battle actually commences is not yet learned.

Many politicians, of course, knew this. Roosevelt himself showed uncanny skill in leading the opposition on to making poorly timed attacks. The difference between Professor Robinson and the politicians was that he could tell better than they the grounds on which the prediction was based. This enabled him to communicate his technique to others who might improve it.

From the Observer's Point of View Law and Economics Are the Language of Institutional Personalities

MR. JUSTICE CARDOZO has said that law is literature. Without changing his essential meaning, I prefer to call it language, because only the best of it (which includes his decisions) can be dignified as literature. Most of it is commonplace language in which very commonplace unliterary men

conduct their disputes. The same observation can be made
of economics. Both of these sciences are the formal means
of expression when institutions are parading in their best
clothes or else when they are fighting battles.

If this is true, it would follow that a parallel could be
drawn between the ordinary language of the time and the
legal and economic language of the time. The methods of
growth should be similar. The struggles between good grammar, whether economic or philological, and the common
and vulgar means of expression should be the same. We
should find the economic grammarian and the language
grammarian both striving to keep unsound constructions out
of their languages and we should expect that they would
always fail. We should expect to find economic and legal
language being constantly enriched by new words taken
over from nonrespectable groups, just as ordinary language
is enriched by words taken over from prostitutes and con-
victs.

An examination of H. L. Mencken's book, *The American
Language,* shows how close this parallel is. Human institutions must talk in the language of their folklore. They do not
invent that folklore. It grows as language grows. Each class
of society from the criminal to the preacher contributes. Indeed, the so-called lawless element of society contributes far
more to economic and legal theory than anyone imagines.

Mencken's book is outstanding because he is not interested
in grammar or the correct use of words. His story of the development of language is told not from the point of view of
how it ought to be spoken, but how it is spoken. In reading
this book, I obtained for the first time a grasp of language as
a living force, reflecting the moods and spiritual struggles of
a people in the strange new words, bad and good, which
were constantly flooding in. Groups which experience the

greatest conflict between respectable attitudes and practical needs are the source of most new words; i.e., the nonrespectable classes, engaged in *sub rosa* but very necessary social activities. Seeking a way to describe themselves, since society has denied them a position of dignity, they create a language of subtle satire and attack. This is the philosophy of one denied a seat in the church who thumbs his nose at the preacher in order to maintain his own morale. Thus a woman became a "moll," a "twist," etc. A thousand dollars, instead of being "money" or something to be invested to insure a respectable position, is correctly described by the importance which its possession gave in a social hierarchy. It is called a "grand."

As one reads this book on language, one learns that the tempo and accent of legal and economic theory ape the tempo and accent of language. In pioneer conditions when language is full of exaggeration and braggadocio, governmental theory follows the same pattern. In conditions of dull and learned respectability, men's common talk becomes dull and learned, full of complicated evasions of facts. So we find the same pattern in their economic and legal theory, or ideology of governmental and industrial institutions. Russia today has the pioneer conditions, together with the language and governmental theory of braggadocio and extreme exaggeration. When new pioneering organizations are striving to become logical and respectable, they adopt the extreme dogmatism of Communism and Fascism. They become violent and untactful in their attempts to prove they are superior to others, and this conceals an inner sense of inferiority. When institutions are content to remain nonrespectable, they use both the language and the economic theory of cynics against those who deny them a place in the sun. Thus the language of *sub rosa* groups is vulgar, but sharp and pointed. It appears new and fresh to the respectable because it reflects a different point of view. Legal and economic theories are in reality nothing more than huge compound words with high emotional content.

The language of medicine, which once was a moral and theological debate over principles, has become to a large extent a pure nonphilosophical tool. So also are most of the theories of medicine. Men are not shocked and enraged at cancer, as they are at civil war in Spain, although the two have curious similarities from an organizational point of view. Men take sides in the one case, and not in the other. Their words and theories reflect this attitude in each case. They are dull, but descriptive. Neither the words nor the theories are fitted for the debate or dinner-table conversation of the "thinking man."

Mencken's book on the American language is a far greater contribution to the study of political institutions in America than Mencken himself realized when he wrote it. It shows how attitudes are reflected in the way men talk about their organizations. And legal and economic theory is nothing other than a way of talking about organizations. It also shows how the words affect the attitudes, crystallize them, make them stereotyped, and finally form the cement which binds the organization together.

Thus we see that new language does not arise and new words never come into currency apart from particular organizations. Esperanto has never been and never will become a current language any more than utopian socialism will become a current economic language. Language comes into being because particular organizations must express themselves and organization does not thrive without some sort of need. The gangster with a racket is an answer to competitive conditions in which current ideals refuse to permit sensible organization. For example, one of the most frequently recurring rackets is in the distribution of milk. Here we have complete anarchy in the distribution of a necessity. Milk companies compete to such an extent that often a number of different companies will send expensive trucks to deliver milk to the same floor of a large apartment house. One man and a horse (which stops and moves on without the driver climbing in and out of the cart) can distribute milk far more efficiently. Only if competition requires that milk be carried long distances with speed to scattered localities are trucks required.

In such a situation, respectable theory refuses to compel milk companies to apportion a city into areas in order to operate efficiently. Practical distribution of milk is supposed to create an inefficient bureaucracy or else interfere with our liberties, solely because it has become burdened with the offensive words "government interference with business." Hence a situation arises where organized *sub rosa* effort thrives. Gangsters are able to gain a large measure of control over the milk business because there is need for some sort of control and no one else will exercise it.

In labor conflicts public government is not permitted to take the necessary control. Therefore, large corporations are found hiring their own gangsters and spies on the theory that one must fight fire with fire. However, it is not a respectable spy system with the romance of the wartime spy. General Motors puts in operation a spy system with a language and a theory and a set of loyalties peculiar to the criminal class since this is the only class which is effective when working against a taboo. Its high officials hate to think or talk about the system in public. They deal with liars and traitors because the lack of scruples of such people makes them more efficient in furnishing strikebreakers. The more respectable elements of the organization are pained by this phenomenon in exactly the same way that the statesman is pained at having to deal with a political machine.

Such conflicts give rise on the one hand to complicated theories to explain and dignify the respectable institutions and on the other to satiric words to give the nonrespectable organizations some sort of standing. Thus the labor controversies in this country have been responsible both for Mr. Justice Sutherland's beautiful theories that minimum wage legislation for women destroys their freedom of contract, and at the same time for the picturesque terminology of the "finks" and "nobles" of the strikebreaking fraternity. The language of nonrespectable institutions is sharp and pungent at best and obscene at its worst. The language of authoritarian institutions is invariably solemn, learned, statistical, dull, and dry at its worst, filled with rhythm and eloquence at its best.

For example, one cannot read the argument of George Wharton Pepper in the famous Agricultural Adjustment Act case without being impressed both by its rhythm and beauty and its complete lack of descriptive meaning. It calls forth dreams of a beautiful past when government and business lay down together like the lion and the lamb. It combines poetry, law, and economic theory the way they should be combined for effective advocacy of a subject which falls equally within all these mysteries. I am not trying to be satirical at the expense of George Wharton Pepper, because I admire his argument immensely and strive to imitate his style when I am before a court. I am trying to show how the final residue of statistics, learning, and law, which constitutes the language of respectable institutions, protects those institutions against the crude, coarse facts which intrude into their imaginary world.

It is important to make clear that throughout this chapter I am not talking about the use of words as a sort of verbal pointing, which is the kind of language found in books full of technical description of concrete things. I am referring to the terms which make up philosophy and convey moods and attitudes.

The difference between what may be called "verbal pointing" and the philosophical terminology is that the former may be used by anyone who is familiar with the objects to which it refers. The latter is an essential part of an organization and has no meaning whatever to one who doesn't know the place which that organization fills.

Therefore, when the conflict between magic words and reality becomes so keen that the words themselves are losing their effect, we find that authoritarian organizations arise to give these words greater force. For example, we have never been absolutely sure about our law. There has always been an uneasy feeling that lawyers are tricky fellows (as compared with economists), and that the language of the law is a devious kind of logic. Therefore, the judicial institution is worshiped because it seems to prove that at least within its priestly portals the language of the law is used with truth, with logical finality, and with authority.

Our economic creed, however, has been usually so implicitly accepted that ordinarily all one has to say is "thrift," or "the law of supply and demand," or "balance the budget," and the evil spirits disappear. Therefore, no supreme court of learning has ever been needed to personify the authority of economics.

However, if the conflict between words and practical needs becomes keen enough, a supreme court of economic theory will appear. This is illustrated in a larger way by the recent unconscious attempt of the Supreme Court of the United States to make the Constitution the final word in economic as well as legal theory. The Court was simply responding to the pressures which demanded authoritative order when the magic words were losing their magic.

In a smaller way this reënforcement of magic words by

magic institutions in times of conflict can be illustrated by two events within the memory of the reader.

The first is found in the great prohibition experiment, which has now receded so far into the past that we can understand it. Here men felt an intense spiritual conflict. They wanted the nation moral and dry in principle and at the same time wet in fact. Prohibition enforcement, which like all legal process had to represent a compromise, became entirely ceremonial. Only in this way could it represent the various conflicting ideals to which men felt they had to cling in the prohibition era. Convictions of highly selected types of bootleggers ceremonialized respect for law. Acquittals of others celebrated individual liberty and the integrity of the home. As a *sub rosa* political organization grew up to fill the practical need, the conflict became keener. Learning was called in. Statistics were collected. Books were written. Finally the conflict reached the stage where it required an authoritarian tribunal. Automatically there arose the Commission for the Study of Law Observance and Enforcement, popularly called the Wickersham Commission. Great lawyers and educators sat on its solemn bench. While this commission was studying everybody felt better. They expected a rabbit would surely appear out of such a high silk hat. For a while this confident expectation resolved the conflict in the same way that the Supreme Court of the United States is continually resolving other like conflicts for us, when we insist on believing two opposite things at once. A rational country, devoted to statistics, was about to apply modern scientific method consisting of reason and statistics to a social problem.

Of course, when the report came out, it simply restated, in more complicated language, the conflict which everybody felt. It was, however, a useful and indeed an inevitable step in the solution of the problem. Reason and dialectic are always called on by government today to supply the prophetic vision that killing geese supplied for Rome, that the Delphic oracle supplied for Greece, and that prayer supplied for the statesmen of the last century. The effect of resorting to prayer was to make men become practical after the emotional fervor had been allowed to dissipate itself. By such ceremonies the gods of prohibition resigned in favor of technicians.

Today we see almost the identical situation in the problems of relief and of unemployment. Everyone insists on pretending that the country must balance its budget. But the literature of budget balancing is one of sorrow and not of hope. There is a very complicated set of absolutely contradictory ideas behind this apparently simple phrase. Budget balancing requires that relief be cut down at a time when there are available goods to be distributed to the needy. Our religion of individualism, which once was strong enough to starve people for moral reasons, has lost this potent magic. Therefore, we must take care of the needy and balance our budget at the same time. As is inevitable, a great literature has arisen out of this conflict. As this is being written there is a religious and mystical war going on in Congress. Roosevelt suggests one and a half billions. This is because he wants to balance the budget. Certain devoted priests want to balance it still more. There must be no compromise on a principle like this because if we compromise the principle flies out the window. Economists argue. Editorials are written. No one seems to be getting anywhere. The Supreme Court, once the great settler of spiritual conflicts through a mystical constitution, is in temporary difficulties. Anyway, the budget is not a legal problem.

In such a situation something like the Wickersham Commission is yearned for. Let us submit the troublesome problem to an oracle. At first this yearning takes the form of a demand for a census of the unemployed. All the intelligentsia take up the cry. Census technicians realize the folly of such an enterprise because the problem is one of distribution of goods, not unemployment. Many persons who are supporting families on an income of $250 a year are "employed." Everyone realizes that the census will not tell us how to balance the budget and also provide for relief. The demand for an authoritarian commission gathers force. Finally the headlines of the *New York Times* read as follows:

BILL FOR JOB STUDY RUSHED TO SENATE TO HALT RELIEF CUT

The Senate Committee on Education and Labor voted today to report favorably the Murray-Hatch resolution calling for the appointment of a Federal commission to study the general problem of unemployment and relief. The action was regarded as an important step preliminary to the expected fight in the Senate over the relief appropriation of $1,500,000,000 which the House will approve early next week (May 23, 1937).

We have thus repeated almost exactly the process by which the conflict over prohibition was resolved. If it were not for this conflict between ideals and practical needs in the question of relief, no one would think of such a commission. For example, if we transfer the same situation to a time of war, the problem becomes only one of organization to get the available goods around. It is not necessary to reconcile the need to distribute food with budget balancing. The only limits are those of supply, production, and transportation.

Once we have recognized that support of the needy is a legitimate social objective, we can become practical about it. Until that time conflict will have to be resolved by learned investigation. If the commission which is contemplated actually sits on the unemployment or relief problem, it will end by representing the same split in opinion now represented in the Congress which asked for the commission. If the conflict is resolved more quickly, there will be no such commission.

Let us examine in more detail the conflicting ideals that whirl around the related problems of relief, employment, distribution of goods, and budget. A page from the *New York Times* on May 24, when the conflict was at its height, will serve as an illustration. In the left-hand column Edith Abbott, dean of the School of Social Service Administration of the University of Chicago, holds forth. We quote portions:

Miss Abbott painted a dark scene of "misery and privation in what we like to call a land of plenty" and took President Roosevelt and Harry L. Hopkins, Federal Relief Administrator, particularly to task for "that tragic decision made by the Federal Administrator and his chief" to withdraw funds for direct relief, with the liquidation of the FERA.

The next column has the following headlines:

HAMILTON CALLS FOR DIRECT RELIEF

_____

Substitution for WPA Would Save 40 Cents on the Dollar, Republican Chairman Says

In the next column we find:

URGES END OF WPA TO SAVE A MILLION

_____

Gebhart of Economy League Wants the States To Share Evenly with Government

_____

Sees 8-Fold Cost Rise

_____

He Says Expensive Works Have Led to That Increase Over Worst Depression Year

And, finally, on the same page, Senator Byrd of Virginia takes the courageous but paradoxical position of opposing a

$1,500,000 appropriation to build houses for mountain families in his own state. They can't afford such nice houses, he says. It is gross waste and inefficiency to build them:

Senator Byrd today called upon Secretary Wallace to investigate charges of "gross waste and inefficiency" in connection with the Shenandoah Park homesteads in Virginia, a $1,500,000 Resettlement Administration project, and, if the charges are sustained, to "salvage what you can of this allocation and return it to the public Treasury to be applied to reduce the deficit in our revenue." (*New York Times*, May 24, 1937.)

All three men agree on the great principle opposing inefficiency and extravagance. However, anyone who thought that these people could agree on any plan of practical action would be badly misled.

We may bring the situation into clearer light by comparing it with one in which there was no spiritual conflict, the attempted rescue of Amelia Earhart. In discussing this situation the writer makes no decision as to whether providing somewhat expensive houses for people in need is a more beautiful ideal than rescuing a national heroine from the ocean. It might be argued that we could not provide all people in need with such good houses. It would be equally true that we could not spend such vast sums to rescue everyone lost at sea. Such discussions are only confusing. We use the illustration simply because the doubts about spending every available national resource in the rescue of Amelia Earhart were confined to very few people. There was no real conflict.

Had there been a conflict, the rescue would have proceeded along the lines of the housing project. First, plans would have been made for the use of the best planes to search the ocean. Then, when this extravagance was attacked publicly, cheaper planes would have been used. By the time that this device had received condemnation for inefficiency, the rescue would have been changed from a practical, efficient endeavor to a public debate about general principles. Everyone would have agreed that people in distress must be rescued. They would have insisted, however, that the problem was intimately tied up with balancing the national budget, improving the character of people lost at sea, stopping the foolhardy from adventuring and at the same time encouraging the great spirit of adventure and initiative and so on *ad infinitum*. They would have ended perhaps by creating a commission to study the matter statistically, take a census of those lost at sea, examine the practices in other countries. What was saved in airplane fuel would be spent on research so that the problem could be permanently solved.

It is that kind of confusion which is illustrated by this page from the *New York Times*. These four people agree on balancing and on the advisability of shelter even for the needy, but cannot agree on any practical plan of action. Let us read further the report of Miss Abbott's speech.

In comment on complaints about the mounting cost of social welfare, Miss Abbott decried "that enormous section of the Federal taxes that goes for the army and navy, the Veterans' Administration, the national debt incurred for war purposes, and all other expenditures for past and future wars.

"Then," she went on, "there is all the money wasted to reward the political friends of the successful party. I am sure you will agree with one that this is the real boondoggling—the truly vast expenditure that brings no useful return."

. . . . .

"Look at the reports of the RFC and read of the billions that went for banks, railroads and all the rest of that vast program. . . ."

She said that the cost of the War and Navy Departments and the cost of past wars was close to $4,500,000,000 a year. The cost of all Federal social welfare activities, including prisons, she added, was about $250,000,000 a year.

. . . . .

"The money so desperately needed for social welfare is already collected by taxation, but it is spent for past and future wars."

. . . . .

"But it is important also that we should continue to take note, as we did last year, of the wasteful expenditures of public funds to take care of political friends of the successful party. . . ."

You will note that Miss Abbott considers the abolition of war expenditures and the removal of patronage and politics from political organizations as somehow connected with the day-to-day relief problem. Such a position, of course, prevents immediate practical action because it complicates the problem by adding a disarmament conference, plus an attack on Mr. Farley, to an already full calendar. Hamilton, Gebhart, and Byrd might agree on Miss Abbott's general principles, but they would quarrel very violently with each other as to the place the social worker should take in the administration of relief. Hamilton would probably remove Democratic politicians, but not all politicians. Byrd would certainly remove social workers, but not soldiers.

Since there is no leadership here, but only a conflict of moral ideas, this means that the resulting administration of relief must be confused. If it moves along in one of the lines suggested, it will get opposition from all the others.

Let us analyze Mr. Byrd's attack on housing. He thinks the housing is too expensive for the poor mountaineers. He denies that houses built in Virginia add to the wealth of either Virginia or the country unless the kind of bookkeeping with respect to these houses accords with his own fiscal ideas. These fiscal ideas are to him more important than the houses themselves. So much for the larger issue.

However, in spite of Senator Byrd's objection, a few houses are built. In the building of them we note the same atmosphere creating the same sort of conflicts all over again. This may be illustrated by describing some of the troubles of the Government Housing Administration. In the first place, the Government must choose the best and most respectable architects on its planning board. If it does not do so, it will be playing politics by not choosing the most patriotic and respectable men. The best and most respectable architects are those who have been building skyscrapers. They want the very best materials used. Their plans for government housing, therefore, are much more expensive than they would be in the case of a private structure, for the reason that the architects can make public speeches if the Government opposes them, which they cannot do in the case of a private employer. A compromise is finally reached. But the houses are all of a more permanent character due to a moral objection to the Government's putting up flimsy constructions, which does not apply to a private construction.

Bids are called for. A group of contractors offers better materials than are specified in order to freeze out competition. They figure that they will make it up later. Architects favor contractors who give the Government more than the letter of the contract requires. This gives the advantage in government bidding to a small group. Once that group has established its position, a curious phenomenon called "price leadership" keeps the members from chiseling on one another. Their influence with the architects is such that outsiders have a difficult time breaking in. There is nothing necessarily corrupt about this process. It just happens.

The fixing of prices by what is called "price leadership" is furthered by another moral idea which arises from the attempt to keep politics out of government. This idea is that the Government cannot be trusted to accept private bids. All bids must be opened in public. Now it so happens that no building corporation in the group likes to start a *public* war against the other building corporations. Therefore, if the bids are public, they all follow list prices and the bids are practically identical. Where bids are private, a member of the group needing the business is very apt to make reductions on many of the articles; where in doing so he invites various kinds of retaliation from his competitors. This process makes the prices which the Government pays for construction a good deal higher than the prices contractors pay for construction. It also tends to create more expensive construction.

In turn these circumstances give support to the argument that the Government should not build houses at all. Building should be left to private business. However, the purchasing power of a third of our population is such that private business cannot build any houses for them at any price. Therefore, we have a situation where no houses can be built. If the demand is great enough, houses will be built by the Government, but the conflicting moral ideas will require them to be built under a blaze of oratory. The administrator who builds them must be not only an administrator but a skilful politician. He cannot concentrate only on building houses.

There is no answer to this problem except to say that as the governmental organization to build houses acquires strength it gets rid of most of the incidents of the conflict. It becomes as efficient as most of the private organizations which do the same thing. Indeed, it probably becomes more efficient because the standards of criticism which apply to it are much higher. In other words, no government project to build anything is ever as bad as the West Side of Chicago, which has been produced by private industry. Nor does it produce anything as foolish as the New York skyscraper. No

one will believe this, however, so long as the standards of
the day judge governmental organizations only by their failures and private organizations only by their successes.

All this lies behind the four theoretical articles condemning extravagance by government and reciting familiar economic slogans to support that attack.

There is a subtle difference between the point of view I
am trying to describe and the realistic or debunking philosophy. The difference is this. The fact-minded observer is one
who realizes that disillusionment about the human race is
a futile attitude. To call a nation stupid indicates an emotional state which prevents effective study of its habits. A
horse breeder does not call horses stupid but takes them as
they are. He refuses to invent a mythical horse in comparison with which his own horses appear in an unfavorable
light. There is today no evidence that the human race is going
to be able to get along without a priesthood, whether it be
religious, or civil, or economic. The fact-minded observer can
recognize this fact and utilize it. Observations which are frequently heard, such as that it is surprising organizations like
the American Bar Association should resist social reform,
simply show the lack of understanding of the forces which
create the American Bar Association. Statements of alarm
because of the so-called failure of "intelligent leadership"
simply prove that the speaker doesn't understand the part
which ideals play in social organization. He doesn't realize
that organizations come first and creeds are built around
them afterwards. The fact-minded observer is not one who
thinks that he can formulate a new religion or a new philosophy for a group. The religion for a new organization may
be selected out of the mass of conflicting ideals which exist
in the culture by processes not unlike the development of
language. It is as impossible to get people to adopt a new
creed as it is to get them to talk in a more convenient lan-

guage like Esperanto. For example, if we lived in an atmosphere of chivalry, we would have no basis for predicting capitalistic economics. On a smaller scale, if we looked at the
financial organizations at the time of the Civil War, we
would have no basis for describing the fantastic symbolism
of the present holding company, which unquestionably has
worked after its fashion.

Nevertheless, the fact-minded observer need not be a pes-
simist. Acting within the limited range of day-to-day possibility, his observations may enable him to make guesses as
to how current symbols may be used to obtain slight advances. The analogy to the breeder of horses may be useful.
His methods improve the speed of his animals little by little.
He would be a failure if he attempted to breed rubber-tired
wheels on the horses.

The fact-minded observer will know that in a rational age
social planning is required in order to convince people that
they are not adrift on tides of time and circumstance. He will
realize, however, that the social plan will primarily be useful only as a slogan and it should be adapted for that purpose. He will not expect logical adherence to it. He will know
that if the attitude toward any organized project changes,
so that social planning is no longer necessary and opportunistic action becomes respectable, the institution will be
enabled thereby to become more effective in reaching its
practical objective.

And, finally, he will realize that this objective platform
is not a universal truth. It is only a tool for diagnosis. Everyone will not become a student of government. Most people
will think in terms of a religion of government. For the public generally, all that is needed to make this point of view
effective is that it be tolerated in those who manage and study
governmental organizations.

To diagnose such conflicting situations requires a realization that there is no particular use in getting angry about it.

Medicine has progressed from the theological attitude of the medieval University of Paris to the practical, nonintellectual technique of the modern hospital, where they haven't time to formulate logical philosophies explaining why they try to cure people. There are signs of the same kind of change in attitude toward the study of social organizations.

As a formula for an objective philosophy of government, a slogan now current in individual conflicts might be used. That slogan is "Be an adult and avoid infantilisms." It symbolizes, as well as a phrase can, an attitude which can face facts.

However, those using it should remember that like all legal and economic creeds it is inspirational and not descriptive. What a truly adult human race would be like the writer cannot imagine. Harry Stack Sullivan once described the adult personality as follows: "And now, when you have ceased to care for adventure, when you have forgotten romance, when the only things worth while to you are prestige and income, then you have grown up, then you have become an adult."

The so-called Copernican revolution had a significance in human culture far beyond the specific astronomical discovery. For the first time, in ceasing to think of the earth as the center of the universe, men began to look at it from the outside. Amazing advances in man's control over his physical environment followed that change of attitude. Discoveries were made which would have been impossible for men bound by earlier preconceptions. Today there is beginning to dawn a similar change in attitude toward creeds, faiths, philosophies, and law. Looked at from within, law is the center of an independent universe with economics the center of a coördinate universe. Looked at from outside, we can begin to see what makes the wheels go round and catch a vision of how we can exercise control, not only of the physical environment, but also of the mental and spiritual environment. When men begin to examine philosophies and principles as they examine atoms and electrons, the road to discovery of the means of social control is open.

CHAPTER VII

The Traps Which Lie in Definitions and Polar Words

IN which we digress for a moment to explain how difficult it is to describe a culture of which you are a part and to point out the traps which lie in polar words.

ONE who would escape from the culture of his own time long enough to view it from the outside, as the historian views the French Revolution, or the anthropologist views a primitive people, must beware of the hidden traps which lie in the terminology of that culture which he must necessarily use. He is confronted with the same difficulty the anthropologist would face if he had to write his observations in the language of the tribe he was observing. He would find all the words used in connection with their sacred institutions so heavily freighted with little mental pictures of the ideals and phobias of the tribe that they would imperfectly describe the actual moving effect of those ideals on the tribe. This is such a dangerous handicap to one who describes modern society that it is necessary to digress from our main theme for a chapter in order to explain it.

We may take an example from the development of physics. In the last century the terminology of physics was tied up with little mental pictures of a world composed of matter and energy. Matter was little lumps, of which the atom was the smallest. Time was a sequence. Space was a frame. These word images were taken from the general images of the day. They could not be used to describe a world in which time was a dimension and matter a form of energy.

Today we realize that word images of ordinary discourse cannot be used to describe the phenomena of physics. They are too hopelessly confused with the view of the universe as made up of little lumps of matter. Einstein's great contribution to science is the fact that he made men realize that mental pictures had their distinct limitations as scientific tools. He escaped from these little pictures through symbols of mathematics which had the advantage of carrying no concrete mental images along with them. The fourth dimension and the Riemann metric, both of which Einstein used, either mean absolutely nothing when translated into language or they become completely absurd. However, when one gets used to them, they appear to have meaning enough to use, just as the symbol for zero is treated as a number in mathematics.

The term "subconscious mind" in psychology has no meaning. Yet we think it has and thus it becomes a handy tool. We never stop to define it. Whenever we stop to define it, we get all mixed up and decide there is no such thing. Then we go ahead and use it just the same. Words which are useful in one kind of discourse are not useful in another. The term "virtue" is an excellent term to use in bringing up a family. It has, however, no more meaning than the fourth dimension. Like the fourth dimension, if we attempt to define it, it resolves itself into a series of confused contradictions. Useful as the term is in daily life, it is a very confusing word for the psychoanalyst in discussing maladjusted personality. If he gets tangled up in the connotations of that term, he becomes an ethical philosopher and not a diagnostician. A great majority of psychoanalysts do this very thing because they begin to weave little mental pictures about their own words and thus become preachers without knowing it instead of diagnosticians.

Therefore, it becomes necessary for anyone thinking objectively about human institutions to realize the traps which lie beneath words. This is a familiar enough idea. What is not so familiar, however, is the kind of trap which lies behind peculiar types of words often called "polar" words. These have no meaning by themselves. They require an opposite term in order to be used at all. Let us illustrate.

The term "up" has no meaning apart from the term "down." The term "fast" has no meaning apart from the term "slow." And in addition such pairs of terms have no meaning even when used together, except when confined to a very particular situation. The realization of this fact in physics is called the principle of relativity. "Up" and "down" are very useful terms to describe the movement with reference to an elevator. They are utterly useless and, indeed, lead us into all sorts of errors when we talk about interstellar spaces. The reason is that these words require a frame of reference which does not work in astronomy. The idea that the sun went "down" and that the sky was "up" was among the great stumbling blocks to astronomical science for centuries.

The observer of social institutions must face a similar difficulty because most of our language about the organization and objectives of government is made up of such polar terms. "Justice" and "injustice" are typical. A reformer who wants to abolish injustice and create a world in which nothing but justice prevails is like a man who wants to make everything "up." Such a man might feel that if he took the lowest in the world and carried it up to the highest point and kept on doing this, everything would eventually become "up." This would certainly move a great many objects and create an enormous amount of activity. It might or might not be useful, according to the standards which we apply. However, it would never result in the abolishment of "down."

The battle between justice and injustice is a similar struggle. It creates activity. It leads to change. It also leads to civil wars. What we call "progress" is a consequence of this activity, as well as what we call "reaction." Our enthusiasms are aroused by these words and therefore they are excellent tools with which to push people around. Both the Rebels and the Loyalists in Spain are fighting for justice. That is what enables them to kill so many people in such a consecrated way.

Since justice is a nice word, we refuse to apply it to people who are struggling for things we do not like. The pacifist will refuse to admit that any war can be a war for justice. The born fighter will say that men who refuse to fight for justice do not really care for justice at all. Each side gets morale from the use of such terms and obtains the confidence necessary to make faces at the other side, knowing that God is with him. However, these polar terms are purely inspirational. They are not guides. Each side always claims to have "justice" on its side. Even organized criminals fight each other in the interest of justice.

All this does not, of course, mean that such words are foolish. They are, on the contrary, among the most important realities in the world. Take the term "efficiency," for example, which is an ideal of the business world. It has no meaning whatever unless there exists something which is called "inefficiency." One does not speak of a mountain as either efficient or inefficient. I recently engaged in a discussion with a newspaper editor, whose paper had a policy of taking care of all its old employees. This editor was very much in favor of an "efficient" society. He therefore wondered whether the policy of taking care of old employees was really "efficient." What was happening in his mind was simply this. Being a man of kindly impulses, he wanted the people whom he knew to be well fed. Being engaged in a struggle for economic power, he liked to see his paper make money. If he had desired to fire some of the older employees, he would have obtained the moral courage to do so by saying that newspaper "efficiency" demanded it. He desired to keep his old employees. Therefore, the word "efficient," with its little mental pictures of making profits, created a conflict. In order to resolve that conflict he had to invent a new term. He was for humanitarianism and against cruelty. Here was another pair of polar words which gave him support because it put him on the side of the nice word. His competitor, who was firing his employees when they got old, would of course have been troubled by this new set of polar words. He would not want to be called cruel. He would like to be considered humanitarian. Therefore, in order to resolve this conflict, he would proceed to prove that in the long run temporary cruelty led to humanitarianism. This is a complicated idea and therefore it takes a great many economic books to prove it. The idea that humanitarianism is better than efficiency is an inspirational idea and can be proved by a sermon. However, it requires a number of learned books to prove that present cruelty results in long-run humanitarianism. Economic theory is always equal to such a task. The humanitarian is shown to be an advocate of "paternalism" and against "rugged individualism."

These arguments never get anywhere in persuading the other side. However, they perform a real function in bolstering up the morale of the side on which they are used. The trick is to find a pair of polar words, in which the nice word justifies your own position and the bad word is applied to the other fellow.

Thus keeping on old employees is not "efficiency." Answer: But it is humanitarian, which is the only proper objective of efficiency. Apparent efficiency which leads to inhumanitarian results is really "inefficiency." Reply: But humanitarianism which destroys rugged individualism is in reality paternalism, which in the long run leads to more suffering than it cures and hence is inhumanitarian. Rebutter: But rugged individualism which destroys the morale of the individual by depriving him of security in the interests of selfish profits in the long run is in its essence Fascism. Surrebutter: Now the cat is out of the bag. You are attacking the profit motive and that leads to Communism.

This sort of thing can be kept up all night. It doesn't get anywhere and it doesn't mean anything. However, it makes both sides feel that God is with them. It is a form of prayer.

If you are really interested in which newspaper will succeed, the one that fires or the one that keeps its employees, look them over from the point of view of habits, discipline, leadership, and so on. Then make your guess. What is true of the smaller organization is also true of great governmental organizations.

The words "budget balancing" and "social cost" contain all sorts of hidden polar terms. They are completely meaningless except as moving forces. "Social cost" is a broader term than "budget balancing." The term "cost of government" is used to prevent the government from entering into the distribution of goods. Private industry is supposed to "cost" no one anything, unless it is engaged in some activity of which people disapprove. It was usual once to hear arguments about the awful social costs of the tobacco industry. Now it is regarded as one of the great helps along the road to recovery. The terms "cost" and "economy" are much like the terms "efficiency" and "inefficiency." From the point of view of one who regards big automobiles in themselves as an unmixed blessing, the automobile industry is one of the most efficient in the world.

Suppose, however, we apply to the automobile industry the standards of efficiency and inefficiency of one interested in the cheapest, safest, and most effective transportation. From this point of view, no more inefficient transportation could be imagined than the hauling of persons around in cars with hundreds of times more power and space than are needed. The building of expensive roads, the enlargement of streets, the hiring of additional traffic officers, the waste of labor in constructing these huge machines, the loss of forty thousand lives a year, a million accidents, and so on, are different elements of cost to society. Any form of amusement can be proved to entail great social cost in the same way. The cost of crime is also a favorite illustration. It is supposed to cost more than the automobile industry, although the toll in lives and property is actually infinitesimal in comparison. Therefore, we should suppress the automobile industry as well as the criminal classes.

Obviously this does not make sense. The automobile industry creates a great deal of activity. Men live and enjoy themselves by activity. There may be some other activity which you prefer, in which case you can talk about it in terms of your preferences. However, the term "social cost" is meaningless in diagnosis. It is only useful in preaching.

Budget balancing is the same kind of polar term. Governmental spending creates a great deal of activity. It builds concrete things such as houses, which the economist calls "wealth." The country is not poorer for each additional house which is built. Yet it is thought to be poorer in terms of budget balancing. The deficit financing of Germany created untold wealth in that country. Nations all over the world contributed goods, built apartment houses, roads, and parks for Germany. Germany emerged from the so-called inflation which followed its governmental deficit a much richer nation in every material respect. The nations which sent the goods over to Germany had less goods than before they sent them. Germany had more. Yet the use of these polar terms made people believe that Germany was "poorer" as the result of the "inflation." The reason why they felt that Germany was poorer is that "budget balancing" is the nice term and "governmental deficit" is the bad term of these two polar words. Therefore, if the bad term can be applied to German deficit financing, Germany must be worse off than it was before.

Failure to balance the German budget is also supposed to be one of the causes contributing to the intolerant rule of Hitler and the reason why the respectable people in Germany are crushed. Actually, if one escapes from these polar terms, one may see that the little pieces of paper which the German middle class possessed at the end of the War were claims on organizations which had lost their morale. Such organizations had been conquered by the War. They did not have the vitality to survive because the people involved could not think in organizational terms and thus caused Germany to flounder among the welter of principles which led to inaction instead of action. These organizations therefore disappeared as an inefficiently managed political machine disappears, and the negotiable paper representing claims on them vanished with them. Political machines do not rise or fall because they balance their budget. Nor does any other form of organization. One of the reasons for the great strength of Hitler and Mussolini is the fact that they paid no attention to balancing the budget. They put people to work. They formed a cohesive organization. The writer is not defending either one of these two intolerant rulers. He is only pointing out the source of their strength. Having put people to work, created loyalties and morale, they became powerful in spite of all the theoretical guesses of observers caught in these polar terms.

Budget balancing, being a polar term, can only be used for purposes of inspirational leadership or for counsels of defeat. It can do just as much harm or just as much good as enthusiasms over virtue and vice, or efficiency and inefficiency. It all depends upon the situation in which it is used. Of course, books must be kept by every organization. However, it is the objectives which are important; the bookkeeping is only a sort of creed. Budget balancing was a marvelously effective creed for our great industrial organizations prior to the depression. S. W. Straus and Company grew to be one of the most powerful financial organizations in the country by proving it had assets in excess of its liabilities. The morale and force of the organization after its structure collapsed were such that it was able to turn around and make great sums of money out of "reorganization" of its properties. This was another use of the slogan "budget balancing." Straus and Company proceeded to convince people that it was the only company which could "balance the budget" of the bankrupt industrial properties on which it had sold securities.

Budget balancing can be used as well to prevent the sale of bonds as to further it. Opponents of the Straus organization pointed out that "the budget is not really balanced." Between two organizations using the same slogan, one on the attack and one on the defense, the success must be predicted in terms of a guess as to the vitality of the institution. The same is true of governmental budget balancing. When the Government balances the budget, it will only mean that the people have accepted the rôle which it has taken among the organized activities of the country. That acceptance will be indicated by the general belief that the respectable end of the magnetic needle represented by the two polar terms will point at the Government instead of away from it.

In other words, in a struggle between two competing organizations, the one which wins and obtains control "balances its budget" in any atmosphere where public acceptance of the place of the organization must be expressed in fiscal terms. The phrase, however, simply means that the organization has won an accepted place. The moving-picture industry did not succeed because it was thrifty and always balanced its budget. After it had grown, and after the period of disorder and anarchy which had been an incident to that growth had passed, people thought it was a permanent part of our industrial feudalism. Therefore, they had faith that the "assets" of the organization were sufficient to meet its "debts." Since the great organizations had won their place, they were automatically endowed with all the virtues of the American Businessman, who balanced his budget and did not "spend" his "assets." The Government is not allowed to have "assets" today, because its place in organized distribution of goods is not yet recognized. Hence it cannot "balance its budget" until (1) it withdraws from these activities, or (2) such activities are accepted as part of its function. The future part that government must play will not be determined on principles of individual thrift.

We are not attacking the use of polar words on the public stage for purposes of creating morale or enthusiasm, because we cannot conceive what the human race would be like if it did not react to them. However, we are pointing out that from the point of view of the diagnostician these terms contain traps which ruin his judgment. They must be used in public, but he should not believe in them. It may be accepted as a fact that men will continue to fight for virtue and against vice, to struggle for justice and against injustice. This applies to the writer as well as to everyone else. That fact should be recognized in making a diagnosis.

Sometimes men are found without moral illusion who are able to create great organizations through the sheer use of power. However, this lack of illusion is itself an appearance, not a reality, because when all other ideals have gone by the board, power itself becomes the greatest of illusions. It becomes a polar term and its opposite is impotence. It is too crude a term and too far away from moral conceptions to last long. Men are incurable moralists and therefore organizations which do not develop such things as constitutions and rules of law and moral inhibitions of a more poetic nature do not last long. Pretty soon someone comes along and reminds the man in "power" that he is really a "slave" to that "power." This mixes him up so much that he hires a priesthood to solve his difficulties and thus law and economics, crushed to earth for a while, begin to rise again.

Polar words are used as concrete realities in mental dilemmas where an ideal and a practical need or impulse conflict. Where no such conflict is felt polar terms are confined to a more practical frame of reference. Ordinarily, men play games without being spiritually troubled as to whether they have an efficient or a moral way of amusing themselves, or whether their amusements do "good" to humanity instead of "bad." Puritanical people who believe that amusement is some sort of sin, however, feel a conflict here and develop a philosophy about which games are efficient and which are inefficient. Thus puritanism has created a lot of literature even in the field of sport. For instance, it was felt necessary to justify football in colleges as something that builds character, since colleges are supposed to be serious places devoted to that aim. The football enthusiast, however, doesn't really worry very much about the characters of the players. He needs the argument only when his favorite sport is attacked.

Once men are caught in these polar terms, they become reformers and sometimes do very queer things indeed. The reform of legal procedure offers a beautiful example of a struggle between these polar terms. The trial of a lawsuit is actually a game like football in which a great many emotions are released and a large number of contradictory ideals are celebrated at the same time. The trial of a bootlegger during prohibition illustrated freedom of the individual and the moral beauty of law enforcement at the same time. It was also a lot of fun for the trial lawyers who, if they were efficient, looked at the thing purely as a game. People who did not take it as a game, however, felt they had to become procedural reformers. They said: "This sporting theory of justice is uncivilized." They decided that the purpose of a trial was really an investigation of fact and therefore attempted to make the procedure live up to that ideal.

A trial cannot be a sensible way of investigating facts because the process consists in having two partisans indulge in mutual exaggerations on their own behalf with the idea that the judge will find the truth in the middle. The detective does not adopt that process. Neither does the scientist refuse to look through the microscope himself in order to listen to a debate between opposing theories about what the atom is made of. Procedural reformers, however, based their recommendations upon the idea that a trial actually was an investigation. They therefore tried to make an investigation out of what really was a combat. The New York Code, under the impact of this sort of procedural reform, became the most complicated legal ritual which the world has ever seen. It is becoming less complicated today only because people are becoming less mystical and more practical about the term "trial." We are not trying to make the trial process do things of which it is incapable.

We may make our illustration of procedural reform clearer by transferring it to another activity. Suppose that a football reformer observed the obvious fact that the object of the game is to make touchdowns. This would lead immediately to the important discovery that if the two teams would only cooperate hundreds of touchdowns could be made in a game, while only one or two are made when each opposes the other. If such a reform were adopted and the game were to continue, it would have to develop a very complicated method indeed in which the teams pretended they were coöperating and at the same time kept on playing.

Or take another example. A reformer wishing to make bridge more "efficient" or more "honest" would instantly observe that the object of bidding was to enable a player to tell his partner what he had in his hand. Therefore, he would make it the rule that instead of the inefficient and dishonest subterfuges now employed, each partner should go over and whisper to his partner what cards he held. In law this is called "getting rid of technicalities."

A good deal of procedural reform is based on this idea. It is neither a good nor a bad thing from an objective point of view. It keeps a lot of people busy. So long as the trial must represent all conflicting ideals which are current, it has to represent the ideal of "efficiency" as well. This keeps a large number of both lawyers and reformers occupied. If these same people were set by the Government to painting pictures or producing books, everyone would accuse the Government of extravagance and claim they were boondoggling. The intellectual atmosphere of the time, however, permits them to make a living alternately producing and abolishing "technicalities" (another polar term). Thus a number of people are kept out of productive enterprise in times when we are unable to distribute our productive capacity. The same phenomenon might be a bad thing if there was not already too much production, but at present it prevents the further extension of the W.P.A.

Of course, in order to make judgments as to whether any activity is a good or a bad thing, it is necessary to have standards. For the time being we are adopting the standard that it is a good thing to produce and distribute as much goods as the inventive and organizing genius of man makes possible. We will not enter into a philosophical discussion as to why we like that kind of society. We will only ask the reader to

agree with us for the time being that maximum production
and distribution of goods are a good thing, because that
assumption offers a platform on which to stand to observe
the slogans and ideals which we are discussing. Battles over
polar terms are one way of distributing goods, because the
combatants are usually highly paid and greatly respected for
their learning and ideals. We realize that there is no ultimate
answer to the argument as to whether medieval civilization
is really better than modern civilization. Both produce heroic
characters and there are no ultimate standards except those
which are emotionally felt by the individual. The standard
which the writer now adopts is that of a society which produces and distributes goods to the maximum of its technical
capacity. He believes that creeds and theories develop automatically from organizations. He judges the desirability of
such creeds by the extent to which they advance his standard.

In judging and observing creeds and philosophies, it is necessary first of all to recognize the fact that life is something
like a drama and that a drama is not successful without a
hero and a villain. No creed can be successful unless someone
is violating it. We must not get caught in the notion that
the efficient dramatist should kill the villain at the beginning
of the first act so that he cannot cause all the suffering which
intervenes before his final death in the third act. Human
beings, including the writer, are moved by inspirational
forces. If one is going to describe the impact of these forces,
he must get outside them in order to look at them. He must
not make the mistake of thinking that he can abolish them.
He must not think that if he himself is called on to take a
part in the drama he does not have to follow its conventional
form. If that form is not followed, no one will sit in the
audience.

In producing that drama it is necessary to have some objective, which the producer accepts on faith. If he is able to

achieve that faith and at the same time treat objectively the faith of others, he may become a powerful factor either in diagnosing or in moving human beings and human institutions. Whether he is an influence for good or evil depends entirely upon the values selected. Nevertheless, in a society where scrupulous people refuse to adopt this technique, the unscrupulous will become the most powerful. Political machines will run the government instead of college professors, because the members of the first are able to look at facts as they are and the second are interested in principles as ends in themselves. They are hopelessly caught in the tangle of polar words. They create much motion, but no direction.

And how may we escape from the confusing effect of such polar terms? The handiest platform today is that suggested in the last chapter; i.e., to assume that human organizations have a sort of subconscious mind. The subconscious mind may thus become useful, like the fourth dimension in mathematics. At least it will be useful until you attempt to define it in words. Then this term also will become a welter of contradictions, just as the old terms were, because "subconscious" mind is also a polar term. "Consciousness" and "subconsciousness" have their own limited application, but one must not try to make universal truths or substances out of them.

And this leads to the second trap which lies in wait for the diagnostician of modern society. That trap consists in a faith in definition. The only purpose of logical definition is to resolve mental conflicts. It is not useful as a descriptive tool because it is ordinarily used as a method of finding out what "things" really are, instead of as a method of conveying thought by the quickest available means. The law, which is above all a method of reconciling conflicting ideals, becomes so heavy with definitions that it is almost unintelligible. Therefore, it becomes a convenient illustration of the traps in which learned people are particularly liable to be caught.

Definition is ordinarily supposed to produce clarity in thinking. It is not generally recognized that the more we define our terms the less descriptive they become and the more difficulty we have in using them. The reason for this paradox is that we never attempt to define words which obtain a proper emotional response from our listeners. Logical definition enters when we are using words which we are sure "ought" to mean something, but none of us can put our finger on just what that meaning is. In such situations priestly-minded men believe that definition will make the meaning clearer. Most of this kind of definition occurs in the use of the polar words which we have just been describing.

We may illustrate by a homely example. There is no conflict in a farmer's mind about the meaning of the words "horse" and "duck." The one is not used as a polar term to the other. If you tell a farmer to bring you a horse, he never comes out of the barn leading a duck.

Suppose that the farmer attempted to define the difference. If he took the task at all seriously, he would find millions of differences. His definition would become so involved that he could no longer talk about the animals intelligibly. He would probably end up by thinking that horses were really ducks and vice versa, because this is an ordinary effect of the close concentration on particular pairs of terms; they tend to merge, and the distinctions between the two grow less and less sharp.

Of course, you say, the farmer would never attempt such a thing. This is true in the ordinary situation. But suppose that a conflict arose between an abstraction and a need which required the use of the words in pairs. We can easily imagine such a hypothetical situation.

Suppose, for example, we had a statute that taxed horses at ten dollars a head and ducks at ten cents. This does not create any conflict, because it seems to be a fair enough classification according to the prevailing folklore of taxation. However, suppose, in addition, that due to the automobile, or some other cause, horses became completely worthless and ducks became very valuable. Suppose that the original statute had been passed by ancestors of such great respectability that it would be tearing down the Constitution to repeal it and use new words. Obviously, if we want to collect revenue in such a situation, we must begin to define the real essence of the difference between a horse and a duck. We set our legal scholars to work. They discover that there are all sorts of immaterial differences apparent to the superficial eye. The mind of the scholar, however, is able to penetrate to the real essence of the distinction, which is value. The horse is the more valuable animal. It is clear that the fathers thought that this was the difference, because Thomas Jefferson once remarked to his wife that his horses were worth much more than his ducks. Differences between feathers and hair were never mentioned by any of the founders. Therefore, it is apparent that the webfooted animals are really horses, and the creatures with hoofs are really ducks. (Such observations are called "research.")

This works all right so far as the taxing situation is concerned. Revenue begins to flow in again. However, scholarly definitions are supposed to go through the surface and to the core of things. Ordinary men feel a conflict, because deep down in their hearts they feel that there is something wrong somewhere. This conflict makes them celebrate the truth of the definition by ceremony. If the conflict is a minor one, a procession once a year in which ducks are led around with halters and equipped with little saddles will be sufficient. A supreme court is also helpful in such situations. However, if the conflict is sufficiently keen, we shall find farmers all over the country forced to feed ducks on baled hay. Ducks will not die because of this, however. They will actually be kept alive by low-class politicians sneaking into the barn at night and giving them the proper food. (Thus a great organization of bootleggers gave us our liquor only a few years ago.) If this situation is finally accepted as inevitable, scholars will be called in to prove that the particular food which is being fed to the ducks is actually baled hay, even though to a superficial observer it looks like something else. This definition will mix men up along some other lines and the literature will continue to pile up so long as the conflict exists. When the conflict disappears, the need of definition will go with it.

The illustration sounds absurd, but the writer has tried many cases involving exactly that type of situation. A plaster company was scraping gypsum from the surface of the ground. If it was a mine, it paid one tax; if a manufacturing company, it paid another. Expert witnesses were called who almost came to blows, such was their disgust at the stupidity of those who could not see that the process was essentially mining, or manufacturing. A great record was built up to be reviewed by the State Supreme Court on this important question of "fact."

A typical piece of theology of this type is the transformation of the due process clause in the fifth amendment from a direction regarding criminal trials to a prohibition against the regulation of great corporations. The word "property" in a like manner has changed from something which was tangible to the right of a great organization to be free from governmental interference. Such changes appear to have something wrong about them, because the older response to the sound of the word "property" is still instinctively felt. A spiritual conflict is created which requires a great deal of literature or ceremony to resolve.

How may the observer of social institutions avoid such traps? The answer is that in writing *about* social institutions, he should never define anything. He should try to choose words and illustrations which will arouse the proper mental associations with his readers. If he doesn't succeed with these, he should try others. If he ever is led into an attempt at definition, he is lost. The writer learned that lesson in the course of a seminar which he attempted to give at the Yale Law School with a great foreign anthropologist. The notion which started this endeavor was that the anthropological point of view would be helpful in talking about the law. We began the seminar on the assumption that the fundamental link between the anthropologist and the lawyer was that they were both concerned with social institutions. Then as a next step we started to define "institution" so that our discussion would be clear. As in all such endeavors, the word "institution" broadened until it meant everything in the world. Someone even suggested that Niagara Falls was an institution, because it had continuity and movement and coherence and whatnot. Then we had to subdivide so that this definition which had grown to include everything could be applied to activities narrow enough to talk about. When we ended we had a definition so involved that it could not be used for any purpose whatever.

For the purpose of making a ceremony which dramatizes two or more contradictory ideas at the same time, the process of definition is most useful. It conceals inconsistencies. It is peculiarly adapted to the law, where ceremony is more important than action. It is not adapted to the administrative process. Thus we find administrative tribunals reverting to practical language wherever their activity is recognized as a legitimate one and accepted without question. A workman's compensation board talks and acts in determining awards in fairly plain English, without elaborate definition. However, when the theological question arises, as to the "jurisdiction" of the compensation board, we find ourselves in the area of conflicting moral ideals. We want to give compensation only to those injured "in the scope of their employment." Suppose that a workman stays over time. Is he within the scope of his employment? Yes, replies the New York Court of Appeals, because otherwise workmen would become clock watchers. The treatment of such subjects requires theological definition.

The process of creating abstract realities out of polar terms and surrounding them with scholarly definition has always accompanied the decline of great religions. It is not surprising therefore that in a time when private property and rugged individualism are more myths than realities we should find law and economics more theological than ever before in our history.

This chapter is a digression, though a necessary one. We do not claim that we can avoid the use of polar terms in the rest of this book, since it is impossible to write without some standard and since standards can never be formulated except in polar terms. The only safety which an objective observer can have is the realization of the kind of traps which such very necessary words contain if used outside of a narrow frame of reference.

CHAPTER VIII

The Personification of Corporation

In which it is explained how great organizations can be treated as individuals, and the curious ceremonies which attend this way of thinking.

ONE of the essential and central notions which give our industrial feudalism logical symmetry is the personification of great industrial enterprise. The ideal that a great corporation is endowed with the rights and prerogatives of a free individual is as essential to the acceptance of corporate rule in temporal affairs as was the ideal of the divine right of kings in an earlier day. Its exemplification, as in the case of all vital ideals, has been accomplished by ceremony. Since it has been a central ideal in our industrial government, our judicial institutions have been particularly concerned with its celebration. Courts, under the mantle of the Constitution, have made a living thing out of this fiction. Men have come to believe that their own future liberties and dignity are tied up in the freedom of great industrial organizations from restraint, in much the same way that they thought their salvation in the future was dependent on their reverence and support of great ecclesiastical organizations in the Middle Ages. This ideal explains so many of our social habits, rituals, and institutions that it is necessary to examine it in some detail.

The origin of this way of thinking about organization is the result of a pioneer civilization in which the prevailing ideal was that of the freedom and dignity of the individual engaged in the accumulation of wealth. The independence of the free man from central authority was the slogan for

which men fought and died. This free man was a trader,
who got ahead by accumulating money. There was something very sacred in the nineteenth-century conception of
this activity. In the 'seventies the most popular text in economics was one originally written by a clergyman, Bishop
Francis Wayland, and revised in 1878 by A. L. Chapin,
President of the Congregational College at Beloit. Joseph
Dorfman, in his brilliant book on *Thorstein Veblen and His
America*,[1] summarizes this philosophy of the holy character
of the trader's function as follows:

1) "God has made man a *creature of desires*" and has established the material universe "with qualities and powers . . . for
the *gratification of those desires.*" Desire is the stimulus to production and invention. 2) To satisfy desires, to obtain pleasures,
man must by "irksome" labour force *"nature to yield her hidden
resources."* 3) *The exertion of labour establishes a right of PROP-
ERTY in the fruits of labour,* and the "idea of *exclusive possession* is a necessary consequence." Originally the object belongs to
the producer "by an intuitive conception of right, and the act of
appropriation is as instinctive as the act of breathing." The right
of property may be conceived as "a law of natural justice," as
Bowen of Harvard put it, because "the producer would not put
forth his force and ingenuity if others deprived him of their
fruits." Thus is established 4) *"The Right of EXCHANGE."*

Here is the beginning of the religion of the essential dignity of an individual's accumulating wealth by trading which
later became the mystical philosophy that put the corporate
organization ahead of the governmental organization in
prestige and power, by identifying it with the individual.
Our fathers breathed this atmosphere in every day of their
schooling. For a pointed summary of their attitude toward
distribution of goods by so-called governmental organizations, we quote again from Mr. Dorfman's book:[2]

[1] p. 23.   [2] pp. 24–25.

Since socialism is the "utter negation" of the right of private property, "man is no more adapted to it than the barn fowl is to live in the water." Philanthropy or any other aid of the poor is a violation of the same laws of God and property. All attempts to "relieve the natural penalties of indolence and improvidence" bring about "unexpected and severe evil." The doctrine that the government should provide for the unemployed "is the most subversive of all social order." Even the claim of Ruskin that "all labours of like amounts should receive the same reward," means the suppression of "commercial law," which is "God's method." If labour and capital are free, as they are in the "order of nature undisturbed" under "the law of competition," then "the flow of each . . . toward an equilibrium, is as natural as that of waters of the ocean under gravitation." In reality the labourer has no complaint against the competitive system. As Perry put it, employer and employee "come together of necessity into a relation of mutual dependence, which God has ordained, and which, though man may temporarily disturb it, he can never overthrow."[8]

Here was the philosophy of the men who came later to dominate our large industrial organizations and also to work for them. There was nothing in that philosophy which justified far-flung industrial empires. Indeed, the great organization in which most men were employees, and a few at the top were dictators, was a contradiction of that philosophy. The great organization came in as a result of mechanical techniques which specialized the work of production so that men could not operate by themselves. Nothing could stop the progress of such organization, and therefore in order to tolerate it, men had to pretend that corporations were individuals. When faced with the fact that they were not individuals, they did not seek to control, but denounced and tried to break them up into smaller organizations. Those

[8] The quotations in the above excerpts are selected from texts and articles current at Carleton College when Veblen was a student.

who did not choose to dissent, however, sought refuge in transferring the symbolism of the individual to the great industrial armies in which they were soldiers.

It is a familiar social phenomenon to see the symbols of the habits of pioneer times transferred as a social philosophy to later institutions to prove that we still are following the examples of our fathers.

The trick of such social philosophies is to justify the hard lot of those who never attain any particular rank in society. Rugged individualism is a peculiarly American creed. Germany, with a strong military tradition, justifies an industrial civilization with a philosophy which has the flavor of military discipline, since the soldier has always been respected above the trader in Germany. Compare the mysticism of private property which we have quoted above with a recent Berlin dispatch, which reads as follows:

The discharge of the old contingent [from the German government labor battalion] was accompanied by a morning festival broadcast by all German radio stations, especially to the 1,300 labor-service camps. The festival was held under the motto, "Blessed be that which makes hard." This motto was repeated by the labor-service chorus, which chanted: "We thank the Führer for the hard life which he bestowed upon us in the labor service." From a Berlin dispatch to the *New York Times* (*New Republic,* June 2, 1937).

The essential military character of this prayer is as marked as the deification of the trader in the prayers recited by American organizations. It is of such stuff that the vital and living economic philosophy of a people is made.

It was this identification of great organizations with the dignities, freedom, and general ethics of the individual trader which relieved our federation of industrial empires from the hampering restrictions of theology which always prevent experiment. Men cheerfully accept the fact that some individuals are good and others bad. Therefore, since great industrial organizations were regarded as individuals, it was not expected that all of them would be good. Corporations could therefore violate any of the established taboos without creating any alarm about the "system" itself. Since individuals are supposed to do better if let alone, this symbolism freed industrial enterprise from regulation in the interest of furthering any current morality. The *laissez faire* religion, based on a conception of a society composed of competing individuals, was transferred automatically to industrial organizations with nation-wide power and dictatorial forms of government.

This mythology gave the Government at Washington only a minor part to play in social organization. It created the illusion that we were living under a pioneer economy composed of self-sufficient men who were trading with each other. In that atmosphere the notion of Thomas Jefferson, that the best government was the one which interfered the least with individual activity, hampered any control of our industrial government by our political government. We were slower, therefore, in adopting the measures of control of industrial organization than a country like England. The Government at Washington gradually changed into what was essentially a spiritual government whose every action was designed to reconcile the conflict between myth and reality which men felt when a creed of individualism was applied to a highly organized industrial world. Government in Washington was supposed to act so as to instil "confidence" in great business organizations. The Supreme Court of the United States, because it could express better than any other institution the myth of the corporate personality, was able to hamper Federal powers to an extent which foreigners, not realizing the emotional power of the myth, could not understand. This court invented most of the ceremonies which kept the myth alive and preached about them in a most dramatic setting. It dressed huge corporations in the clothes of simple farmers and merchants and thus made attempts to regulate them appear as attacks on liberty and the home. So long as men instinctively thought of these great organizations as individuals, the emotional analogies of home and freedom and all the other trappings of "rugged individualism" became their most potent protection.

The extent to which freedom of restraint of great industrial government was dramatized as individual freedom is illustrated by the fact that it was possible for John W. Davis, as late as 1936, to rouse his audience to a high pitch of indignation against an act regulating holding companies by speaking as follows:

There is something in this act that arouses me far beyond the scope and tenor of the act itself. In one respect it is unique in the history of our legislation; in one respect it constitutes the gravest threat to the liberties of American citizens that has emanated from the halls of Congress in my lifetime. That is strong language. But I mean to make it so. (*New York Times*, August 26, 1936.)

It was the personification of the corporation as an individual which gave moving force to such remarks, which otherwise would seem almost incredible. Anyone who actually struggled for the liberties of actual individuals, rather than idealized ones, was greeted with the hostility that greets anyone who tears the veil away from a great symbol. Thus Felix Frankfurter of Harvard, fighting for Mooney and for Sacco and Vanzetti, was a distinct handicap on the endowment drive of that great institution. Roger Baldwin, head of the Civil Liberties Union, served a term in jail and was always regarded as a suspicious character. This is not surprising, nor should the observer become indignant about it. It is simply an illustration of how the personification of the great corporation actually worked to monopolize completely the mantle of protection designed for the individual. The Civil Liberties Union thus contained less respectable people than the American Liberty League.

The mantle of protection which this attitude threw over corporate government is illustrated in the popular reaction to the sit-down strike when it was first used as a weapon against General Motors Corporation by John L. Lewis. So firmly fixed in popular imagination was the belief that General Motors was a big man who "owned" the plant that the public became alarmed over possible dangers to their own homes because of this method of conducting a strike. Many sincerely felt that this insult to the sanctity of property justified the shedding of blood and that Governor Murphy's conciliation of the General Motors strike in 1937 was a compromise with the Devil that endangered individual freedom. If General Motors had been pictured as a governing organization, exercising the governing power over thousands of people, the right of these people to security in their jobs might have been recognized as on somewhat the same level as the rights of security holders in the corporation. The concept of the "ownership" of General Motors prevented that attitude from developing. The sit-down strike, though much more orderly than the strikes in past depressions had been, actually gave the impression of greater disorder and anarchy because it could be dramatized as the taking away of property from an individual. This kind of dramatization was, of course, more keenly felt by the respectable people than by the masses, with whom the personification of the corporation as an individual was disappearing. For example, a temperate and impartial analysis of the principles of labor law by Dean Landis of the Harvard Law School in 1937 during the initial activities of the C.I.O. provoked outspoken hostility among the alumni of that great institution.

This entire volume could be filled with the queer effects of the personification of industrial enterprises in mixing ceremony with the production and distribution of goods. Control of great organizations drifted out of the hands of those who knew the techniques of the business and into the hands of bankers. Stock manipulation became more important in control than efficiency of production. Organizations competed with each other in building magnificent structures for pure show and in order to gain dignity and prestige in the company of their peers. Great law offices grew up in New York to supply the infinitely complicated logic needed to keep the separate individuality of parent and subsidiary or affiliate corporations apart. Theological disputes produced a great literature as to what the "real nature" of a corporation was which was assiduously studied in law schools.

A similar complication of philosophy and dialectic attended the ceremonies of chivalry when the institutions which this mythology once described so vividly were disappearing. Such things are familiar in times of social change.

When the actual world is not at variance with men's belief, it is unnecessary to write or think much about it. People are not troubled by doubt in such times; therefore doctrine is not needed. When symbols or beliefs have no relation to what men see before them, regularity of doctrine becomes of paramount importance. Since observations in such a situation create only paralyzing doubt, men must drown their observations in doctrine and philosophy. Therefore, ceremonies grow in number and mystical literature increases by leaps and bounds, becoming more and more abstract as it grows. That this has happened to economic theory is obvious. The reasons why it has happened lie in the fact that where the fiscal religion becomes completely undescriptive of what is going on, ceremony is the only way of giving force to the creed.

This symbolism made practical legislation legalistic and complicated so that it would not contradict fixed beliefs. For example, the Social Security Act was drawn to resemble an insurance corporation, because insurance corporations were supposed to be very pious and respectable individuals indeed. The Government put money in a huge reserve. This reserve had to be invested in its own bonds and therefore had no meaning whatever, except to make social security legislation look like an old-line insurance company. In other enterprises the Government found that by adopting the device of a government corporation it gave its activities a little of the freedom which was enjoyed by private corporations and escaped the rules and principles which hampered action when it was done by a government department instead of a government corporation. In other words, it gave the Government some of the robes of the individual.

There seemed no limit to the size of these industrial empires masquerading as individuals. Laws against monopoly and restraint of trade were easily evaded in the fairyland where men pretended that organizations were men who owned property. Nothing in the Middle Ages compares for sheer fantasy with the holding company, or with modern security manipulation by which control of large organizations may be obtained without investment risk. Equally fantastic was the notion that a corporation had the rights of a citizen of the state which incorporated it. This permitted the use of the sacred doctrine of states rights to hamper regulation of industrial empires which had no connection with any particular state.

Organizations which exercise governing powers of a permanent character do not maintain their power by force. Force is entirely too exhausting. They do it by identifying

themselves with the faiths and loyalties of the people. Therefore, the picture which people see of a society is always in
terms of these faiths and loyalties. They do not examine anything, however obvious, which contradicts those faiths. Few
educated men who opposed the holding-company bill could
actually describe the structure of any of our great holding
companies, but this did not interfere with their belief that an
attack on that form of corporate structure was an attack on
individualism.

In the brief filed by the Government in the Electric Bond
and Share case[4] a typical holding company is described as
follows:

In the United States the Bond and Share system embraces utility
properties in no fewer than 32 states, from Pennsylvania to Ore-
gon and from Minnesota to Florida. The system serves 2,487,500
electric customers, 10 percent of the total electric customers of the
United States, deriving therefrom in a year $214,600,000 in reve-
nues. This exceeds the annual income of any state in the United
States, with the exception of New York (*Financial Statistics of
State and Local Governments* [1932], p. 10, compiled by the
United States Department of Commerce, Bureau of Statistics).
In 1934, 85 billion kwh of electric energy were generated in the
United States. Of this amount the Bond and Share system gen-
erated 11.8 billion kwh, or approximately 14 percent, and han-
dled 14½ billion kwh, or 17 percent. The system owns 23,460
miles of transmission lines (i.e., lines of more than 40,000 volts),
or 30.2 percent of the total miles of transmission lines in the
United States.

•   •   •   •   •

[4] *Securities and Exchange Commission* v. *Electric Bond and Share Co.,*
18 *Fed. Sup.* 131; brief for the Government prepared by John J. Burns,
General Counsel, Securities and Exchange Commission; Robert H. Jackson,
Assistant Attorney General and Special Counsel, Securities and Exchange
Commission; John J. Abt, Special Counsel, Securities and Exchange Com-
mission; Benjamin V. Cohen, Special Assistant to the Attorney General;
Thomas G. Corcoran, Special Assistant to the Attorney General; and others.

These gigantic gas and electric utility enterprises over which the Bond and Share companies hold sway represent tremendous aggregations of capital belonging to investors throughout the world. Of the huge investment in these enterprises, seventy-five to eighty percent is represented by the senior securities of operating companies, purchased for the most part by the investing public. The interest of Bond and Share or its intermediate holding companies in these operating companies (as represented by their common stock holdings) usually did not exceed 25 percent of the total stated capitalizations of the operating companies. When these capitalizations reflected, as they nearly always did, ledger values substantially in excess of the cash paid into the operating companies or the original cost of the properties to their predecessor companies, Bond and Share's real equity in these properties became even smaller, and the public's larger. Write-ups in the capital accounts of the operating companies, in other words, served as the book basis for the securities issued. . . . It is a fair conclusion, even though possibly not susceptible of exact proof, that in light of the write-up policies pursued by Bond and Share, the common stocks of its operating companies, which its intermediate companies hold, represent substantially less than 20 percent of their *bona fide* capitalization. The real owners of the operating properties in the Bond and Share system are not Bond and Share (which owns, in its intermediate holding companies, only a minority interest sufficient for control); nor are the real owners the intermediate holding companies which own substantially all of the common stock of the subsidiary companies. The real owners are the senior-security holders of the operating companies. It is they who have contributed substantially more than three-fourths of the capital. Yet they have been deprived of any real representation in the management of their properties, and for them Bond and Share has no mandate to speak.

. . . . .

A holding company is distinguished from an investment company by the control it is in a position to exercise over its subsidiaries. In the complicated field of corporate finance, that control may be exercised in many ways, sometimes loosely and sometimes rigidly, sometimes openly and sometimes covertly. Where voting stock is widely distributed, actual control may be exercised by a very small percentage of common stock, yet a large minority interest may be unable to exercise control if a still larger interest is possessed by another organized group. It is relatively easy for a company charged with controlling another company to prove that it in fact exercises no control, but it is extremely difficult for an outside agency, which must draw its facts from unwilling witnesses, to assume the burden of proving actual control. The use of voting trusts and of agents and nominees with undisclosed principals may conceal the real source of control

. . . . .

The dealings between Bond and Share and the serviced companies are conducted on an informal basis. Not only are its recommendations normally and usually followed, but when a request is made by a serviced company for a particular service, that request as frequently as not originates in a suggestion of Bond and Share's representative. So unified and harmonious has been the Bond and Share plan of management that the serviced companies and Bond and Share in dealings with each other, employ the same New York law firm. And the serviced companies have never had occasion to employ legal representation separate from that offered by Bond and Share or Bond and Share's New York counsel. The Bond and Share group has always been one happy family.[5]

And, finally, the personal control of the holding company which controls all those companies is in itself a minority operating without any formal violation of the competitive ideals which accompany a fiscal way of thinking—just as a great central organization at Rome, which was no longer military, operated under the folklore that every Roman was a soldier.

The main purpose of the fiscal symbolism in this country as it existed after the World War was to preserve the inde-

[5] pp. 47–48, 50–51, 62–64, 96–97

pendence of the great organizations which controlled the production and distribution of goods. It supported the notions that to manage the currency and credit of great organizations led to inflation and repudiation of debts, stifled individual initiative, destroyed the home of the poor man, turned his future security over to wicked politicians, compelled regimentation, and ended in dictatorship. In such an atmosphere the Supreme Court of the United States in declaring unconstitutional the minimum wage law for women[6] emphasized the idea that it interfered with the freedom of women, rather than the fact that it protected large organizations from added expense.

The proof of these propositions could be made by either legal or economic learning. The arguments often appeared nonsensical, but it should be remembered that for the purpose of binding organizations together nothing makes as much sense as nonsense, and hence nonsense always wins. If the reader does not believe this, let him substitute for an impressive and moving ritual in any organization to which he belongs, a series of factual and practical observations. If he does, he will see the organization crumbling for lack of the emotional drive which comes only from ceremony. Tears and parades, not factual psychological discussion, are the moving forces of the world in which we happen to live; and this is true even for psychologists.

Thus we find a great deal of literature along the general lines of the following, which we quote from President Hopkins of Dartmouth College. President Hopkins is speaking of the probable effects on national character if men look to governmental organization instead of to industrial organizations for support in a temporal world.

[6] *Morehead* v. *Tipaldo*, 298 *U.S.* 587, reversed in *West Coast Hotel Co.* v. *Parrish*, 300 *U.S.* 379, after Roosevelt had proposed his famous plan to rejuvenate the Court.

Initiative, courage, hardihood, frugality, and aspiration for self-betterment are to be penalized, and the fruits of these are to be taken from those who have undergone self-sacrifice to attain them and bestowed upon those who have never developed the qualities to possess themselves of rewards. . . . The necessity for struggle, by which men have developed strength, and the discipline of hardship, through which they have achieved greatness of mind and heart and soul, are to be replaced by a specious security.

.   .   .   .   .

But it is the effect of the New Deal on the imagination and aspiration of youth that I most dread. I am desperately afraid of it because it teaches young men and women to unlearn the lessons of America which school and college have striven so earnestly to teach. It encourages weakness and penalizes strength. It diffuses throughout the masses of our people the spirit of acquisitiveness which it condemns in groups of them. It punishes accomplishment and persecutes individuals and industrial enterprises alike simply on the basis of the magnitude of their achievement without regard to the social value of the imaginative and creative talent which brought them into being. (*Atlantic Monthly,* October, 1936.)

The periodical literature of the time was full of these forebodings. Walter Lippmann led the crusade for the individualism of corporate enterprise, which meant that men should not become dependent upon that kind of organization which admitted it had public functions to perform. These people did not think of the dependence of men upon great industrial organizations as interfering with individualism. If the decreasing independence of actual individuals was called to their attention, they insulated themselves against this obvious fact by pointing to a complicated literature of economics and law. The fact that every individual in the country had become absolutely dependent on great organizations, including the student body and the professors of Dart-

mouth College, did not disturb President Hopkins so long
as the organization was not called the Government, and
therefore did not disturb the smooth process of accustomed
ritual.

Yet from the short quotation set out above, it is easy to see
that President Hopkins was worried by facts which were
making current mythology less and less tenable. Hence he
felt called upon, in his capacity as educator, to do what he
could about dictating the social philosophy of the future by
pointing out the danger of deserting the old-time religion. It
is a phenomenon which will be found repeated over and
over again in every era.

As the symbolism got farther and farther from reality, it
required more and more ceremony to keep it up. The business corporation built more elaborate cathedrals and endowed greater colleges to keep its theology moving along
the right lines. This, of course, was an unconscious process,
just as the great era of cathedral building in the thirteenth
century was unplanned. It was these influences which created
a separate science of economics, designed to prove that it was
not organizations but principles which were operating in
the field of the production and distribution of goods. Of
course, it *seemed* important to these economists just what
principles they thought up and advocated. Actually, however, the only important thing was the little pictures in the
back of the head of the ordinary man. So long as they existed
the great organization was secure in its freedom and independence.

In this situation people described difficulties in which organizations found themselves solely in terms of individuals
competing for money and became, as a result, extraordinarily
mixed up in their diagnosis. Instead of guessing on the
strength and stability of the organization as one guesses on
the future of a political machine, they made their predictions

on the basis of a system of bookkeeping which pretended that claims against organizations were tangible private property having a money value set by the laws of supply and demand.

Hence, in estimating what organizations could or could not do, people talked only about whether the organization could "make money." This method of thinking, of course, prevented the governmental organization from doing anything in the distribution of goods. The Government could not "make money" since it was not supposed to be actuated by the profit motive. Hence it could not efficiently engage in the distribution of goods. Therefore, we could not "afford" to have the Government maintain our supply of skilled labor during the depression or preserve our resources, because the Government did not "own" the labor or resources. For this reason it could not "spend money" on such things without going bankrupt—just as an individual could not spend money on his neighbor's property without going bankrupt.

Guesses made by experts on these assumptions were almost invariably wrong. An amusing book during the depression entitled *Oh Yeah*[7] collected the predictions of the most prominent financiers, monetary experts, and economists and created uproarious laughter, so absurd did these predictions appear in the light of what followed. Guesses on the future of particular industrial organizations were not much better. It was easy to prove that if a man followed expert market advice he would consistently lose money. The best predictions came from men who were not using current fiscal symbols but who were thinking in terms of organization. Floyd Odlum of the Atlas Corporation rose to a position of immense financial power by engaging in financial undertakings at the time when most experts had determined that financing was unsafe because of the Securities Exchange Act and other

[7] By Edward Angly (Viking Press, 1931).

governmental interferences with business. He was successful because he thought in terms of control of great industrial armies.

In the current mythology a group of individuals were supposed to be competing with each other in an effort to produce
wealth and exchange it for a vague thing called capital. Capital theoretically consisted of ownership of every sort of useful productive property. But private ownership of this kind
of property disappeared with the great organizations. By a
gradual transference capital came to mean the ability to control bank credits, which had no particular relationship to
productive property. Control of bank credits came more and
more into the hands of those who controlled the banks. If a
corporation could get a respectable bank to say that its property (the habits and disciplines of its organization) was
worth a given amount of money, it became automatically
possessed of that sum because it could get the bank to tell
the public that its shares were worth that money. From 1920
to 1930 capital began to be the money value which respectable banks would put on the hopes of an enterprise. Financial institutions began to rely on an institution called the stock
exchange to create capital for them. They went through a
process called "floating" loans or stock issues. This consisted
in creating a market for engraved pieces of paper so that they
were almost as readily exchangeable as currency.

A new philosophy called "liquidity" sprang into being.
The idea was that capital goods could be made almost like
currency. Material wealth was supposed to be back of the
pieces of paper, just as gold was supposed to be back of the
government issues of currency. It was, of course, realized that
if very many people tried to cash in on these pieces of paper,
they would lose their exchange value, but it was supposed
that this would not happen. Material wealth behind these
pieces of paper gradually included all sorts of intangible

things, such as "good will" which had been obtained by advertising campaigns and "going concern value."

Gradually the process of "capitalizing earning capacity" grew to be the rule. This meant that a share in an organization was worth any amount on which the earnings would be a reasonable rate of interest. This meant that the organization itself was the "wealth" or the "property." The law was not slow in following this make-believe and the circle was complete. Physical property came to be an unimportant element of capital. Values were based on what organizations could be expected to pay each year.

Curiously enough in this reification of organization as a form of property, the value of skilled labor as an asset received no legal and very little economic recognition. It was possible for corporate organizations to spend money to keep their physical plant in repair during times of idleness. However, it was not possible to educate or maintain skilled labor for future use. Bonds could be floated on hopes that organizations of executives would earn dividends in the future. No matter how ridiculous those hopes were, the public always bought. But a reservoir of skilled labor could not be capitalized. Labor organizations could not incorporate and raise money on their probable future earnings. This was not because the future earnings of labor were less speculative. Nothing could have been more absurd than at least half of the investments in industrial concerns. It was because nothing in the fiscal symbols of the time provided any mystical place for such an organization.

This folklore which denied that labor had a moral claim on an industrial organization produced most interesting results. The textile industry in New England had a supply of docile labor which it exploited for years. Then it took the so-called "capital" thus accumulated and invested it in the

South where labor was still cheaper. This enriched a few trust companies in Boston but left whole communities impoverisℓed. Nevertheless, under the creed of rugged individualism, primitive-minded conservatives of New England fought to the bitter end to preserve this manner of doing things.

The relationship of governmental organization to industrial wreckage of this sort was entirely confused. Necessity compelled government action; theory denied it. In a certain town in New York prior to the depression a large factory was growing larger. Homes had to be built for new workmen. Water, lights, and paving had to service these homes. Pressure was put on the municipality to service new additions. Municipal expenditures went up to supply factory labor with a place in which to live. Everyone was happy since it was a "growing town." Workmen were paying for their homes.

When the depression came these workmen were discharged. They could no longer pay taxes. The burden on the balance of the community became greater. Not only did the municipality have to keep up the additional expense, but thousands were thrown on relief. The situation became so bad that the Federal Government had to finance relief. Thereupon the manufacturing plant threw all its political force into an attempt to make the Government reduce the level of subsistence of the men as much as possible, so as to balance the national budget and not put false ideas in the heads of the workmen. The efficiency of private charity, as compared with government interference, was made the subject of all industrial sermons. Unemployed were relentlessly persecuted on moral grounds, in spite of the fact that there were plenty of material goods to feed and clothe them. It was thought sound economics to reduce them to the lowest level of subsistence and make the taking of that pittance as humiliating as possible. Every move the Government made was accompanied by hostile oratory and blind irritation.

This was not done by ill-will. It was simply the result of thinking in terms of a fiscal fairyland in which industrial organizations were individuals and government was supposed to protect their property.

Since corporate property had come to mean the right of an organization to distribute goods, the Government could not engage in such distribution without damaging the whole structure. Government itself could not be efficient because it did not operate for profit, which was an essential element of efficiency. If a man did not work for profit, he became bureaucratic, unless he happened to be a minister of the gospel, a professor, or perhaps a scientist. Hence, government clerks could not fail to be bureaucratic. This extended down to the lowest governmental units. Municipal light plants were bad in principle.

Even charity could not be administered by the Government because the Government would not know where to stop. Needy and unemployed people would get the idea that the world owed them a living. This was supposed to ruin their characters. Thus in the great drought which occurred in the Southwest at the end of President Hoover's administration, money could be raised for the farmers only by the Red Cross. Government money could go only for crop loans, which was not thought to be such a dangerous use of the funds and would not have such a bad effect on the character of the farmers.

In any event, the fact that government organization could not be put to practical use was tied up to character, the home, religion, law, and the science of economics. Any counter-proposal was some form of Socialism, which led to both bankruptcy and bureaucracy.

On one occasion only could the Government step into the temporal world of corporate organization and that was in time of war. Then all questions of where the money was coming from disappeared. Then the great corporate personalities were supposed to subordinate their rights to a greater cause.

This book is not concerned with the unsolvable problem of whether America would have progressed faster or slower under some other set of myths. It does not attack the use of the corporate personality in folklore. The results have been the creation of one of the greatest productive machines that the world has ever known, and this perhaps is justification enough if anyone is interested in justifying what has happened. This book is concerned only with diagnosing the present difficulties which have come upon us now that the industrial feudalism is no longer protecting large groups of our citizens who demand security, and with trying to explain the ideological difficulties which prevent the creating of organizations which will give that protection. We cannot be practical about social problems if we are under the illusion that we can solve them without complying with the taboos and customs of the tribe. The corporate personality is part of our present religion. We must continue to refer to corporations as individuals in public discourse so long as the words have emotional relevance. Since, however, we must use the words and ceremonies, it becomes important that we be able to use them intelligently. It becomes necessary, therefore, to analyze a few of the principal rituals connected with the personification of corporate organization which are generally completely misunderstood.

The two most important ceremonies which have dramatized the rugged individualism of business organizations are those which surround the antitrust laws and the reorganization of insolvent corporations. The one is useful in times of prosperity. The other is called on in times of adversity. Both are designed to perpetuate the illusion that it is men, and not organizations, with whom the Government at Washington is dealing. We will consider them in the next chapter.

CHAPTER IX

The Effect of the Antitrust Laws in Encouraging Large Combinations

In which it is shown how the antitrust laws enabled men to look at a highly organized and centralized industrial organization and still believe that it was composed of individuals engaged in buying and selling in a free market.

W E have seen that the growth of great organizations in America occurred in the face of a religion which officially was dedicated to the preservation of the economic independence of individuals. In such a situation it was inevitable that a ceremony should be evolved which reconciled current mental pictures of what men thought society ought to be with reality. The learned mythology of the time insisted that American industry was made up of small competing concerns which, if they were not individuals, nevertheless approach that ideal. "Bigness" was regarded as a curse because it led to monopoly and interfered with the operation of the laws of supply and demand. At the same time specialized techniques made bigness essential to producing goods in large enough quantities and at a price low enough so that they could be made part of the American standard of living. In order to reconcile the ideal with the practical necessity, it became necessary to develop a procedure which constantly attacked bigness on rational legal and economic grounds, and at the same time never really interfered with combinations. Such pressures gave rise to the antitrust laws which appeared to be a complete prohibition of large combinations. The same pressures made the enforcement of the antitrust laws a pure ritual. The effect of this statement of the ideal and its lack of actual enforcement was to convince reformers either that large combinations did not actually exist, or else that if they did exist, they were about to be done away with just as soon as right-thinking men were elected to office. Trust busting therefore became one of the great moral issues of the day, while at the same time great combinations thrived and escaped regulation.

This phenomenon is a familiar one and is constantly recurring in the growth of all social institutions. The simplest example is the institution of prostitution. We celebrate our ideals of chastity by constantly engaging in wars on vice. We permit prostitution to flourish by treating it as a somewhat minor crime and never taking the militant measures which would actually stamp it out. The result is a *sub rosa* institution which organizes the prostitutes after a fashion, at least to the extent that there never seems to be any shortage in our large cities. It is the writer's observation (which cannot, of course, be proved by statistics) that the more violent the wars on prostitution in a city whose population has a peculiar need for this sort of enterprise, the greater will be the control and discipline in the organization which supplies this need. Under the pressures of moral attack it will drift into the hands of ruthless and determined leaders. The privates in the army will endure harder lives while a battle is going on. The white-slave trade was the product of an exceedingly puritanical era.

A curious situation is presented. Everyone knows that vice will never be "suppressed" in New York. Nevertheless, everyone thinks that we ought to keep on trying. Therefore, we hire preachers and policemen to do this job for us. In the meantime we continue to patronize vice and our best young people treasure among their most exciting experiences incursions into the underworld. It becomes a fascinating subject for movies, novels, and plays for people who prefer to live their lives vicariously. The institution of prostitution continues to thrive after its peculiar fashion.

The phenomenon of the political machine is similar, though the moral conflict is not so keen. Preachers and investigators are constantly employed in removing politics from politics. They do this by denouncing the politicians on the other side. The politicians on their own side are reluctantly accepted on the ground that one must fight fire with fire. Prohibition offered another example, in which we turned the liquor trade over to bootleggers. Under the enforcement campaign, powerful organizations to distribute liquor grew up in self-protection, with disciplines like those of an army in war. No bartenders' union ever had the strength and morale of these courageous men who supplied whisky to a thirsty populace in that interesting era when good church people were justifying themselves in putting poison in liquor to prove to the sinful the eternal lesson that the wages of sin is death. I realize that it will be a shock to many readers to apply the word "courageous" to criminals, because it is a polar term and not supposed to include any form of bravery which is not manifest in a respectable cause. In the late war the Germans were not supposed to be courageous men fighting for an ideal. They were called "Huns." Criminals in a similar situation are called "rats," on the theory that they fight only when in a corner. A distinction is made between "courage" and "brute force" on the theory that those on the other side are like animals who have no souls.

These illustrations seem a far cry from the antitrust laws, but actually they are both examples of the same sort of psychological reaction. Granted an insistent social demand, which opposes a deeply felt ideal, and a conflict of this kind between two institutions—one respectable and moral, exemplifying the ideal, the other *sub rosa* and nonrespectable, filling the practical need—is as inevitable as the reaction of a man sitting on a hot stove. Without a grasp of this principle, it is impossible to understand the antitrust laws, because the discussion centers around whether the antitrust laws *should* or *should not* have been passed. People sit up all night writing books to contradict each other on whether the antitrust laws have done any "good." They become blind to the fact that they were part of the total cultural situation which tolerated great organizations in the face of a deeply felt ideal that there was a curse to "bigness." Corporations (before the era of public-relations counsel) were pictured as fat, greedy men preying upon the poor. Therefore, there had to be a crusade against them. That crusade resulted in the antitrust laws.

The old trust-busting era was a time when corporations were big men who were almost as wicked as criminals. Their actions were actually ruthless in the extreme and quite in keeping with the type of personification in the public mind, as anyone may note who reads the financial history of the period. However, in observing this development, it should not be forgotten that organizations are a product of the forces of practical needs and ideals. If the conflict is keen, less respectable and less scrupulous persons are more efficient, because the activities have to be of a *sub rosa* character. Institutions, by a process of natural selection, achieve the character given to them by society. So it was with corporations in the nineteenth century. Unscrupulous men were demanded in order to make the corporation conform to the picture men had of it. Therefore, unscrupulous men rose to power.

By unscrupulous men, of course, we mean men who were not caught in the common ethics with regard to "bigness," and who were therefore ready to use practical means to avoid the handicap which such ethics put upon the formation of organizations. We do not mean unkindly men. The careers of Carnegie and Rockefeller show that they had a strong sense of social obligation which asserted itself after the conflict over their methods had died down. The term "unscrupulous," being a polar word, is full of traps. It has no meaning other than describing an individual who is not caught in any particular set of scruples. It means nothing in a vacuum, other than a realization that the most effective means are the best to obtain a given end.

In this atmosphere the antitrust laws were the answer of a society which unconsciously felt the need of great organizations, and at the same time had to deny them a place in the moral and logical ideology of the social structure. They were part of the struggle of a creed of rugged individualism to adapt itself to what was becoming a highly organized society.

Thus in those days anyone who attacked the "Trusts" could achieve the same public worship as a minister of the gospel who had the energy to attack vice. It was this that made Theodore Roosevelt a great man. Historians now point out that Theodore Roosevelt never accomplished anything with his trust busting. Of course he didn't. The crusade was not a practical one. It was part of a moral conflict and no preacher ever succeeded in abolishing any form of sin. Had there been no conflict—had society been able to operate in an era of growing specialization without these organizations—it would have been easy enough to kill them by practical means. A few well-directed provisions putting a discriminatory tax on large organizations would have done the trick, provided some other form of organization were growing at the same time to fill the practical need. Since the organizations were demanded, attempts to stop their growth necessarily became purely ceremonial. As fast as one cloak was stripped off and declared illegal by the courts, other cloaks were manufactured and put on. The antitrust laws, being a preaching device, naturally performed only the functions of preaching.[1]

The actual result of the antitrust laws was to promote the growth of great industrial organizations by deflecting the attack on them into purely moral and ceremonial channels. The process was something like this: Since the corporation was a person, mere bigness could not make it a bad person. One cannot condemn his neighbor simply because he is big and strong. Therefore, the courts soon discovered that it was only "unreasonable" combinations which were bad, just as any court would decide that a big, strong neighbor should not be incarcerated so long as he acted reasonably. In various other ways the actual enforcement of the antitrust laws was completely emasculated by the courts,[2] not because the courts

[1] "Moreover, a half century of experience has been so inconclusive and uninstructive that business today does not know what policy it wants the government to pursue. A part of the business world vigorously demands laws to protect, preserve, and extend competition. Another part complains of the effects of too vigorous competition which it is the purpose of our laws to maintain. Most men who come to the Department of Justice, complaining of someone's else price-fixing, implore us to tell them how to 'stabilize' their own industry, which is a polite term for restraining of competition that they find it difficult to meet. Businessmen disagree violently whether it is too much competition, or too little competition, that causes most evils in business.

"Results show, however, that the policy to restrain concentration of wealth through combinations or conspiracies to restrict competition have not achieved their purpose. Concentration of ownership and control of American industry was never greater than today. We cannot deny that it fell to lawyers at the bar, on the bench, and in administrative posts to execute the policy which has thus resulted in disappointment."

(Speech of Robert H. Jackson at Sea Island, Georgia, May 28, 1937.)

[2] *Ibid.* "A failure to enforce the Antitrust Laws would have been bad enough but they were not merely ignored, they were perverted. In 1908 the Court discovered (*Loewe* v. *Lawlor*, 208 *U.S.* 274) that labor unions were monopolies in restraint of trade if they attempted to boycott the goods of any firm that was engaged in interstate commerce. Those who enjoy comparative studies of the judicial process will find it interesting to note the elasticity of the interstate commerce conception in the cases where it was

were composed of wicked and hypocritical people, anxious
to evade the law, but because such a process is inevitable
when an ideal meets in head-on collision with a practical
need. The process is just as unconscious as was the toleration
of speak-easies in dry communities during prohibition.

utilized against labor as compared with the narrow interpretation when
the sugar trust was under consideration.

"After experimenting for many years with efforts to enforce the Antitrust Laws through the Court, the Congress enacted the Federal Trade
Commission Act, which was designed to add to the existing remedies
against monopoly proceedings before an administrative body. It was
thought, apparently, that if the Courts would not enforce the laws themselves, they would let someone else do so. This hope was in the main
disappointed.

"The Federal Trade Commission has had its powers whittled away and
has been cramped by Court interpretations and judicial constructions. It
was directed to prevent unfair methods of competition. Of course it was
impossible to define by statute the multitude of unfair practices. The Commission was expected, after investigation, to determine what practices were
unfair methods of competition. But the Supreme Court promptly decided,
'It is for the Courts not the Commission ultimately to determine as a matter of law what they include,' and it went back to its old precedents for
the definition (*Federal Trade Commission* v. *Warren*, 253 *U.S.* 420). The
Court next decided that it would not only define the terms but that it
would also examine the whole record in any case and ascertain the issues
presented and whether there were material facts in evidence not given
sufficient weight by the Commission (*Federal Trade Commission* v. *Curtis
Publishing Company*, 260 *U.S.* 568). Chief Justice Taft filed an opinion,
the substance of which is that he was unable to decide just what it was
that the majority was deciding. It was apparent, however, from the outcome, as the Chairman of the Commission stated, that the Court had
claimed the power to frame an issue of its own, and to support it by its own
findings of fact.

"Another blow to the Commission was dealt in *Federal Trade Commission* v. *Klessner* (280 *U.S.* 219) and *Federal Trade Commission* v. *Rala-
dam* (283 *U.S.* 643). Professor Bates describes the effect of these two decisions to be that when the Commission 'attempted to check monopoly it
found that public deception was the essential and when it attempted to
check public deception it found that monopoly was the essential,' of its
power.

.   .   .   .   .

"At the end of this long road we read like an epitaph Senator Wagner's

In this way the antitrust laws became the greatest protection to uncontrolled business dictatorships.[3] The process by which this was accomplished needs further explanation. If the practical need of these great organizations had not violated a current taboo, men would never have tolerated the abuses which grew up around them. For example, there was no sense whatever in their methods of levying tribute on investors through issues of securities which worked in the long run not unlike the numbers racket in New York City—that is, the persons on the inside gave out no more prizes than was

statement that 'no one can state authoritatively what our national policy is.' The Senator spoke with characteristic restraint. He might well have added that no one can state authoritatively what our national policy *can be* under the attitude of the Court.

"I am bound to say that this is a record in which I, as a lawyer, can find little satisfaction. No group in the United States is louder in its demands for democratic government than the Bar. It is always issuing pronouncements in which it fears dictatorship, and always professing fear lest fundamental institutions be impaired or undermined. At the same time, no group in the United States has so consistently thwarted the efforts of the democratic government to establish and enforce a policy concededly within its constitutional power as have the lawyers, on the bench and off. They have systematically denatured and sterilized every statutory policy designed to repress monopoly."

[3] *Ibid.* "While the country has forbidden monopoly it has also been subsidizing it. Monopoly has had tax advantages that have aided its rise. While the sale of a small business to another who wished to continue it as such would be subject to a capital gains tax, if it were absorbed by a big business the matter could be arranged in the form of a tax-free 'reorganization.' The tax-free reorganization privilege has been a powerful incentive for the concentrating of business. The advantage in single transactions, at the cost of the Treasury, has often exceeded the whole annual appropriation for antitrust enforcement. Enforcement has been and is inadequately financed.

"Moreover, the privilege of paying dividend profits free of tax from one corporation to another operated as a subsidy for the holding companies one of the most favored forms of creating and operating monopoly. The recent repeal of this privilege and the substitution of an intercorporate dividend tax have already proved highly effective in dissolving holding companies, and undoubtedly an increase in that tax would prove an automatic discouragement of that particular type of antitrust violation."

absolutely necessary to keep the country interested. There was no common sense in the bitter wars between these great organizations, or in their failure to recognize any responsibility which government from time immemorial has recognized toward its retainers. But neither the public nor the organizers thought of these industrial organizations as "government." The trick of personification veiled this obvious fact from their eyes. Since the organizations were persons, they should be treated as if they had free will and moral responsibility. Regulation was bureaucracy and tyranny over individuals.

Therefore, when corporate abuses were attacked, it was done on the theory that *criminal* penalties should be invoked rather than control. Senators could always adopt the side of the people on the corporation issue and demand prosecution of the great enterprises under the antitrust laws. Since they had no direct responsibility for such prosecutions, this method gave them the advantages which go with complete lack of responsibility for results. Theirs was but to point the way. In this manner every scheme for direct control broke to pieces on the great protective rock of the antitrust laws.

The confused results of antitrust law enforcement on the practical control of organizations were not recognized because men did not think of great corporations as public organizations like an army. Yet in fact the effect was the same as if courts in time of war should lay down and clarify the principles of what were reasonable or unreasonable combinations of troops. Under such a theory generals making unreasonable combinations would be prosecuted, but of course given the benefit of counsel to prove that their particular combinations of troops were reasonable. The theory of this process would be that while it might delay things a bit at the time, the principles of strategy would become clearer and clearer as time went on and thus the army would become more efficient. Generals who understood these principles would rise to the top following the great fundamental principles of *laissez faire* army organization. If the process failed to achieve results, it would be the fault either of the antitrust division of the army or else of the courts.

Of course, when this is applied to an army it sounds like obvious nonsense. That, however, is only because we think of the army in terms of human organization and not of principle. Had we thought of the great industrial enterprises in terms of organization, the results would have been far different in terms of governmental regulation. Since we thought of them in terms of individuals to whom correct principle should be taught by the precept and example of the judicial process, the antitrust laws, designed to offer some sort of regulation, actually became the great bulwark of defense of these organizations against any regulation whatever. They offered an escape valve through which the energy of reformers was dissipated, permitting the organizations to go on undisturbed.

Within the organizations themselves, men were not theoretical but intensely practical. They did not follow economists and lawyers. They used them. Realizing the advantages of a respectable position in society, they employed public-relations counsel, skilled in the use of propaganda. After the War, cartoons showing corporations to be great, greedy men became fewer and fewer. Gradually they changed themselves from bad to good men in the public eye. They took the rôle of the sinner who had repented and become a saint. Men reading Josephson's *Robber Barons, The Great American Capitalists, 1861–1901,*[4] were able to say: "Once unenlightened corporations used to do these bad things, but now they have reformed and do not do them any more." The era of

[4] Harcourt, Brace, 1934.

trust busting disappeared. It was still good for an occasional battle cry, but as the industrial empires grew in power their symbols became more and more respectable. The words "tainted money" as applied to corporate donations went out of common use. Theodore Roosevelt, with his big stick that never hit anybody, accomplished two things. First, he convinced the public that if we would only drive politics out of the Department of Justice the laws were sufficient to make these big individuals really compete. Second, he convinced corporate executives that it was a good thing to hire public-relations counsel and show that they also were followers of the true religion.

The antitrust laws remained as a most important symbol. Whenever anyone demanded practical regulation, they formed an effective moral obstacle, since all the liberals would answer with a demand that the antitrust laws be enforced. Men like Senator Borah founded political careers on the continuance of such crusades, which were entirely futile but enormously picturesque, and which paid big dividends in terms of personal prestige. And, of course, people like Borah were sincere in thinking that the moral answer was also the practical answer. Thus, by virtue of the very crusade against them, the great corporations grew bigger and bigger, and more and more respectable. This is not an attack on the process. It was an inevitable one in such an intellectual and moral atmosphere. It allowed the organizing ability of the American people to develop. Whether it would have developed faster or slower under other conditions is a question which it is not the province of a descriptive analysis to answer.

In any event, the Federal antitrust laws, since the 'nineties, have stood as a great moral gesture which proves that in a nation of organizations individuals really are supreme; or, if not, they are going to become so very soon through the intervention of the Federal Government. Plenty of individual economists have written and talked about the trust problem as one of organization and control. Yet the general tenor of public debate about great industrial organizations, both conservative and radical, has been based on the conception that the only proper type of society is composed of unorganized competitive individuals. In each great depression the attack on industrial organizations is renewed, coupled with the demand that they be dissolved—a demand which is always defeated because of the forces which make such organization essential. In *Thorstein Veblen and His America,* Joseph Dorfman reviews the debates which attended the depression in the 'nineties. The following quotation from that book[5] could be used as descriptive of the recent depression with only a few changes in names.

The Populist Party had its first national convention at Omaha in July 1892. Donnelly again delivered the preamble, with a ringing arraignment of the corporate interests, and the delegates staged a tremendous demonstration. One unsympathetic critic wrote: "No intelligent man could . . . listen to the wild and frenzied assaults upon the existing order of things, without a feeling of great alarm at the extent and intensity of the social lunacy there displayed. . . . When that furious and hysterical arraignment of the present times, that incoherent intermingling of Jeremiah and Bellamy, the platform, was adopted, the cheers and yells which rose like a tornado from four thousand throats and raged without cessation for thirty-four minutes, during which women shrieked and wept, men embraced and kissed their neighbors, locked arms, marched back and forth, and leaped upon tables and chairs in the ecstasy of their delirium—this dramatic and historical scene must have told every quiet, thoughtful witness that there was something at the back of all this turmoil more than the failure of crops or the scarcity of ready cash. And over all the city during that summer week brooded the spectres of

[5] pp. 88–89.

Nationalism, Socialism and general discontent." Southern agrarians characterised the nomination of Grover Cleveland "as a prostitution of the principles of Democracy, as a repudiation of the demands of the Farmers' Alliance, which embody the true principles of Democracy, and a surrender of the rights of the people to the financial kings of the country." A Western agrarian leader spoke of Cleveland as a "fossiled reminiscence."

In Minnesota Donnelly was nominated for governor at a meeting addressed by the socialist Robert Schilling of Milwaukee. Donnelly declared that a horde of millionaires expected to become titled aristocrats and, if their progress were not arrested, they would fulfil their wishes. The farmers of Minnesota and the Dakotas, according to Donnelly, were defrauded of a billion dollars by an organised conspiracy of railroad men and grain speculators. The Carnegie Steel Company sent for the hated Pinkertons in an attempt to break a strike at its plants in Homestead, Pennsylvania, and there was a bloody battle when they arrived. The entire state militia was called out, martial law was declared, and the strike leader was held for murder. Alexander Berkman, an anarchist, attempted to kill H. C. Frick, one of the most hated anti-union employers in the country, and a private in the militia was tortured by his officers for publicly expressing sympathy with the act. Davis Rich Dewey declared that the conflict "gave rise to grave forebodings as to the stability of republican institutions." In Congress, in the press, and on the public platform "the Pinkertons, branded as mercenaries and hirelings, were charged with treason and were said to be employed not only to protect the property of employers, but to . . . provoke [the populace] to violence . . . as an excuse for the calling-out of troops." The strikers declared that "the public and the employees aforesaid have equitable rights and interests in the said mill which cannot be modified or diverted by due process of law. . . . The employees have the right to continuous employment in the said mill during efficiency and good behaviour." Laughlin denounced this "inalienable right to continuous employment" and attributed the doctrine to the "one-sided reading" of the strikers, particularly to their exclusive attention to Henry George. So-

cialism made converts on the apparent evidence "that the individualistic system of competition had broken down." The courts
ordered the Standard Oil trust dissolved, but a new device, the
holding company, made its appearance.

And note particularly that the paragraph closes with a
reference to the dissolution of the Standard Oil trust and the
beginnings of the holding company. As this is being written,
a crusade against the Aluminum Company of America is in
the first stages of its long struggle through the courts.

This was the procedure of attempts to control the great industrial organizations of this country in the interests of
democratic and humanitarian service to those dependent on
them. Attempts to reform usually ended with an appeal to
the old creed under whose protecting mantle these institutions had grown, the creed of rugged individualism, with the
organizations personified as individuals.

The reason why these attacks always ended with a ceremony of atonement, but few practical results, lay in the fact
that there were no new organizations growing up to take
over the functions of those under attack. The opposition was
never able to build up its own commissary and its service
of supply. It was well supplied with orators and economists,
but it lacked practical organizers. A great coöperative movement in America might have changed the power of the
industrial empire. Preaching against it, however, simply resulted in counterpreaching.

And the reason for this was that the reformers themselves
were caught in the same creeds which supported the institutions they were trying to reform. Obsessed with a moral attitude toward society, they thought in Utopias. They were
interested in systems of government. Philosophy was for
them more important than opportunism and so they achieved
in the end philosophy rather than opportunity.

Edward Bellamy saw in the corporation itself a step toward Socialism. He thought of a future world of nationalized industry. He was the forerunner of the N.R.A. and the attacks on his preaching resembled very much the attacks on the recent National Recovery Administration. His failure in diagnosis was much the same as that of the N.R.A. He believed that change in social institutions occurs when right-thinking, intelligent men get together and plan to change them. He saw in political argument over principle, not a symptom of spiritual conflict, but a positive directing force.

When the spiritual conflict died down after the panic of the 'nineties, the old religion reasserted itself. The antitrust laws became the great myth to prove by an occasional legal ceremony that great industrial organizations should be treated like individuals, and guided by principle and precept back to the old ways of competition and fair practices, as individuals were. This was then, and is today, the principal utility of that massive moral philosophy known as antitrust legislation.

One great change, however, did come over corporate activity because of the philosophy which produced the antitrust laws. Since everyone thought of these great enterprises as individuals which should be moral and gentlemanly in their dealings, they came gradually to conform to those standards. This is in accordance with the principle of political dynamics which makes it inevitable that an institution will, in the long run, conform to the character which men give it. The antitrust laws were based on a popular conception that great corporations *could* be made respectable. Following that ideal, great corporations *did* become respectable.

The old days were marked by ruthless suppression of competitors by any means available, including discriminatory freight rates, locally ruinous prices, and any sort of undercover tactics to drive out small competitors. Men like Rockefeller did not hesitate to use devices which were illegal and immoral according to the standards of today. Today the corporate practices which most effectively give great organizations their positions of dominance follow, with the greatest fidelity, the current moral concepts of what an individual should do. The most important among those methods are (1) the manipulation of securities; (2) the pooling of patents; (3) price leadership and control. A brief analysis of these practices will illustrate how great organizations, operating in a folklore which refused to think in terms of organization, nevertheless obtained respectability.

1. *The manipulation of securities.* Here we have a device which current morals consider respectable so long as investors do not lose money. The wrecking of great organizations to make money on the stock violates all our standards. The securing of control in order to "build up" an organization is considered one of the higher duties of our industrial leaders. It is well known that owning a small percentage of stock gives substantial control, provided that no one else has a large percentage. This minority stock control, aided by the holding company device which we have already described, permits individuals to rule vast empires without any substantial investment whatever. Popular magazines like the *Saturday Evening Post* hail control acquired in this way as a great achievement. Control is obtained mostly by bankers, a class which in the long run has always occupied a position of the highest dignity and respectability. All the myths surrounding bankers fortify them better than any other class against radical attack. This is at least one of the reasons for the acceptance of banker control and for the power which lies in the slogan, "Government must not interfere with business." To illustrate, we quote an incident described in the syndicated columns of John T. Flynn:

Now the Mid-America Corporation controls the Allegheny Corporation and the Allegheny Corporation, thru a series of holding companies, controls a vast network of great railroads and all kinds of important industries. There is over three billion dollars invested in these vast properties. This money is not the money of the Allegheny Corporation or of the Mid-America which controls it. It is the money of countless investors, most of them small investors. Furthermore, the properties themselves are touched with a well-organized public interest.

They were dominated until the crash by the Van Sweringens. Then they fell into the hands of a New York bank. Then, thru an investment of a few million dollars, they were thrown into the hands of an Indiana fruit jar manufacturer. Now they have toppled into the basket of two young unknown stock brokers with an investment of not more than 10 million dollars in this vast empire. Is it unreasonable to ask that it is about time that these great properties and these extensive business investments cease to be kicked about?

Robert R. Young, one of the young stock brokers who, with a handful of pennies, now sets out to rule and reorganize these giant properties, seems to have been doing very nicely down in Washington. On the witness stand before Sen. Wheeler's committee he conducted himself smoothly and with tact. When, however, he was pressed on the question as to whether, with his pitifully small investment, he should be permitted to settle the fate of these immense public properties, he became a little annoyed.

The proposal was actually made to him that the public interest and the interest of investors seem to require that the holding company stock which he has now managed to get hold of and which thru a series of slick holding company schemes of the Van Sweringens dominates these properties, ought to be put into trust, perhaps into the hands of a committee of trustees named by the I.C.C. Young then lost his smoothness altogether and announced somewhat wrathily that "there was too much Government in business." (*Washington Daily News*, May 31, 1937.)

The respectability of such devices was constantly under attack by liberals; yet they failed to make any appreciable headway against the mythology. The reason, of course, was that since logic did not create that mythology, logic could not destroy it. It was a product of the conflict created by great organizations struggling and finally achieving a place in the mystical hierarchy of rugged individuals. Liberals, caught in the same religion, usually ended by supporting the oracles of its authority.

For example, John T. Flynn, whom we quote above, wrote much about corporate manipulation, always in a state of amazement that such things could exist in a country of thinking men. Therefore, he shared the ultimate fate of all liberals who think that reform lies in trying to make institutions live up to their creeds. He testified with great earnestness against Roosevelt's proposal to change the personnel of the Supreme Court in order to stop its constant interference with legislative and economic policy on the part of the Government. This very institution which had dramatized and given vitality to those little pictures of the corporate personality which were responsible for making the holding company even in its most fantastic forms acceptable, was defended by a man who crusaded to make society conform to those pictures. The Court, which had thrown the mantle of the individual around the great corporate enterprise by identifying those who attempted to regulate it as attackers of freedom and the home, had become in his mind the actual protector of freedom and the home. The reason he defended it was that he needed the little pictures of a society of individuals which the Court was dramatizing in order to carry on his business as a reformer.

That general point of view, shared by most liberals, was expressed by the philosophy underlying the antitrust laws. It provided a ceremony in which the efforts of reformers could be dramatized, and through which opportunistic practical control could always be defeated, because liberals always disliked political control which was in opposition to principle.

2. *The pooling of patents.* Here we have an interesting example of one individualistic symbol used to avoid the logical consequences of another. The patent law became one of the most effective devices for emasculating the antitrust laws.[6] Patent law was supposed to protect the individual inventor against exploitation. An obviously effective way of doing this would have been to guarantee the inventor a proportion of the fruits of his invention. This, however, would have been paternalism and not individualism. Hence the inventor was given the right to sell his patent to another individual. Protection was accorded to those inventors who were good businessmen. Those who were not obviously did not deserve consideration. To give them protection which no one could wheedle out of them would have been as great an interference with the sacred right of contract as minimum-wage laws for women, according to the thinking of the time.

Since the patent laws obviously were designed to protect "owners" of patents rather than inventors, it became possible for an industrial organization to own all the patents necessary for an entire industry, which they could license to others on terms which gave them control of prices. This made the corporation appear as the heir of the individual inventor. Naturally, there were limits to this, as the confused line of decisions on the pooling of patents shows. However, those limits were vague and offered little resistance to the inventive genius of lawyers who were able to invent new rituals to achieve these results as fast as the old ones were outlawed.

[6] *Ibid.* "While the nation has forbidden monopoly by one set of laws it has been creating it by another. Patent laws, valuable as they may be in some respects, often father monopoly. Unless we are prepared to reconsider the conditions upon which we will extend patent protection, we can have no consistent antimonopoly policy."

In addition to this, it was never quite clear just what was an invention which could be patented and what was not. Infringement suits were costly and always uncertain. The patent law, operating under forces which made it one of the instruments of organized control over industry, became one of the most intricate mysteries of the law—a combination of law and mechanics under which almost any results might be achieved. Patent lawyers became a class apart. The great men in this specialty represented great organizations. Poor, struggling inventors could obtain only poor, struggling lawyers whenever they opposed corporate interests.

And finally the practice grew up of corporate enterprises hiring men to make inventions as their agents. This, under the familiar doctrine of agency, made the organization itself, rather than the individual, the "inventor." And thus the patent law, designed to protect poor inventors and at the same time treat them as rugged individuals, became one of the most effective instruments to escape the disorganizing force of too logical an application of the antitrust laws.

3. *Market dominance and price leadership.* In the old days the methods of building up large organizations and suppressing competition were crude and direct. Men met in secret sessions and planned their campaigns with the frankness of military leaders. The antitrust laws took away respectability from that way of combining and made it somewhat dangerous. Agreements in restraint of trade were hard to prove; even when proved, they must be shown to be unreasonable. However, coöperation in its essence could not be unreasonable, since it was not an agreement. It was simply the tendency of free men to get along with each other. The difference between combination and coöperation is hard to define, so the word "intent" was used to distinguish them. Results achieved with one intent were legal which would have been illegal if another kind of intent had been found. Thus the results became unimportant and the law confined

itself to the philosophical problem of the state of mind at the time. The great principle of competition was not violated even where men did not compete, provided that they did not intend to agree not to compete.

Thus the phenomenon known as "price leadership" became the dominant factor in establishing control on the part of great organizations. If men refused to follow the practices of the recognized and respected members of their industry, they were regarded as "chiselers." Various pressures were put on them to follow published prices. These pressures could seldom be proved. Members of an industry did not have to "agree" not to indulge in "cutthroat" competition. All that was necessary was the general belief that such competition was not proper and would lead to retaliation.

Trade associations became an important part of business organizations. They formed committees and drew up codes of ethics. These codes did not mention any principles of price leadership. Such a thing was not included within the admitted objectives. The codes were concerned with coöperation and fair dealing between Christian men, who assumed a sort of moral obligation to be friendly. They affected prices, not because of any specific agreements, but because they took away the respectability of sharp competition among their members. It was impossible to attack anything as subtle as this sort of price control under the antitrust laws.

And so the antitrust laws, instead of breaking up great organizations, served only to make them respectable and well thought of by providing them with the clothes of rugged individualism. The N.R.A. expressed the change which had come over men's thinking when it permitted corporations to combine in order to eliminate "unreasonable" competition. The profit motive, which at one time was a respectable justification for any sort of price-cutting, had become a somewhat immoral thing because of the competing symbol of coöperation.

The net result of the antitrust laws was to make the most
effective forms of competition, i.e., competition that hurt, appear to be a lack of a coöperative and Christian spirit. They
did this by eliminating the more brutal practices of great organizations. Without these laws we might have had the car-
tel system, adopted in Europe, which raised prices immoder-
ately without much regard for the public. On the other
hand, if the antitrust philosophy had not been developed, it
is doubtful if the great organization could have achieved such
an acceptable place in a climate of opinion in which rugged
individualism was the chief ideal. In any event, it is obvious
that the antitrust laws did not prevent the formation of some
of the greatest financial empires the world has ever known,[7]

[7] Industrial Holding Companies—Gross Assets as of December 31, 1935,
of Fifteen Important Companies:*

Company	Date of Or- ganization	Gross Assets as of Dec. 31, 1935
Allied Chemical and Dye Corp.	1920	$400,100,000
American Radiator and Standard Sanitary Corp.	1929	159,100,000
Crown Zellerbach Corp.	1928	101,300,000
Eastman Kodak Co.	1901	168,300,000
Gulf Oil Corp. (of Pa.)	1922	430,200,000
International Paper and Power Co.	1928	881,400,000†
Koppers Co.	1924	177,300,000
Loew's, Inc.	1919	129,300,000
Pullman, Inc.	1927	258,600,000
Sinclair Consolidated Oil Corp.	1923	331,100,000
Standard Oil Co. of New Jersey	1882	1,895,000,000
Texas Corp.	1926	473,800,000
Tide Water Associated Oil Co.	1926	182,800,000
Union Carbide and Carbon Corp.	1917	336,500,000
United States Steel Corp.	1901	1,822,400,000
Total		$7,747,200,000

* List selected from Bonbright and Means, *The Holding Company*, p. 77. Gross
assets obtained from *Moody's Industrials*, 1936.
† 1933 figure.

held together by some of the most fantastic ideas, all based on the fundamental notion that a corporation is an individual who can trade and exchange goods without control by the Government.

CHAPTER X

The Ritual of Corporate Reorganization

IN which is explained the doctrine of vicarious atonement through which the debts of an industrial organization are forgiven.

T HE antitrust laws, which we have been discussing, were the platform from which industrial enterprise could be viewed as a collection of competing individuals in times of development and prosperity. The ritual of corporate reorganization performs the same service for great enterprises in adversity. It is perhaps the most interesting of all our legal rituals from a ceremonial point of view, because it is the most complicated mystery of all. In the celebration of this ritual great law firms are able to maintain staffs and offices which give a magnificence to the legal profession known at no other time or place. The fees charged have been fantastic. The literature has been almost incomprehensible, but the result reached has been most impressive. A corporate reorganization is a combination of a municipal election, a historical pageant, an antivice crusade, a graduate-school seminar, a judicial proceeding, and a series of horse trades, all rolled into one—thoroughly buttered with learning and frosted with distinguished names. Here the union of law and economics is celebrated by one of the wildest ideological orgies in intellectual history. Men work all night preparing endless documents in answer to other endless documents, which other men read in order to make solemn arguments. At the same time practical politicians utilize every resource of patronage, demagoguery, and coercion beneath the solemn smoke screen.

The purpose of all this is (1) to prove that when corporations cannot pay their debts they must surrender all their property to their creditors like other individuals, thus vindicating inexorable economic law; (2) to permit a practical treatment of a political situation without violating this folklore. The practical methods are clearly those by which a political machine maintains itself in power against opposition.

Although to the casual observer the complications seem most forbidding, actually the dialectic of this process is very simple. It consists in the endless repetition in different forms of the notion that men must pay their debts, in a situation in which neither men nor debts in any real sense are involved.

In order to understand this it is necessary to analyze the creed of the relationship of debtor and creditor in a society of fairly self-sufficient individuals, which has been gradually transferred to the relationship of great organizations to each other and to their retainers and subjects. The original picture of debt was that a thing had been loaned as a horse is loaned. If a man borrows another's horse and kills it by wanton misuse, he should be punished severely. On this analogy men who did not pay their debts were put in jail. The notion persisted long after it became apparent that jailing a man for debt was a cruel and useless thing to do, and that it hampered, instead of encouraged, trade. It put hazards on the taking of credit risks which strangled expansion. Nevertheless, long after it had become an economic absurdity, imprisonment for debt continued as a moral lesson.

Gradually, however, it became harder to put men in jail for debt. The notion that a debt was a thing which the defaulting debtor had wantonly destroyed gave way to the idea of the creditor making an "investment." "Risk" and "investment" are words which go together and when men began thinking of debt in terms of risk, they were willing to let the creditor suffer in an individualistic world for his bad judgment. The moral responsibility is thus not entirely on the debtor. The old moral lesson, that of the debtor's culpability, is now dramatized by the fact that men can theoretically be put in jail in most states for debts *fraudulently* contracted. Fraud, however, is a difficult thing to define in the ethics of trading, which are essentially the ethics of deceiving the other side. Therefore, in this country today it has become practically impossible actually to keep a man in jail for any other kind of debt than alimony, to which the ideology of an investment risk had never been attached. Marriage is not the sort of thing in which the bride is supposed to consult her banker, nor is she supposed to be punished for lack of judgment if she makes an obvious mistake.

The little picture of debt as an investment in which the creditor must use good judgment carries with it the notion that the creditor has the right to make himself "secure" by relying on the value of the property which the debtor possesses. This in turn involves the corollary idea that the creditor can take whatever property the debtor has. To this ideology legal procedure gradually conformed; levy of execution took the place of punishment. Where a debtor did not have enough property to go round, there grew up rules of a war to get that property. In this game the underlying folklore of an individualistic society insisted that "natural justice" give the prize to the swiftest creditor. This caused the development of elaborate legal formulas to determine symbolically which creditor really was first in getting the "property." The writer recalls a lawsuit in which his client was engaged in a race between creditors to "attach" railroad ties which had been cut and were scattered about the woods. They had to be reduced to "possession" in order to give his client a prior attachment. Metaphysical questions as to what was "possession" were argumentative weapons. Must the sheriff post a notice on each pile of ties or would a series of notices tacked on trees near the pile of ties be sufficient? Or was it necessary to go to the expense of gathering up the ties and putting a padlock on a fence enclosing them? Law schools taught courses on the nature of possession. Words like "constructive possession" were invented to plug ideological holes. It was all done to celebrate the great individualistic principle that the early bird catches the worm. This metaphysics, while complicated, was still manageable because the things which were attached were concrete and there were actual living individuals who could be classified as debtors and as creditors.

The ceremony dramatized two important ideals: first, that the race was to the swift; and, second, that a man who could not pay his debts must surrender his property and start all over again. Another little picture complicated the drama—the ideal of bankruptcy. This ideal represented the pacifist notion that creditors should not have to fight each other and that an equal division of property was preferable. It also involved the humanitarian idea that a debtor who had surrendered all his property had sufficiently atoned for his sins to be allowed to start over again. Therefore, debtors were "discharged in bankruptcy." There was, of course, a spiritual conflict present in this ideal of bankruptcy. The "honest" man (whose disappearance has been commented on by the prophets of each successive generation) was not supposed to take advantage of the bankruptcy laws. The occasional merchant who worked all his life for creditors was given a halo for his suffering.

This conflict was represented in the law by the fact that both the bankruptcy game and the creditors'-race game existed side by side. Complicated rules were involved to determine when the creditors' race stopped and the bankruptcy game began. A great literature arose to define where the border line was.

When the large organizations, wearing the garments of

rugged individuals, replaced actual individuals, the conflict
of the ideals and the political practical techniques of organization created the law of corporate reorganization. This
game became a good deal like three-dimensional chess. In
the old game, at least, the words "individual" and "property"
described some of the pieces which were moved about on the
chessboard. With the rise of great organizations, both of
these terms became ceremonies. The property of a railroad
doesn't exist in the old sense of property because it cannot
be bought and sold as a tangible thing. Its value is inseparable
from the habits and disciplines and morale of the organization which operates the railroad. Since "property" meant
anything with a money value, it became necessary to put a
money value upon the habits and disciplines of organizations
and to call them property.

Therefore, such things as "going-concern value" and "good
will" had to be called property and given a money value. The
money value of these things, like the money value of all property belonging to individuals, was supposed to be determined
by the laws of supply and demand.

This worked beautifully as a slogan to keep the Government from stepping into the situation, since all sound men
agreed that bureaucracy cannot try to change the laws of
supply and demand. (They proved this by such examples as
the experience of Brazil with coffee and the failure of attempts to control the world market in sugar. It was also frequently pointed out that governmental price-fixing caused
the fall of the Roman Empire.) However, these notions did
not work so well when it came to "selling" the "property" of
a large corporate individual to settle its debts. There was no
demand. This was explained on the theory that no individual, corporate or otherwise, had enough "money" to "buy" a
railroad, or an enterprise like Paramount Publix, which controlled about a third of the amusement industry of America.

The real reason was that since the "property" consisted in
the unity and coherence of an organization, only organization itself could "buy" it. The organization itself was the
only "property" which the organization "owned." The notion of buying this sort of property in the open market was
as unreal as it would be for the Republican party in New
York to "buy" the very successful Vare machine in Philadelphia so that they could beat Tammany Hall, and to fix
the price of the Vare machine by capitalizing its earning capacity.

Of course, in reality the struggle which attended the "in-
solvency" of a great organization could be nothing other than
a struggle for political control of that organization. The symbols were debts and credits and sales, and men had to plan
their practical campaigns in those terms. This created a situation in which the rules of debts and credits became like the
platforms in a political campaign. They didn't mean anything. They were full of contradictions. They could never
be successfully followed if political considerations dictated
otherwise, and yet they were supposed to be followed to the
logical end even if it meant loss of the battle. The conflict
could only be resolved by a public drama where the rules pa-
raded in dress clothes, while a political machine directed the
play from behind the scenes.

The central idea in that drama was the personification of
industrial enterprise as individuals who must pay their debts
or else atone for not paying by giving up all their property
and starting over again. The verbal currency was taken from
the old sale on execution, but of course the words had to acquire new meanings while seeming to keep the old. It was
done in this way: A friendly creditor, representing all the
creditors, sued the corporate individual. Instead of levying
execution on its property, he crossed an imaginary line into
a court of equity (which was supposed to possess principles

which relieved litigants from the harsh logic of the law). Once across this line, he told the judge that if the property were "sold" at public sale the creditors would all suffer, because the sale would destroy the going-concern value, which was an important "asset." He therefore asked that a receiver be appointed to hold the property together as an operating unit, while the creditor hunted for purchasers. A purchaser would finally appear and buy the property. The corporation would then be stripped of everything it had and cast into outer darkness as a lesson to other corporations not to incur debts which they could not pay. Thus the vicarious atonement for the sin of getting into debt was accomplished.

Actually, however, no one could operate the property but the organization. Hence a political combination, composed of the winners in the struggle for control, took over the management by calling itself the purchaser.

The creditors were divided into all sorts of classes. Some were secured and others unsecured. There were always conflicting claims on securities, but the first in time was supposed to have the preference. There were also a lot of different kinds of stockholders, who had different kinds of preferences, but none of whom were supposed to get anything until the creditors had been paid. Matters in this area became very complicated indeed, because lawyers would try to draw up elaborate instruments which would give the rights of both creditors and stockholders to the persons they represented. However, the central little picture of a hierarchy of claims, sharply divided into two great classes, creditors and stockholders, was very clear and simple.

This process was called an "equity receivership." It obtained the same results as bankruptcy, so far as the division of the "assets" equally among creditors was concerned, by using the imagery of a philanthropic creditor selling the property, not only for his own benefit, but for the benefit of all.

"Throwing" the corporation into bankruptcy was a little different from an equity receivership, though it is impossible to say exactly where the difference lay. Lawyers, however, felt that the equity receivership was a little better because they themselves had invented all the rules in this procedure, and they were not bothered by the legislature as in bankruptcy. Hence the equity receivership was preferred, but if a student wanted to ask a lawyer just why, he got no such simple explanation. Instead he was referred to a large number of books. The subject was simply too colossal to be talked about simply. That would be like trying to reduce military strategy to a formula. Both bankruptcy and equity had their advantages in different kinds of tactical situations. Each dramatized the same ideal—the atonement of the corporate individual for its failure to pay debts by stripping it of its insignia and casting it into outer darkness.

All of this drama was played before the court. It was like a Chinese play, in that it was endless, and very highly stylized. No one was permitted to talk naturally about the facts of financial life and politics on the stage.

Behind the scenes a different game went on. Here men realized that it was a question, not of sale, but of obtaining control. Those already in control had an enormous advantage. Symbolically, the stockholders were below the creditors. Actually, the management, who usually controlled the stock, could no more be ousted than the head of a political machine can be ousted. The scene became one in which different conflicting interests traded and negotiated for strategic position within the enterprise, much as rival military cliques might struggle for the control of an army. The secured bondholders had the advantage of rank. The natural-born leaders who gathered the private soldiers together had the advantage of power. It therefore often happened that the stockholders, who were usually on the side of the former management, got a position because of their strategic advantage which a logical application of the principles of debt did not give them. Attempts to reconcile this with the theology that "secured bonds must be paid first" resulted in the utmost confusion. No one ever knew how the "law" stood on any of the points about which the conflict raged.

The battle behind the judicial scenes was further complicated because it had its own symbols, which were not those of a large individual selling another large individual's property on execution, but those of democratic government, in which the majority was supposed to rule. Thus a majority of the shares was supposed to control the management. The power of the majority of the bondholders was more complicated. It could not legally control the minority (as in the case of shareholders) because bondholders were supposed to have separate independent claims which could not be taken away by a majority. However, another device made of these bondholders a sort of democracy with a very limited suffrage. The security was generally held by a corporate trustee who "represented" the bondholders. Actually, as the investigations of the Securities and Exchange Commission showed, the corporate trustee assumed practically no responsibility.[1] The written documents which were his authority were mostly composed of clauses relieving him from all liability so long as he did not do anything. There was much criticism because the duties of the corporate trustee for bondholders were purely formal. However, this fact was actually not surprising since the only purpose of this trustee was to personify the bondholders, and thus to allow the courts to think of them as a single character in the play, instead of a mob. Within the symbolic bondholder personality represented by the corpo-

[1] *Report on the Study and Investigation of the Work, Activities, Personnel and Functions of Protective and Reorganization Committees*, Part VI, "Trustees under Indentures."

rate trustee, the symbols of democracy again were supposed to govern to a limited extent. But it took a very *large* majority instead of a bare majority of secured bondholders to compel the trustee to act. The proportion depended on the "trust indenture" by which the trustee received his title. The courts worried somewhat as to how large a majority would be legal and equitable for such an instrument to require. They never came to any very definite conclusion on this, however.

And thus the whole phenomenon was very complex. It started as a drama of an execution sale. Then if you looked at it long enough it became a democracy, with a constitution. You never could tell with any certainty in which rôle it was appearing because the players always took different sides on this question. After you were acclimated to this, however, you discovered that it was actually a *sub rosa* political machine using patronage, demagogic appeals, and all the favorite devices of such machines to influence and control the vast unorganized mass of individual creditors.

The techniques used were the same as those of any political organization. The various parties did not call themselves political machines, but used the words "protective committee." Numerous "protective committees" were formed which competed for favor among the creditors by advertising, making speeches, and sending out campaign literature. As is usual in political campaigns, the "ins" had the advantage of the "outs" because they controlled the political machinery. Therefore, an alliance between bankers and management would nearly always be successful. The banking group had the lists of creditors and the prestige. The management had the experience. This made the appeal of other protective committees doubly difficult.[2] In the first place, they did not have the same control

---

[2] "By and large, control over committees has been in the hands of the management and the bankers. Their feeling has been and is that the committee field is their preserve and that outside interests (at least those whom

of the means of communication to the creditors. The situation might be compared to one where a political party in
power controlled the press and the radio. In the second place,
the bankers' protective committee was composed of men who
were regarded as solid and substantial citizens, thus making
the other groups appear as radicals. (The term actually used
was "strikers.") Yet the "outs" usually got some reward for
their energy.[8]

The "outs" in conducting the campaign used the identical
symbols as in a national election couched in financial terms.
In doing this they followed the inescapable principles of
all public debate. Thus, they always charged the "ins"

the bankers do not sponsor or approve) have no just cause for 'poaching'
on it. This has been conspicuously true of the bankers, who, to a great extent, have been the spokesmen and strategists for the management in reorganizations." (*Idem,* Part I, "Strategy and Techniques of Protective and
Reorganization Committees," p. 342.)

[8] "Such powerful outside interests [like that of Wallace Groves in Celo-
tex] have had no previous connection with the company. They merely
seize upon the chaos of reorganization for the purpose of entering and taking possession of the company. In some respects, they are like the striker-
lawyer who similarly is devoid of financial stake or previous economic
interest in the company. But they differ significantly in composition, resources, tactics, and generally in objectives. The outside banking groups
have money, power, and prestige which the usual striker cannot command.
Their objectives are usually not the comparatively insignificant profits which
a striker gets by way of fees for services or as a settlement. The outside
banking groups are generally willing, if advisable, to sacrifice such trifles.
They are seeking control of the corporation and the possibilities of the great
power and profits which control entails. And for this reason, as well as
because of their prestige, position, and superior resources, they use weapons
other than the threats and suits of the striker. They resort to the market
place. They buy up strategic claims and securities, and with these in their
possession, they gain control of the company. Sometimes, for the purpose
of strengthening their own position, they will form a protective committee
and solicit the support of security holders; sometimes they will work without a committee." (*Idem,* Part I, "Strategy and Techniques of Protective
and Reorganization Committees," p. 757.)

with corruption,[4] dominance by selfish financial interest, extravagance, failure to balance the budget, use of public funds for their own political advancement, and failure to protect the interests of the "small" investor. (Both parties always expressed intense concern for the "little fellow.") The "ins" always charged the "outs" with being radicals, advancing "unsound" schemes, and following unsound economic theory. They pointed with pride to their past record as financial governors.

The "ins" usually won, but not always. Sometimes the elections resulted in divided control. However, after the election was over the politicians stopped calling each other names and the new administration was accepted. The voter had about the same knowledge of what was going on as in the ordinary municipal election.

An example of this kind of political fight is found in the famous Kreuger-Toll reorganization.[5] In this fantastic story of American finance, Kreuger, one of the most brilliant swindlers of history, had succeeded in extracting colossal sums of money from honest but gullible American bankers of the highest prestige and standing. When the crash came a vast army of investors who had entrusted their savings to the advice of these bankers found itself subjected to an involuntary capital levy. Had the United States Government subjected its citizens to such a levy there would have been a national scandal which would have wrecked the party in power. The symbolism of our industrial feudalism deflects that indignation where the levy is made by some financial principality. The financial corporation is an individual who

---

[4] *Idem*, Section III, "Outside Groups and Their Techniques," Part I, "Strategy and Techniques of Protective and Reorganization Committees."
[5] *Idem*, Part I, pp. 237–240, 777–791, 809–837.

has unfortunately gone wrong, not an organization which
we desire to control.

There followed the formation of a protective committee
by the bankers who had sold the securities. They were actuated by the highest motives. No ruler desires to lose power
because he has made mistakes. He wants to continue to rule
because he naturally feels that he has been endowed with
gifts in that direction not given to ordinary men. Sometimes
this conclusion is justified; sometimes not. The trouble with
such groups in industry is not lack of ability but their refusal
to recognize that the organization has a public purpose. In
any event, the bankers assumed control because they felt it
was their duty.

In the Kreuger-Toll reorganization the scandal had been
so notorious that the ground was ready for the formation of
an opposing party.[6] This party represented what in politics

---

[6] A committee was formed headed by Bainbridge Colby and represented
by Samuel Untermyer to oust the bankers of control. The effect of this
committee was described by the Securities and Exchange Commission as
follows:

"These attacks had a pronounced effect. One of their results was to
evoke a public response from the Murphy committee denying that deposit
with it would involve loss of 'personal claims,' and announcing an amendment to its deposit agreement 'clarifying' this point. The Colby committee
retaliated with a circular again calling attention to the importance of retaining rescission rights, and asserting that neither the original nor the
amended deposit agreement of the Murphy committee preserved these
rights. Continuing in bold-face type, the circular declared that the bankers'
committee had attempted to preserve these rights:

" '* * * in a manner, however, which in the opinion of our Counsel is
wholly inadequate and insufficient for that purpose. The very fact that they
have made this eleventh-hour (though inadequate) amendment is in effect
a confession of their failure to safeguard your rights.'

"Even Colonel Murphy admitted the effectiveness of the publicity of Mr.
Untermyer:

" '* * * Now, we were terribly hampered in what we were trying to do,
and owing to the fact that anyone as vocal as Mr. Untermyer was against
us. He changed a large amount of public opinion on account of commanding a large amount of publicity, and he is very able, and when we tried to

would be called the liberals. It was opposed to banker control, in the same way that the West is opposed to Wall Street.
It was fully as idealistic in its purposes and intent as the more
conservative group. It included in its membership university
professors and high-minded lawyers. It retained Samuel Untermyer as its counsel and started the political fight to get the
investors to send their securities to it, instead of to the other
committee. It should be said in passing for the benefit of the
layman that such a campaign required funds. Such funds
were, of course, provided by an agreement on the part of the
security-holders who sent their bonds to the committee that
the bonds could be used to pay for all expenses of the committee. This is called a deposit agreement and a court finally
passes on the fairness of the charges.

This particular campaign was bitter.[7] All sorts of charges

do anything with the court for instance, to get an American trustee in
bankruptcy appointed, and when we tried to get a Swedish liquidator
appointed and Mr. Untermyer opposed, these people were afraid to act, because they didn't know who on earth was qualified to speak for the securities.' " (*Idem,* Part I, "Strategy and Techniques of Protective and Reorganization Committees," p. 783.)

[7] Mr. Dulles, attorney for the bankers' committee, testified as follows:
"Everything was being grabbed by everybody else, and because Mr. Untermyer and I had gotten into a state where anything he wanted to do I
opposed in principle, and everything I wanted to do he opposed in principle. There was just absolute inaction throughout the whole Kreuger &
Toll side of the picture. We couldn't get a trustee in bankruptcy that we
could agree on, we couldn't get a successor trustee, we couldn't get representation on the board of liquidators, we couldn't get enough deposits of
bonds from any one quarter so that there would be sufficient credit or interest to speak with authority, and the whole situation was being sacrificed to a personal—what had become more or less a personal feud between Mr. Untermyer and myself, and I felt very strongly that the duty
which I owed to my clients overrode any personal considerations of trying.
to have a fight with Mr. Untermyer and defeat him as a matter of personal prestige, and in doing that sacrifice the duty which I owed to my
clients, and there was only one solution for it, and that was to come to cooperate with Mr. Untermyer and get the situation cleared up." (*Idem,*
Part I, "Strategy and Techniques of Protective and Reorganization Committees," pp. 812–813.)

were made by the liberal committee. However, not being in possession of the lists of security-holders, and not having the financial prestige of the conservative group, they were able to get hold of only one fourth as many bonds as were deposited with the conservative party. They did not, however, entirely lose the election. Such was the strength and violence of their charges that they were given a share in the management of the reorganization. The firm of Sullivan and Cromwell, consisting of about sixty lawyers, agreed to consult with Mr. Untermyer's large firm. Fees were charged by everyone.

After the coalition it was noticeable that the charges and countercharges suddenly ended. Mr. Untermyer developed the greatest respect for the firm of Sullivan and Cromwell, which the firm reciprocated, as was evidenced by their testimony at the investigation conducted in 1935 by the Securities and Exchange Commission. At first Mr. Untermyer's position was that the other side needed watching. After the compromise the necessity for his services was occasioned not by any need for supervision but because of the magnitude of the task and the superior character of Mr. Untermyer's qualifications, which, added to those of Sullivan and Cromwell, made an almost perfect combination.[8]

[8] Mr. Dulles testified:

"Q. Did you agree that in considering the amount of the fee, which Mr. Untermyer would be entitled to, the insignificance of the Colby deposits as compared with the Murphy deposits, would not be considered?

"A. No. It would perhaps be helpful if I added to that statement this: That it was implicit in our arrangement to cooperate, that we would not throughout these proceedings take the position that because we had alone sixty percent of the bonds, and they had a small amount of the bonds, we would take the position that we were to dominate the situation.

. . . . .

"Q. Well, now, when you speak of the value of their work, you were thinking in terms of the respective fees that might be accruing to counsel to the Colby committee were you not?

"A. No, not in terms of fees. I was thinking in terms of where there

There was probably nothing hypocritical in this change of front. It was the normal reaction of people engaged in a political campaign to picture the other side as corrupt, wrong headed, impractical, and without thought for the "little fellow." It was also quite normal to have these same people work in harmony when the political strife was ended. However, no more wasteful way of distributing the assets of a corporation can possibly be imagined, than conducting a long and expensive fight over who is to distribute them. Nevertheless, the situation under our present industrial feudalism makes such a fight unavoidable. There is not the slightest sense in blaming anyone.

We will not confuse our description here by throwing a scheme for reform into the discussion, because such situations do not lend themselves to sudden reforms. We will only point out that if we think of the situation in terms of organization, rather than in terms of money and *laissez faire,* we may be able to come to some sensible conclusion; if we think of it in terms of a free fiscal economy which emphasizes the benefits of a competitive struggle for money as the best

was work to be done, and work which could competently be done in this situation by Mr. Untermyer or Mr. Hartman, that they would not be excluded from the doing of that work merely because we would say that we have forty times as much bonds as you have.

"Q. There was a gentleman's understanding that just by reason of the fact that the Colby committee had a relatively small amount of bonds on deposit, Mr. Untermyer and Mr. Hartman would not be precluded from any legal retainers that might arise in connection with this situation?

"A. Assuming that they were qualified to do the work. In other words, Mr. Hartman, as I recall, said to me: 'If we do cooperate, it will end up by your getting all of the bonds and we won't have any. Now, it isn't a fair basis of cooperation for you to turn around and then say because you have got all of the bonds, therefore you are entitled to dominate the whole situation to the exclusion of us. It is our cooperation that will have brought about that situation, and therefore it should not be capitalized against us.' "

(*Idem,* Part I, "Strategy and Techniques of Protective and Reorganization Committees," pp. 825–826.)

principle, no sensible solution is possible. All changes will be aimed at making the system conform to its ideals. Thus the reforms will not be a change of organization methods but a moral reform. We have pointed out as the principle of political dynamics that moral crusades are simply methods of adhering to ancient practices, and, at the same time, of resolving the spiritual conflict which we feel because we adhere to them in the face of practical needs which these practices do not meet.

The issues in the thousands of fights for control of these great organizations are as numerous as in a series of municipal elections. The organizations are built up by patronage, money, loyalties, desire for prestige, ambition to do a creditable, workmanlike job. In an interesting book, *The Investor Pays,*[9] Max Lowenthal describes the reorganization of the Milwaukee Railroad. The book is illuminating on the techniques used. However, it is written with a strong undercurrent of moral indignation which one who takes an objective point of view cannot share. It is difficult to see how the thing could be done otherwise so long as corporations are regarded as individuals without public responsibility, instead of as an integral part of our government. There are likely to be many attempts to reform, but no real change until the general folklore on this subject changes.

The ethics of the group controlling reorganizations were no better or worse than the ethics of our great municipal machines, like Tammany Hall. Contrary to popular mythology, political machines, both financial and municipal, contain a very large number of unselfish and highly moral people. They are thrown into a situation, however, in which the penalty of not fighting fire with fire is often failure. Since the advantage is to those who step over the border line of

[9] A. A. Knopf, 1933.

what is called ethical conduct, the picture presented by an investigation (such as that conducted under Commissioner W. O. Douglas of the Securities and Exchange Commission) is always shocking.

We will illustrate this by a typical paragraph or two from the Securities and Exchange Commission's report, Part III, "Committees for the Holders of Real Estate Bonds."[10]

4. USE OF THE SLOGAN: "——YEARS WITHOUT LOSS TO ANY INVESTOR."

For a decade all the wiles of advertising, all the arts and exhortations of salesmanship, had been directed to and had succeeded in identifying real estate bond issues in the minds of investors solely by the underwriters concerned. A bond was judged as a "Straus" issue, not as the obligation of the particular individual or corporation liable upon it. So, if a "Straus" issue was considered a sound investment, it was not primarily for the possible reason that conservative appraisal of values had come to be the rule in all Straus underwritings. Though the various factors necessary for sound analysis of securities were sometimes given, their assertion had minor significance in the sale of these securities. Their truth or falsity was unimportant; it did not matter that a stated appraisal reflected a wish-fulfillment instead of sound judgment. The bonds sold because the investor had been taught that the name "Straus" connoted securities from a distributing source whose clients had suffered no loss in forty years or more. The underwriter's name and its attendant slogan were the distinguishing marks of the real estate bond. Little else counted.

This was a theme with many variations. It was used in the form stated by S. W. Straus & Co.; it had its counterparts among the other real estate bond houses of issue. Greenebaum Sons' Investment Co., for example, utilized: "Greenebaum Bonds—100 Percent Safe Since 1855"; "69 Years' Proven Safety." . . .

Investors suffered no loss because interest and principal pay-

[10] pp. 70–71, 72–73, 85, 86, 152–153, 198.

ments due on bonds would be met, as we have already related, from the pockets of the underwriters if mortgagors defaulted. As a corollary the underwriter concealed the occurrence of default. . .

.   .   .   .   .

This indefensible practice, most highly developed by underwriters of real estate investments, supplies the key to an understanding of the activities in the years 1926–1931 which led ultimately to their collapse. . .

.   .   .   .   .

7. Protection of the House of Issue by the Committee

The customary justification asserted by houses of issue in the hearings before this Commission for their formation of protective committees was their feeling of "responsibility" to the holders of the securities which they had underwritten and sold. . .

.   .   .   .   .

On the other hand, control of the committee—whether exerted by placing members of the house of issue directly on the committee or by insuring the selection of men acceptable to the house of issue—means control over the version of the situation presented to the bondholders through committee circulars, advertisements and answers to inquiries. It also means, as more fully developed in the ensuing sections, that if a friendly and cooperative plan of reorganization were worked out, the true facts as to the value of the property and the relation of the houses of issue to it could be kept permanently in their possession and not brought to light. It also means that there will not be a thorough investigation of possible causes of action against the houses of issue nor will there be litigation by the committees against them.

In this manner the houses of issue will minimize the risk of their own liability to bondholders. In this manner they will also "save face." Through their mouthpiece—the protective committee—they can minimize the seriousness of the situation. They can blame mortgagors, depressions, and business cycles. They can divert criticism to those causes. They can perhaps completely prevent the searching light of publicity being cast on their own misdeeds. . .

. . . . .

Control over a reorganization means, as we have indicated, control over a large amount of business patronage. Much of this patronage can be reserved for those in control or may be dispensed to their affiliated interests, as they desire. Much of it can be dispensed as the occasion may require, in order to afford protection from desired quarters or favor where good will may be needed.

1. S. W. Straus & Co.

The clearest example in point is the system set up by S. W. Straus & Co., whereby it dominated the reorganization of the numerous bond issues which it had sold. From its position of dominance Straus distributed the business patronage to itself and its affiliated interests. In reorganization the bond trustee and the protective committee are the two principal distributors of this lucrative patronage. . . . In effect the Straus organization during this period was engaged in the business of reorganizing these properties.

S. J. T. Straus testified before this Commission:

Q. Is there any function connected with reorganization which Straus did not perform at one time or another in connection with one issue or another? Can you think of any single function which Straus did not perform?

A. At a certain stage of the reorganization, that is true.

. . . . .

One common form of reorganization results in a new corporation owning and operating the property. Quite commonly its stock, instead of being distributed directly to the former bondholders, is held in a voting trust. With like conformity in such cases, it will be the committee which designates the voting trustees. And almost invariably one or more of the committee members will be among the voting trustees who are chosen. Thus it

is that committees may perpetuate their control over the properties even after the reorganization job appears to be done. Another common form of reorganization results in title to the property being acquired by trustees under a liquidation trust, certifi-
cates of beneficial interest being issued to the old security holders
and the liquidation trustees having full power of management
and control. This is an adaptation of the older Massachusetts
"business trust." Here again committee members or their affiliated interests will be found among the liquidating trustees.

Results of this kind are as commonplace in our industrial
structure as the *sub rosa* activities of political machines are
commonplace in our political structure. They follow an inevitable law of political dynamics. Given a situation where
the ideals are in contradiction to the needs, a *sub rosa* organization must develop. That organization gets the job
done after a fashion, but only with an accompanying moral
war to justify the ideals. The result is confusion of purpose
and inefficiency. It is inevitable so long as the ideals and the
needs are in complete conflict.

In such a situation the public shuts its eyes to violations
of its ethics with the same unconscious response which makes
the individual ignore the so-called "lower side" of his own
nature in public. Thus it was that the disclosures of the protective-committee study which we have quoted were given
little publicity. People simply did not want to think of them.
They insulated themselves against what was under their
noses by means of the symbols of fiscal theory. Their reasoning was very simple:

1. These results are unusual because economic theory
teaches us that "credit" can be obtained only by fair dealing.

2. It was the fault of the investors that they lost their
money. They have learned a valuable lesson and will not do
it again because in a capitalistic system nearly everyone follows his enlightened self-interest.

3. If the investors are caught again they will deserve it again.

4. A recognition of the public responsibility of a great organization to provide security to its retainers and distribute goods would be Communism.

5. Our financial organizations are not an industrial or temporal government but individuals, and to control them is to invite a dictatorship.

6. Industrial organizations are not themselves dictatorships because they are individuals exercising their own free will.

7. All sound learning tells us this is the best way to run a financial government.

And so the slogans run which protect the dreamworld of fiscal thinking from the actual world of social conduct.

We have said that the general ethics of industrial organization are no worse than those of the political organization. This is true, but the takings of the industrial politician are very much greater. Such financial rewards, however, are not regarded as graft, so there is no need for concealment. Further than that, there is a settled belief that the money extracted from the public "belongs" to the organization and it is therefore no business of the public what becomes of it. The great financial rewards of our industrial world have come to financiers as a charge on production and management for assistance in using financial symbols.

For example, David Schenker, examining Wallie Groves in an investment trust study conducted by the Securities and Exchange Commission in 1936, showed how that individual had obtained control of a group of investment trusts, owning stock in all sorts of enterprises without any investment whatever. The method was a masterpiece of financial fiction. Groves sold the investment trust companies stock in corporations which he himself dominated at a fictitious profit. He then used this profit to buy control of the investment trusts. The various devices by which those skilled in the manipulation of debts and credits obtained control are a fascinating study. In a very large area of American industrial life the control is not with those who are conducting the business of production and distribution, but with those who are financing it. It is worthy of note to find that in the protective-committee study made by the Securities and Exchange Commission, few witnesses connected with the control of great organizations had anything to do with the actual production or distribution of their products. The great organizing work of industry today is done by bankers rather than manufacturers.

Modern problems of organization have mostly consisted in the coördination of already existing productive plants into larger units. This has involved two elements:

1. The development of new techniques.

2. The reconciliation of these new organizations with popular mythology.

It is the second element that has claimed all the rewards because it is the priestly function, and priests always have a prestige superior to practical men. The burden of this priesthood is illustrated in the following summary of the fees charged in the reorganization of Paramount Publix, described rather objectively in the *New Yorker* of August 3, 1935:

A REPORTER AT LARGE

Boy, Go Out and Get Me a Shingle

Last week, fuller of zeal than of sound common sense, we threw ourself into the face of the legal profession. Nothing happened. It was like throwing ourself at a featherbed. Not bruised, though slightly beaded up, we are just where we started, but it must be confessed that we have a new and slightly reverent admiration

for gentlemen who can resist all inquiries into their strange ways
with so much frustrating, dignified politeness.

.   .   .   .   .

Paramount Publix, which manufactured and distributed and
exhibited motion pictures, went into receivership on January
26th, 1933. Not so long before this, its issued securities had a
market value of $200,000,000, but this lordly treasure had gone
zingo with the depression, and creditors had reached the last
notch of their patience.

Lawyers got busy with the effort to reorganize the company:
to let Paramount dramas continue their march across the screens
of the land and to recover a little cash from the wreckage. They
finally did effect their reorganization, with the setting up of an
enterprise called Paramount Pictures, Inc. And one of their first
chores was to place on the balance sheet of the new company, in
the liabilities column, an item of $2,500,000, listing it as "unpaid
expenses" in conjunction with the receivership.

Now the bills against that item are in: not for $2,500,000 but
for $3,650,000, which amount, say the gentlemen of the law, is
only a reasonable compensation for their learned assistance.

The bills came along in this fashion: Every lawyer who managed to get himself associated with the case decided what proportion of the $2,500,000 should rightly belong to him. He made out
his claim, and filed it with the Federal Court. As I write now, the
Court, in the person of Judge Alfred C. Coxe, has before it the
question of the validity of these bills—whether they should be
paid in full out of the earnings of the new corporation, whether
they should be pared down, and whether some of them should
be disallowed altogether.

Some of the bills can be understood at once. At the outset of
the receivership, there naturally had to be a trustee or a company
of trustees, and so, after a hearing or so in Federal Court, Charles
D. Hilles, Eugene W. Leake, and Charles E. Richardson were
named for the job. No particular amount of pay was named at
the time, but now the three gentlemen say that, with expenses
thrown in, they have earned, between them, $449,866. Of this
amount, Mr. Hilles claims $180,000—which pays him at the rate

of approximately $6,200 a month for the time he served. He did not, of course, devote his whole time to the affairs of Paramount. This much he vouchsafed before a Congressional investigating committee last year. Mr. Leake and Mr. Richardson are more modest, saying that they have earned, respectively, only $150,433 and $119,433 for their labors.

Other items out of the handsome total do not explain themselves so readily to the lay mind. We glance, for example, at the bill of Messrs. Bibb, Dederick & Osbourne, attorneys at law. It reads: "For acting as attorneys for the holder of a debenture bond of the debtor, who intervened in the involuntary proceedings and questioned the equity receivership and the voluntary bankruptcy proceedings—$25,000."

Also, there was formed a committee of people who held debenture bonds. Mr. Frank A. Vanderlip was named the head of this committee and got down to work to protect its interests. He wants $50,000 for his work, and the other members of the committee want, between them, $30,000 for their work. Dr. Julius Klein did some sort of labor for the committee, and asks $52,390 in payment of compensation and expenses. The committee itself says that its necessary expenses (looking up things and going over matters with creditors, it is to be supposed—trips and whatnot) amount to $90,863. But the committee could not work the thing out all by itself. It needed, of course, lawyers. So it hired on the firm of Davis, Polk, Wardwell, Gardiner & Reed. These distinguished counsellors want $150,000.

Likewise: Mr. Peter Grimm, recently called in by Washington as special adviser to the Treasury Department on real-estate matters, was the chairman of a committee representing certain holders of debentures in the Paramount Broadway Corporation, a subsidiary. His committee wants $40,000 for salaries and $40,000 for expenses. But once again the lawyers had to help. Messrs. Stroock & Stroock, who led the committee through its legal mazes, have put in a bill for $100,000 plus $57,000 for expenses.

Now you see what questions we began asking the lawyer gentlemen: How did these committees get going in the first place? Did they just name themselves, saying "Let's be a com-

mittee," and start worrying over things, and employ lawyers to
help them? Was anybody consulted before these big bills against
the new corporation began to pile up? And should the new corporation—the stockholders of the new corporation—be expected
to settle up?

We suppose you see, also, what sort of answers we got. It
was all something we couldn't be expected to understand. Anyway, the case was in litigation, and it is not quite cricket for
lawyers to talk about a case before it is decided. Ladies and
gentlemen, for vagueness that is charming almost to wistfulness,
we commend you to the profession of the law when its own fellows are straining toward the money bags. We finally went to
see a lawyer friend and asked him about it.

"I don't know anything at all about the case," he said, "but I
can make some general explanations which might apply to any
case of a similar sort." That was further than we had got during
three days of inquiry.

"When a corporation has issued debentures," he said, "and
then goes bankrupt, it is to the interest of the debenture-holders to
keep the business going, to try to set up a new corporation which
can take over the assets and liabilities of the ruined one: dispose
of the liabilities somehow or another, and start all over again.

"It is better for the debenture-holders to form committees and
pool the sum of their holdings, so that when they approach the
trustees or the referee in bankruptcy, with proposals to the
creditors, their combined interests will have more weight. Naturally, they need lawyers, and naturally they spend some money
interviewing people like creditors and other stockholders."

We said, "Let's take the two attorneys, Malcolm Sumner and
former Judge Edwin Garvin. They represented a committee of
three bondholders whose bonds were worth a total face value of
$15,000. Now they put in a bill of $150,000—apparently for their
services in protecting this $15,000 investment. How about it?"

"Sounds reasonable," he said. "They automatically became
petitioners for all the security-holders when they took on that
committee of three."

"Reasonable?" we asked.

"Sure," he said.

"O.K.," we said, and left him.

We looked up the Sumner-Garvin claim a little further. They set forth, in this claim, that they had, through their efforts, "wrested control of the corporation from Kuhn, Loeb & Co." But they had nothing much to say concerning the desirability of wresting it from Kuhn, Loeb & Co. Anyway, Kuhn, Loeb & Co. have claimed $100,000 for their services—possibly in resisting the efforts of Sumner and Garvin. And Kuhn, Loeb's lawyer men, not to be outdone by all the Sumners and Garvins of the world, demand $150,000 for *their* labors. Firm of Cravath, de Gersdorff, Swaine & Wood.

But the most intriguing episode of the entire business must have been on that day when the head man at the offices of Root, Clark, Buckner & Ballantine turned to his ranks of lawyers and said, "I guess about three dozen of you had better get out to work on this Paramount case."

God knows how many lawyers are enlisted in the firm which has Elihu Root and Emory Buckner as members. There must be a sizable crowd if three dozen of them can be turned into one case. And they must be men of conspicuous ability, too—all of them—for they certainly earn the jack.

Root, Clark, Buckner & Ballantine have offered bills to the amount of $957,000 for their services in the cause. A million dollars (virtually a million dollars) is considerable money to ask of a corporation just emerging from the holy fire of bankruptcy and trying to struggle toward a newer and finer destiny. But the firm was very careful to show why the money was due.

It served, in the first place, in several different capacities. It was attorney for the Equity Receivers, the Trustees in Bankruptcy, and the Trustees of the Debtor. It occurs to our ill-trained mind that there must have been some black looks from one desk in the office toward another desk in the office when one of the crusaders for the Trustees in Bankruptcy got to arguing with a colleague who was devoting his soul to the Trustees of the Debtor. Be that as it may, none of the boys was starving.

I liked the fine frankness of Mr. Grenville Clark, appearing for the firm in the initial hearing, when Judge Coxe said mildly that the claims seemed "a little steep" to him. Mr. Clark said that he and thirty-five associates, aided now and again by other members of the firm, had put in a total of 72,000 hours on the case. Therefore, he went on, the $957,000 total represented an average hourly wage of only $13.17 for each of the lawyers of his company engaged in the litigation.

He made that $13.17 seem a trifling amount, but our pencil began to scribble. Figuring an eight-hour day and a five-day week—fifty-two weeks in the year—it appears that Root, Clark, Buckner & Ballantine have in their offices at least thirty-six lawyers whose services are worth, each, $27,393.60 a year.

As we suggested at the beginning, our notion was to get some high-class legal opinion on the way these things happen, because goings-on of such nature come under the head of big business, and a lawyer is the only man we would trust to explain anything about big business. We even called upon the attorney for the new Paramount corporation, former Judge Thomas D. Thacher, who is protesting the size of the fees demanded. He appeared at the hearing in the Federal Court last week and argued against the "exaggerated notions" of the lawyers who are asking these fees. We presented to him a rather plaintive request that he tell us more about the reasons for his protest—it was, of course, none of our business how much he will charge the corporation for entering the lists in its behalf. But Judge Thacher rebuked us, gently, however firmly. He did not regard it as a proper thing, he said, to discuss a case with anybody as long as it is in an unsettled condition, and in the hands of a court.

We fell back, at last, upon our lawyer friend again. He is a little lawyer—not one of those $27,393.60-a-year men—and he probably couldn't even get a job with Stroock & Stroock, much less Root, Clark, Buckner & Ballantine. He said, "Look. The lawyers for the new corporation put aside $2,500,000 for the lawyers in the bankruptcy to take a cut at, didn't they? The newly organized firm earned $5,000,000 that year, didn't it?

Did the stockholders do anything to deserve all that money?
They did not. When there is a sure $2,500,000 to shoot at, you
don't shoot short, do you?"

· · · · ·

Morris Markey.

The total of these fees was drastically reduced by the
United States District Court to about $870,000, many of the
claims being disallowed entirely. It seems odd that reputable
attorneys of high standing should have presented bills which
later could be held so immoderate. Had the bills been for
any other type of service, one would have suspected extor-
tion. No such standards can be applied to the situation here.
The ritual which these lawyers were conducting in this free-
for-all combat could be subjected to no pecuniary standard
of value. It was essentially a priestly function. The lawyers
considered these enormous sums their just due.

Large fees in such situations are the rule rather than the
exception. Generally counsel fees in reorganizations consti-
tute the largest single item for all services and usually exceed
the compensation of the officers or groups which the attorney
represents. The fees represent high-class boondoggling and
bureaucratic red tape of so complicated a nature that it is almost impossible to say at what point they are unjustified.[11]
Moral judgments can scarcely be made. In addition to fees,
key places in any reorganization offer opportunities for distribution of valuable patronage. The stakes of participation
in reorganization have become so high that they often are a
greater objective than the reorganization itself.

The situation is very similar to the control of a municipal
government by a political machine, with the possible excep-

[11] The remuneration of those taking part in reorganizations is analyzed
in the Report of the Securities and Exchange Commission, Part I, "Strategy
and Techniques of Protective and Reorganization Committees," pp. 99–218.

tion that public opinion does not permit politicians to take any such percentage of the income of the municipality which they control. Politicians are not protected by any respectable symbols. Fees and patronage in industrial organization, however, are protected by two myths which work together as follows: (1) Nothing that great American businessmen do with their own property can be other than helpful. (2) Great organizations are in fact American businessmen. It is the combination of these two myths that creates an anarchy which makes ethical conduct on the part of socially minded businessmen almost impossible. This can be illustrated by concrete examples.

In 1933 a group of New York bankers closed 280 stores of the McClellan chain, which were operating all over the United States.[12] The means used was shutting off their credit for running expenses. The reason was probably sheer fright, since subsequent events showed that McClellan Stores were solvent. The bankers' action frightened other banks and the McClellan organization stopped functioning. The effect of this uncontrolled use of an arbitrary power was felt in far-distant cities. The security of employees was gone. Investors found that a capital levy had been made when the stock lost practically all its market value. Landlords found that their leases were without present value. The social reverberations can be imagined.

The company went into bankruptcy. Competing protective committees were formed to get hold of the securities and thus control the reorganization. Persons who had inside information bought the stock, thus completing the capital levy on the former stockholders. After a prolonged battle the organization, with the same president, survived. The stores operated again. What actually happened was the transfer of securities

[12] *Idem*, Part I, "Strategy and Techniques of Protective and Reorganization Committees," pp. 65–99.

and thus of purchasing power from people in widely separated cities to people in New York. Had the Government in
Washington made any such transfer, it would have been a
national scandal. However, this was regarded as only a case
of an individual who had become bankrupt. Some persons in
New York, however, had levied a very heavy tribute on a
large group scattered all over the country.

An enterprising young financier named Hedden, knowing
the condition of the company, had bought up claims of landlords on leases with a probable face value of millions of dollars for $160,000 plus $67,000 for legal services. He did this
by taking advantage of their ignorance and fright and his
own superior opportunity to obtain information.[18] "Taking
advantage" is probably too strong an expression, because
what he did was well within the limits set by economic ethics
for traders. After acquiring these claims he sold them to the
McClellan Stores Company at a net bonus of 35,000 shares
(six per cent of the entire capital stock). The shares were
then selling at $12, making a profit of $420,000. His superior
boldness and ingenuity netted a great advantage both for

[18] "Mr. Hedden having determined exactly how necessitous each landlord was, his agents traded with the advantage of knowing to what extent
each landlord 'had to have money.' He testified:

"Q. You mean there were occasional cases of hardship where a man
needed $5,000 now rather than $40,000, ten years from now?

"A. Not only occasional cases, but that was the real reason for every
one of these sales. They had to have money. 1933 was a low period. These
fellows had obligations. I made it my business to try to find out what
their obligations were, to find out how far they could afford to trade with
me, and it was their necessity for immediate cash that forced them to make
a deal.

"Q. It would be their necessity for immediate cash in those cases upon
which you would trade, by which you would get the benefit of a good bar-
gain; is that correct?

"A. That certainly helped me get good bargains." (*Idem,* Part I,
"Strategy and Techniques of Protective and Reorganization Committees,"
pp. 81–82.)

himself and the reorganized company, but at the cost of a drastic capital levy on the landlords scattered from Montana to Florida. However, they did not consider it a capital levy, but took it with the resignation with which one accepts acts of God. Assuming McClellan Stores was a big individual, this attitude was natural enough. Had it been considered as a governmental organization, such political profits would never have been permitted.

The capital levy on the shareholders arose out of the complete anarchy of the situation. There is no reason to believe that had Hedden not been in the picture the wreckage would have been any less unless he had been a philanthropist. On this possibility he testified as follows:

Q. The picture, as I get it, is something like this: when a corporation goes into bankruptcy, the property is treated, in effect, as lost and found property, and the landlords and the stockholders and everybody are entirely dependent upon a champion who happens to come along, and they are protected only insofar as that champion happens to be a decent fellow, that there is no regulation—no legal way—of judging either the ethics or the cupidity of those champions, and it approaches anarchy, doesn't it?

A. It approaches pretty close to it, and when you have high minded committees you have a workable situation. When you have self-seeking committees, you do not. (*Idem,* Part I, "Strategy and Techniques of Protective and Reorganization Committees," p. 87.)

Out of such complete anarchy the laws of credit and an uncontrolled fiscal economy were supposed to make sense. Never since the decline of the Roman Church just before the Reformation had the dreamworld of learned men been so completely at variance with the world of fact. Under the glow of the setting sun of the fiscal world of 1932 men invented new kinds of paper currency and credits by means of which the more skilful of them achieved great power. The story of the knights errant of those days is a fascinating saga. Unfortunately, the creed of currency is a stranger language than the creed of chivalry and the story is harder for most people to listen to. However, Insull, the Van Sweringen Brothers, the House of Morgan, S. W. Straus and Company, whose investors never lost a cent, Odlum of the Atlas Corporation, Wallie Groves, and a long line of greater and lesser men, some good and others bad, struggled to build up power without being burdened by any public obligation after they had acquired it. Such a process, men thought, was the way of God and anything else led to destruction. There was only one threatening danger to the independence of these industrial knights errant and that was the United States Government. In the year 1937 the poll taken by the Institute of Public Opinion showed that two thirds of the people of the United States did not have a decent living wage to support their families according to what they considered the minimum standards of the time. They saw a productive plant which was not running to its full capacity and did not understand why more goods should not be distributed to them. They looked to the Government for relief. The greatest psychological factor which kept the Government in its place and compelled it to render unto Cæsar the things that were Cæsar's was found in the symbols of taxation by which it could be proved that government activity always cost money whereas private activity "made money."

CHAPTER XI

The Benevolence of Taxation by Private Organization

In which it is shown how taxation by industrial organizations is a pleasanter way of paying tribute than taxation by government.

THE folklore of the day thus protected any expenditures, however fantastic, from investigation or criticism, provided they were made by great industrial organizations. Such spending was considered that of a free individual spending his own money. The same folklore hampered government expenditure by correlating it with the unpleasant symbol of the taxgatherer. The difference in attitude was caused by the emotional reaction to these underlying little pictures, not by any rational process of argument. The actual verbal explanation of the difference was, like all creeds, a series of contradictions. Government spending was dangerous because the government would keep on spending "other people's" money. Such continued spending, however, was supposed to be a virtue in private organization because it was private money.

It was also bad for men to become dependent on governmental organization; but it was a good thing for employees to become completely dependent on industrial organization, which was supposed to foster initiative and independence down to the lowest worker. Everyone had a chance to become a high business official. Government employees were supposed to have no similar incentive because friendship and patronage controlled under the name "politics." These factors did not control in industrial organizations, except in bad corporations, and the thinking man refused to judge the good corporation by the bad.

Another difference between government spending and the spending by private organizations was that when the government wasted, it was wasting the taxpayer's money. When a railroad, or a public utility, wasted, it was wasting its own money—which, of course, every free individual has a right to do unless you are willing to change your "system of government" and adopt "Socialism." Of course, the great industrial organizations collected the money which they spent from the same public from which the government collected. However, in the case of a public utility, or textile concern, or a building corporation, the collection was voluntary, since men could go without clothes, light, or houses. Indeed they *should* go without them, if they had no money to pay for them because if they didn't they would become dependent on the government. When the government collected, the collection was an involuntary tax, which in the long run fell upon the poor, because of the great principle that it is unjust to tax the rich any more than you happen to be taxing them at the time, and that the rich will refuse to hire the poor if taxed unjustly.

One method by which private organizations collected revenue was through offering opportunities for investment. Investors were supposed to be protected from losing their money due to the fact that there were always sound bankers to give them advice. If they picked an unsound banker, that was their fault and it was supposed to be a lesson to them, not a tax on their families. In such cases it was said that the investor had voluntarily "lost" his money. It was not considered good form for him to complain. Thus we found great educational institutions whose endowments had suffered heavily because of their investments declining to advertise such "misfortunes" and spending all their time worrying about the calamities of high taxation. When the public generally lost its money, it showed a regrettable lack of judgment on the part of the public. It was not considered as taxation by private organizations.

It was, of course, possible for an investor to lose his money without its being his own fault. For example, government interference in business was thought to be capable of achieving just that result. It made businessmen timid and ineffective and destroyed business confidence, so that even good investments became bad. The depression obviously was not caused by government interference in business. It was one of the results of the War, which had made businessmen overconfident and greedy. However, most sound businessmen were not the kind of men who would get overconfident and greedy, and if they did, the government could put brakes on by delicately manipulating the re-discount rate. This hadn't done any particular good prior to the last depression, but no one exactly understood the causes of the last depression, except the most learned economists, and they could not explain it to anyone because it was so complicated. However, that very complication proved that nothing should be controlled by the government because no one could be trusted with that much power, since power always led to tyranny. It was thought that there were men who could run the government scientifically. Such men, however, would never be selected because of politics, which selected automatically only people who appealed to popular emotion. Therefore, it was dangerous for government to interfere in the taking of money from investors by private organizations, even in cases where it was not the investors' own "fault." Government control was supposed to be limited to setting moral standards for good corporations, so that the investor would have a free choice between good and bad investments.

A realization that a certain amount of claims against great

organizations were bound to be bad gave rise to the theories of "liquidity" and "diversification" of investments. This was the reconciliation of the conflict between the notion that a wise man could select "sound" investments and the fact that every wise man was bound to select a number of bad corporations. In a society where the chief source of security is productive land, no farmer considers it a good thing to own little pieces of a hundred farms in order to get diversification of his investments, nor does he think that these little portions of farms should be "liquid" so that he can unload them at any time on someone else in order to preserve that diversification of investment. Instead he thinks of his farm as a productive plant which he can operate himself to make a living. As society is at present organized, however, wealth and property do not consist of things which individuals can use productively, but in claims on organizations. The wealth of these organizations in turn consists in part in claims on other organizations, which in turn have claims on still other organizations. Those seeking position, control, or security in that situation must be able to jump around rapidly as conditions change. Shifting allegiances become imperative because sticking to one organization is accompanied by unforeseeable hazards.

To describe this scene in terms of private property required a new term, which was supplied by the word "liquidity." The term filled the emotional need for pretending that place and privilege with organizations were like the old tangible property of our traditions. At the same time, by using the analogy of running water, it conveyed the notion that this kind of "property" could flow away very easily. The connotations which surrounded the word "property" prevented control by government. The connotations of the word "liquid" justified the operations of the stock exchange and the various types of

manipulation by which men obtained control of vast industrial empires. This justification was naturally expressed in a
phrase which pointed out its advantage to the investor rather
than to the manipulator. "Liquidity of property" was the
means by which "diversification of investment" was the
means by which a wise man could achieve security in his old
age.

Everyone was supposed to understand the advantages of
this diversification. Those who didn't understand it and put
all their eggs in one basket deserved the consequences. A
proper economic system was one which encouraged wise investments and discouraged foolish ones. Anything else was
paternalism and destroyed character. If a man who had a
thousand dollars to invest lost it foolishly, this worked out
for the best because it tended to eliminate the unwise. People
were supposed to learn from experience. Of course, they
never did, but this was on account of human nature, which
never changed.   .

So much for corporate tax levies under the term "investments." The other method of tax collection was called "purchasing." Rents, light, heat, transportation to and from work,
were regarded as services purchased *voluntarily*. Police protection, libraries, parks, were paid for *involuntarily* by taxes.
Therefore, the real danger to the income of the small man
was supposed to be taxes and not prices, because he had a
choice in the matter of purchases. Therefore it was *public*
waste of funds that had to be watched. *Private* waste of funds
would take care of itself, since the profit motive prevented
businessmen from wasting. Government had no profit motive and therefore was bound to waste more because of the
extravagant theories habitually entertained by those who do
not work for profit. And then, anyway, private funds, when
wasted, only affect the individual who wastes them (and

corporations were individuals), whereas the waste of public funds affects posterity, since they will have to be repaid by the taxpayers of the future.

Therefore, the money taken from the public by advertising and high-pressure salesmanship for useless and even harmful articles was not to be compared with the money which the government would waste trying to regulate it, since funds taken from the public by a selling campaign which misrepresents the article are not public funds, and funds taken from the public by *taxes* are. The public had the free will to resist selling campaigns, but they were *forced* to pay their taxes.[1] If they didn't resist selling campaigns, then it was their own fault, and character deteriorates if people are not punished for their own fault. Even the fraudulent selling of food and drugs could not be effectively controlled, so deepseated were the little underlying pictures which we are describing.

By means of this folklore a curious set of mental habits grew up. People grew to distrust service rendered them by that type of organization called the State, because they felt they would be "taxed" to pay for it. They preferred the services of great industrial organizations because they did not consider their contributions to such corporations as taxation. Men in America were so conditioned that they felt differently about taxes and about prices. The former was an involuntary taking; the latter a voluntary giving. Prices were something a person could pay or not pay as he chose.

Thus all government activity became associated with a very unpleasant symbol, that of forced contributions. Business activity was correlated with the pleasant symbols of a free man going into the market place and buying what he chose.

[1] In a book which is both accurate and interesting (*The Popular Practice of Fraud*, New York, Longmans, Green & Co.), T. Swann Harding analyzes our national sales methods. The notion that selling is a free-will affair based on judgment is very effectively destroyed.

So it was that men opposed government efforts to furnish them with light, power, housing, credit, and looked with suspicion at government efforts to solve national problems. Everything that the government did meant higher taxes, involuntarily paid.

No one observed the obvious fact that in terms of total income of an individual it made no difference whether his money went for prices or taxes. Men believed there was a difference because prices were automatically regulated by the laws of supply and demand. If any great corporate organization charged too much, in the long run it would be forced out of business by other corporations which did not charge so much. This might not be quite so true if the corporation had a monopoly, but our antitrust laws protected us from any situation like that (or if they didn't, it was the fault of the politicians who could always be removed from office by right-thinking individuals). So men convinced themselves of automatic protection with respect to prices by showing that where such protection did not exist it was due to following some unsound principle which could be corrected by "thinking men."

The exact contrary was true with respect to taxes. Here men were at the mercy of politicians and no sound principle operated in this field. Laws of supply and demand were constantly being set aside by politicians. They were interested only in their own personal profit. If it were observed at this point that the selfishness of businessmen interested in their own personal profit might have the same effect, the answer was that the selfishness of businessmen was a different kind of selfishness, because we operated under a profit economy in which business profit always worked to a good end and political profits always worked to a bad one. This was all explained in the books on economics and it was guaranteed by the Constitution of the United States. Thus loyalty to

business leaders and distrust of political leaders was fundamental to the religion of all right-thinking men, who trusted
prices and feared taxes.

Economic learning was based on the theory that this folklore was the only folklore which a reasonable man could
hold. It was of two kinds, practical and philosophical. Philosophical economics was a ceremonial literature which reconciled the conflicts. Practical economics often was a set of
formulas which worked out pretty well in narrow fields, in
which people reacted to their folklore in the customary way.
Thus it was useful in explaining events in a time when competition between actual individuals actually existed. It was
of course unsuccessful in predicting the character and the
extent of the depression, because that event occurred in a
world of specialized organization where men were losing
faith in their folklore. Hence predictions made on the assumption that the reaction to symbols in that new world
would be the same as it had been ten years ago were all
wrong. In such times economic learning leads us astray.

Returning to our main theme, the symbols of taxation, it
is apparent that the result of this intellectual atmosphere was
to endow corporate enterprise with all the pleasant methods
of collecting public funds. Its ways of collecting tribute were
the ways about which no right-thinking individual was supposed to complain. Consequently it was inevitable that so-
called "private" government should become a greater factor
in the distribution of goods than public government.

Efficiency has nothing to do with this. No one can say
what the term means. People who are able to produce co-
herent organizations develop superstitions which aid those
organizations to function. Americans could have organized
just as "efficiently" had the folklore developed differently,
under the term "public" government. Of course, there would

have existed conflicts and some ceremonial body would have arisen to reconcile those conflicts. The conflicts might have been less violent; but that is sheer speculation. England *appears* to have met internal problems with less degree of turmoil and conflict by giving "public" government more responsibility. But England went through a similar ideological struggle. It is easy to recall almost the same conflict and discouragement when England first went on the dole (that is, when governmental distribution of goods was first struggling for recognition). It is not the concern of this book to speculate what might have happened in a different climate of opinion.

Methods of Private Taxation

THERE are many methods of levying industrial tribute, just as there are all sorts of governmental tax schemes. It is impossible to formulate a rounded philosophy for either set of methods, because both represent the results of practical men engaged in perfecting organization and at the same time seeking to conform to a philosophy by emphasizing now one of its contradictory ideals and now another. Therefore we will have to describe their methods, not by generalizations, but by illustration.

We have already noted that one of the principal methods by which industrial organizations levied tribute is known as "investment." The operation of that method may be illustrated by the sale of foreign bonds in this country since the War. The method is interesting because this particular levy was made almost exclusively for the benefit of foreigners. It reached its apex in 1927 and 1928. A list of the amounts levied in this country for the improvement of other countries from the beginning of the War is given in the following table, reprinted from *American Underwriting of Foreign Securities in 1931,* Trade Information Bulletin No. 802, published by the United States Department of Commerce. It lists the foreign capital issues, both governmental and corporate, publicly offered in the United States from 1914 through 1931.

Period	Number of Issues	Total Nominal Capital	Estimated Refunding to Americans	Estimated New Nominal Capital
1914	26	$ 44,670,288	$ 655,000	$ 44,015,288
1915	80	817,529,272	13,675,000	803,854,272
1916	102	1,159,601,264	5,700,000	1,155,901,264
1917	65	720,297,150	37,650,000	682,647,150
1918	28	23,465,000	2,600,000	20,865,000
1919	65	771,044,700	379,257,300	391,787,400
1920	104	602,937,986	105,500,000	497,437,986
1921	116	692,412,963	69,105,083	623,307,880
1922	152	863,048,284	99,421,300	763,626,984
1923	76	497,597,350	77,000,000	420,597,350
1924	120	1,217,217,937	247,993,500	969,224,437
1925	164	1,316,166,150	239,700,000	1,076,466,150
1926	230	1,288,459,182	162,978,000	1,125,481,182
1927	265	1,577,414,260	240,654,000	1,336,760,260
1928	221	1,489,361,680	238,410,413	1,250,951,267
1929	148	705,767,681	34,536,875	671,230,806
1930	121	1,087,560,214	182,227,000	905,333,214
* * * * *		* * * *		* * *
1931	41	285,199,500	56,365,000	228,834,500

The year 1931 marked the end of this era of foreign long-term lending (Madden, Nadler, and Sauvain, *America's Experience as a Creditor Nation* [1937], p. 68).

This table of foreign capital issues from 1914 to 1931 shows a steady yearly increase in the amount of the issues after 1920 with the exception of the years 1923 and 1926, until the peak year of 1927 was reached. The two succeeding years show reductions. There was a spurt in 1930, followed by a precipitous decline in 1931.

Foreign Bondholders Protective Council, Inc., *Annual Report, 1934,* p. 9, states: "It has been estimated that during the years 1920 to 1931, inclusive, there were floated in the United States approximately $10,500,000,000 of foreign dollar bonds." Statistics for this period compiled by the United States Department of Commerce show the aggregate amount of all foreign capital issues including refunding issues, the stock of foreign corporations, and certain other issues not strictly foreign bond investments, as $11,623,143,187.[2]

Several interesting things are disclosed by this table. It appears that ten years after the War private taxation to send goods abroad exceeded in amount even the levies during the War.

Let us examine the mental pictures under which these levies were made. Of course, they had no "security" behind them. There was no international court which could foreclose. Nevertheless, people believed that there was some sort of economic law which made it impossible for foreign governments to repudiate their bonds because this would damage their credit. Their own self-interest created a compulsion on them to pay to maintain that credit. This was in accord with the general economic idea that in the long run men work for their self-interest.

The particular countries on which this self-interest would have the greatest effect were selected by bankers. Only radicals suspected that the judgment of great bankers was not wise. There was supposed to be a direct connection between the soundness of government and its ability to float loans, which the bankers knew all about because they had studied the matter so thoroughly.

The relation of this theory to fact is shown by tabulating

[2] The above paragraphs are a paraphrase of footnotes 6, 7, and 8, p. 4, of the *Report on the Study and Investigation of the Work, Activities, Personnel and Functions of Protective and Reorganization Committees*, Part V. "Protective Committees and Agencies for Holders of Defaulted Foreign Governmental Bonds."

the amounts loaned to various countries and comparing
them with the size of the defaults. Such a comparison illustrates how little the past credit record of foreign countries
has to do with their ability to obtain loans from conservative
bankers. The record of South American countries has been
consistently bad. Yet you will note that more debts were
outstanding in 1935 from South America than from Europe,
whose credit record at the time the loans were made was infinitely better. A little higher interest rate did the trick. Incidentally, Germany had no difficulty in obtaining goods and
services from the American public by this method of taxation just before her complete and utter financial collapse.
During the same years, sound municipalities in this country
were told that if they did not balance their budgets, they
would never be able to obtain credit from private bankers
(who were then thought to be the only source of credit permitted by a sound system of government). On December 31,
1935, the amounts of foreign bonds outstanding and the defaults were as follows:[3]

	Outstanding	In Default as to Interest
Latin America	$1,538,431,980	$1,175,383,400
Europe	1,489,553,200	567,614,600
Far East	531,573,200	5,500,000
North America (Canada)	1,785,891,210	400,000
	$5,345,449,590	$1,748,898,000

The levy represented by these defaulted bonds was widely
distributed. It was estimated to include between six and
seven hundred thousand "investors." They were the people
of thrift, who had consulted sound bankers, as is evidenced
by the fact that the norm of the amount invested was estimated to be $3,000. These taxpayers included every kind of

[3] *Idem*, Part V, "Protective Committees and Agencies for Holders of Defaulted Foreign Governmental Bonds," p. 6.

individual or society which customarily has any funds. We quote from the *Annual Report* of Foreign Bondholders Protective Council, Inc., for 1935,[4] with reference to a single defaulting country, the Republic of Chile:

The Committee of Bondholders for the Republic of Chile Bonds has included in the registrations with that Committee individual bondholders, banks, trust funds, schools, colleges, universities, theological seminaries, churches, church societies, libraries, hospitals, memorial homes, foundations, orphanages, Y.M.C.A.'s, and cemetery associations. Every State in the United States, one territory of the United States, the District of Columbia, and thirty foreign countries are represented in the registrations so far received. While a number of the registrants hold substantial amounts of bonds, the average holding is very small, showing an extremely wide distribution of these bonds. 96% of the bondholders who have registered represent holdings of less than $20,000 worth of bonds per person, and the average holding of this 96% of registrants is $800 worth of bonds per person. The 4% of the bondholders who have registered holdings over $20,000 represent an average holding of $142,000 worth of bonds per registrant. The average holding of all categories is $5,830 worth of bonds per person.

You will note that the "tax base" of this corporate system of taxation was much broader than any which the government would be permitted by the folklore we have been describing. Imagine the government collecting large sums of money from hospitals, educational institutions, or orphanages to build public works in backward mining areas. Government is supposed to leave thrift alone, so that these funds may be collected by private enterprise for its own expenditures. Private organization is supposed to take all the money saved by the thrifty and in return promise them security for their old

---

[4] *Idem*, Part V, "Protective Committees and Agencies for Holders of Defaulted Foreign Governmental Bonds," pp. 6-7.

age. These promises are kept better by some types of organization than others, notably life insurance companies. However, the respectability of the private organization represents only a current guess, which is bound to be wrong a certain percentage of the time. The reason for this is that once an organization has become so respectable that it is a proper one for widows and orphans to trust, great pressures exist to use that respectability to get all the funds possible. Then, at the height of its power, when it is most respected, it becomes the worst organization for widows and orphans to trust. This is a common development among respectable institutions. It happened just before the depression in the case of banking and investment houses. There was no limit to the money which they could collect because of the faith people had in the names of the great financial institutions which distributed to the public such investments as these defaulting foreign bonds. It is always the most respectable organizations which levy the heaviest tribute. Frankly speculative organizations collect money from a different source and cause much less suffering. It was Insull, not Capone, who wrecked the financial structure of Chicago.

In any event, the myth that the great corporation is "wise" in its expenditures, and therefore safe to trust with funds, is what has given the corporation its power to make these public levies. It has built slums and skyscrapers and created the civilization that we see before us. The writer has no complaint about that civilization. He realizes that reverence on the part of its members is what gives it its strength and when that reverence falters, the institution falters. It is essential to the success of any social organization, or creed, that it *must* represent the *true* and the *only* proper way of society. For the purpose of diagnosis, however, we are here temporarily abandoning our habitual attitude of respect for all respectable things, in order to see better how the wheels go round and how it happens that the levy of tribute by private organization has become so firmly accepted as "right" and "natural."

Where Did the Money Go?

Such were the little pictures behind these private levies. The next question is: Where did the "money" go? Were the expenditures "wasteful" or "wise"? The last question is hard to answer. There are no standards of waste or wisdom of expenditure from the point of view of society as a whole, except the preferences of the individual as to what activities he desires to encourage. Is a painting more wasteful than a football game, or is either wasteful? Are the movies a "waste"? Such questions will not be debated here. Men require something other than food and drink and they will gladly starve themselves for such wasteful things as love, war, or churches. The concept of "wasteful" expenditure has little relevance in the broader field, except as a method of keeping the government from entering the field of production of goods. Here it fits in with the mythology of the times and can be used with telling effect.

The question of where the particular "money" went which was raised by the foreign-bond method of levy is less abstract. Actually, it represented goods for the most part sent to the foreign governments for use in building up their own countries. The sale of foreign bonds in this country for the benefit of South American republics may be likened to a great public-works campaign. It built schools, and parks, and roads, and armies in South American countries. Of course, not all of it went to public works. Some of it was used for bribes and all sorts of *sub rosa* activities which are an inevitable part of public activities. But in its larger aspects it meant that the United States had worked and schemed to improve South American republics, collecting for that purpose taxes on institutions in this country, including orphanages and hospitals.

This public-works program had none of the psychological hazards attending public-works projects promoted by the Government. For example, nobody worried about the character of South Americans. Their characters were not highly regarded, and we felt no responsibility for them as we did for our own people. Therefore, if Chileans leaned on their shovels or sat in the shade while building roads in Chile or El Salvador, no outraged newspaper editors filled their columns with protest at the wastage of American money. No one worried about where the money to pay for these improvements was coming from, because the taxes to pay interest on the bonds had to be met by foreigners and hence were not a burden on our own posterity. Indeed, all the symbolic handicaps which prevented our spending money to improve the West Side of Chicago were absent when we improved Chile, or Peru, or Germany. Therefore, it was possible in those curious days to do things for others which we could not do for ourselves, to collect a billion dollars a year as a great bonus for foreign countries because we regarded them as individuals who would pay us back and at the same time to neglect soil erosion and flood control in this country because they would be a burden on the taxpayers of the future.

Government Waste Compared to Private Thrift

As typical of this kind of thinking we quote from a column by Dorothy Thompson, selecting her because she followed so closely the opinions of conservative, respectable people who liked to think of themselves as a bit on the liberal side. This particular column deals with tax evasion and spending. After expressing grave doubt as to whether we are getting our money's worth for the money which the Government spends in this country, Dorothy Thompson continues on a note of rising indignation:

> We have had increasingly little to say about it, even through our elected representatives.
>
> Great gobs of it are just handed over to the administration to spend as they see fit, and if they want to buy piccolos to improve the musical sense of mountaineers or settle families in a deserted village, attended by nurses in the form of social workers, to take their economic temperatures three times a week and record in interminable card catalogues their ways of feeding the baby and dressing him they can't expect enthusiasm from the contributors.
>
> People with country estates have paid their income taxes and dismissed their servants in order that the servants might go on the relief rolls and be worse paid for doing worse work. It's patently against the spirit of the law to incorporate a pleasure estate and write off its luxuries as losses; on the other hand, it was suggested to me some months ago by a New Deal official that I might buy myself a few thousand acres of eroded land for a song and have it reforested by the C.C.C. boys at Government expense, and that seemed to me a rather more immoral procedure.

It would never have occurred to Dorothy Thompson to complain because our representatives had increasingly little to say about the expenditure of the billion dollars invested in foreign bonds. And if it had occurred to her, no one would have paid any attention in 1927, when the bonds were being sold, or very much attention in 1937, after the crash had occurred. There is something immoral to Dorothy Thompson in using government money to aid landowners in planting trees on eroded land, in spite of the fact that it results in a permanent source of future wealth and taxes. Cultural advantages given to mountaineers at government expense also fill her with a fine satirical scorn, because they come from "taxes." We infer that she has no objection to Mr. Rockefeller's benefactions, because they come from people who pay prices and from investors, rather than taxpayers.

She ends, as every columnist with a moral purpose should end, on a note of warning:

This column hopes that all tax evaders are caught and forced to cough up. But it also hopes that the Government will encourage more honesty and willingness on the part of the taxpayer to meet his obligations by spending the money in a more careful fashion. Otherwise the task of the Treasury Department will become comparable to the task of enforcing prohibition. (*New York Herald Tribune*, June 4, 1937.)

She would have hesitated a long time before spreading the notion that if a public utility did not watch its step people might stop paying their bills. Such an action would have been like the sit-down strike, illegal, leading to anarchy, and not to be "condoned."

We do not wish to criticize Dorothy Thompson, who is the favorite columnist of most of our friends. We use this excerpt only because it was typical of the instinctive reaction of everyone writing and thinking on the subject of government expenditures, as opposed to private expenditures. A columnist who was not caught in current folklore as Dorothy Thompson was would not have achieved her popularity. Thus the implicit belief that nothing but efficiency could result from uncontrolled private organization, and nothing but inefficiency could result from government organization enabled us to spend vast sums as bonuses to improve every other country but our own.

Foreign Bond Issues as a Method of Taxation in Order To Dump Surplus Goods Abroad

WHAT were the forces which led these respectable bankers to distribute these bonds and thereby effectuate this levy on our own citizens? Were they corrupt or just misled? Why was it that they failed to see the inherent weakness of this type of investment which was sold not because of any intimate knowledge of foreign countries on the part of the investors, but because of faith in the expertness of the great houses that underwrote the bonds? May we not in the future expect that this type of banker will be eliminated and this kind of capital levy will cease?

If these questions are answered in terms of the prevailing folklore, the average man will answer that they were bad bankers but that bankers have "learned their lesson" and are different today. True the Government is playing a very large part in the distribution of goods, but this is an abnormal situation. It will have to stop because of governmental waste and extravagance, and then a purified private business will collect money from the public and give it real security and not act as it did in the past. All bankers need today is more confidence. They will get that confidence when the Government stops interfering with their business. Bankers will not abuse that confidence any more.

If the same questions are asked from the point of view of one thinking about the habits and political pressures on organizations, the answers will be entirely different. It will be seen immediately that it is not a question of praise or blame of bankers but a response to pressures, which if they were exerted again would produce the same results.

For example, there were plenty of bankers who realized the insecurity of foreign issues. The reports on the advisability of any particular South American loan always reveal a number of adverse opinions. However, the adverse opinions did not prevail. Why? Was it stupidity or something else? Let us look back at the situation at the time these bonds were issued. Under pressure from great private organizations we had adopted a tariff policy which was opposed to most of our accepted economic principles (though of course it developed its own economic principles in defense). This tariff policy compelled us to sell goods abroad without buying goods in exchange. It had become impossible to distribute our goods at home, not because we did not need them but because our own population could not "buy" them. The mythology of the day furnished no symbol by which money could be loaned to farmers as it was loaned to foreign governments. There was no personification of farmers as a group and money could be loaned only to persons.

According to the folklore of the time, loans to governments were supposed to be like loans to big, strong individuals. We had a number of "governments," state and municipal, in this country, but with few exceptions (like Coral Gables) they refused to borrow money in a big way. Public works never escaped the atmosphere of extravagance and waste. Therefore, when wasting goods was required, we turned naturally enough to foreign governments. We had surplus goods. We wanted to get rid of them. The best way was to send them abroad. This cost money. The best way of raising this money was from the public, by selling them these foreign bonds. If we had not sold these bonds, the factory wheels used in turning out these goods might have been idle. Banks are supposed to "finance" industry and to keep these factory wheels turning.

Under these pressures all sorts of social institutions cooperated. The State Department was interested in developing "trade" with South America, in spite of our tariff policy. The only way that could be done so long as actual exchange of goods was prohibited was by loaning the money to South America. Therefore, the State Department did what it could to give the illusion of security and in a few instances the United States Government lent its support to the bondholders to establish an agency to collect the revenues of foreign countries.

In addition to this, comfort was obtained by creating a symbol of a "secured loan" by the pledge of specified foreign revenues. That this was pure ritual in response to a demand for a symbol is indicated by Professor Borchard's testimony before the Securities and Exchange Commission:

Q. That is, it is only in the rare case that creditors have the ability or the opportunity to reduce the security to possession?

A. That is true. Where they speak of a pledge, it is not really a pledge, because the creditor, as a rule, gets nothing. It is a misnomer, therefore, to use the legal term "pledge."

Q. That term, however, was used in foreign bond prospectuses?

A. Yes; by courtesy.

Q. You think that the use of the word may have tended to mislead the public?

A. I really could not say on that. People who know something about it are not misled, but perhaps the uninformed might be.

Q. Do you not think these foreign bonds were, to a very large extent, purchased by the uninformed?

A. I fear so.[5]

Thus this symbolic pledge created the necessary illusion of a debt secured by mortgage. In this situation those who were skeptical about the loan always lost and the bonds were issued. If one investment house turned them down, there was always another to take them up. There was a need to turn the wheels of industry by dumping goods abroad. There was a handy ceremony by which that need could be filled. Therefore, the goods were dumped. A social demand, plus

[5] *Idem,* Part V, "Protective Committees and Agencies for Holders of Defaulted Foreign Governmental Bonds," p. 20.

a respectable symbol, creates a situation in which respectable men can rise to power by filling that demand. It creates the necessary institutions in cases where old organizations refused to participate in meeting that demand.

In contrast let us examine another situation in which an even greater need to dump surplus goods existed during the same period in which these bonds were being issued, but which failed because of the lack of respectable symbols. There was a great surplus of agricultural products in terms of purchasing power. Farmers demanded that a levy be made on the public to dump these goods abroad. They were discriminated against by the tariff. Their only answer was a subsidy which would enable them to give these goods away. The subsidy, however, had to come from the Government. Farmers had no great organizations with the techniques of levying tribute.

Therefore, in spite of a powerful political demand from the farm states, the McNary-Haugen bill never became a law.[6] The thing that stopped it was the fact that government was supposed to be able to collect money only by taxation. The Government was not permitted to sell bonds to the public for investment in order to obtain money to ship agricultural products abroad. This was a function which could only be performed by private industry, because the losses of the seven

[6] The plan of the McNary-Haugen legislation was to provide by taxation for a stabilization fund which would make up to the farmers the difference between domestic and foreign prices when they sold their products abroad. The idea was that farmers should produce to the limit. What the purchasing power of this country could absorb at prices protected by a tariff would be sold here. The balance would be sold abroad for what it would bring and the farmers compensated for the difference. The fight over this general idea was at white heat during the agricultural depression in 1924–25, and support for the plan has continued to the present day. Nevertheless agricultural relief has never taken that form.

For an excellent history of agricultural relief, see Black, *Agricultural Reform in the United States* (New York, McGraw-Hill Book Co., 1929).

hundred thousand investors in foreign bonds were not considered as taxes.

The Protective Coloration of Taxes Privately Levied

THE final step in the foreign-bond picture is the method by which the investors were finally convinced that their money had not been taken from them by an involuntary levy, but that they had "lost" it. This process was carried on by private organizations which had an interest in making profits out of it. A governmental organization having public responsibility would not have served the purpose. It would have taken a different attitude toward the transaction from the beginning, and thus would have been a disturbing element in the whole machinery of bond selling. It would have had a tendency to expose the realities behind the ceremony. Since one of the purposes served by the final liquidation was to justify the whole process from the beginning and prove that it was only a minor unfortunate incident in the operation of financially sound institutions which in the long run gave good advice to investors, the best organizations to justify that belief in times of disaster were these organizations themselves. Therefore, naturally enough, they struggled to keep their control over the machinery of liquidating investments. They did so because, had they lost control over that machinery, the realities of the situation would inevitably have been exposed. This was not the result of planning, but rather of instinctive protective impulses.

The public justification for giving the control of the liquidation of bonds to the same financial group which had issued and distributed them followed the mythology of the times. Government organizations did not operate on the profit motive and therefore private initiative was more efficient. Government organizations could only be operated at great cost to the taxpayers, whereas private organizations made profits and hence "cost" no one anything. The process was practically the same in all corporate reorganizations. We will analyze it with respect to the foreign-bond situation because most of the machinery will be found duplicated wherever any securities issue is liquidated.

The first step was for the houses which issued the bonds (or for a group with similar attitudes which wanted to oust them from control) to form a protective committee to represent as many of the vast number of scattered bondholders as they could induce to deposit with them. There were no rules about this sort of thing. Anyone who could get hold of a number of bonds could act as a protective committee. The field was open to all. The house issuing the bonds usually felt that the formation of the committee was its special prerogative. Therefore, in the competition between the different committees to obtain bonds, the issuing houses had a great advantage because they had the lists of former purchasers to whom they could send circulars. The advantage did not prevent the formation of other committees because there was always a chance for energetic men to collect bonds. Important names were a drawing card.

A typical way in which the committees were organized is illustrated by the following excerpt from testimony taken by the Securities and Exchange Commission:

A. . . . I can tell you very quickly how we got organized; at this luncheon—

Q. . . . We are back at the India House?

A. While we were discussing this, Colonel Hayes says "Here are two friends of mine coming over for lunch. One is Mr. Bedford, of the Standard Oil of New Jersey, and the other Harry McCann, President of McCann-Erickson.

Q. What is that?

A. An advertising house—"They are good friends of mine, what do you say I ask them"—

Q. You ask them?

A. Colonel Hayes asked me, "There are two friends of mine," he said. "Maybe they will go on. Shall I ask them?" I said, "Certainly." It sounded like they would be well qualified to go on there.

Q. Why do you think they would be well qualified?

A. I think a Director of Standard Oil would speak for itself. I had never met him before. I thought if we were forming a bondholders committee and could get a Director of Standard Oil of New Jersey on there, it would be a credit to the committee.

Q. A credit to the committee?

A. Yes.

Q. Were you thinking of the publicity value of that?

A. No; that didn't occur to me at the time.

Q. Were you thinking of Mr. Bedford as a man specializing in the foreign field?

A. No.

Q. How would it be of value, if not publicity?

A. I have been in a great many businesses in America, and I have understood and known in any kind of business, if you get a Director of the Standard Oil of New Jersey to associate himself with you, you were very fortunate.[7]

Such committees were called the self-appointed type and were not highly regarded. However, since all committees were voluntary organizations, it was difficult to determine the difference between the appointed and the self-appointed, as is evident from the following testimony of Dr. Max Winkler, a distinguished expert on foreign bonds.

"I see no advantage at all to the holders of these bonds to deposit with protective committees, most of whom seem to be of the self-appointed and self-anointed type."

[7] *Idem,* Part V, "Protective Committees and Agencies for Holders of Defaulted Foreign Governmental Bonds," pp. 101–102.

Concerning this statement, Dr. Winkler testified:

Q. . . . Is that an expression of your personal point of view?

A. Yes.

Q. That is, you are opposed to protective committees of the self-appointed and self-anointed type?

A. Yes, sir.

Dr. Winkler proceeded to expound his definition of a "self-appointed" committee.

A. I would designate a self-appointed and a self-anointed committee as one which is composed of men who are not sufficiently familiar with the . . . cases of foreign bonds in general, and that particular bond issue especially, which they are organized to protect.

Q. That is, it is not a question of who appoints the members; it is a question of whether they are qualified or not?

A. That would be my definition of the self-appointed.

Q. That is not a definition, is it?

A. That is my definition.[8]

Out of ten committees listed in the report by the Securities and Exchange Commission, only three included members who were bondholders or representatives of bondholders.

What were the motives which induced men to serve on these protective committees? Houses of issue insisted that they owed a moral responsibility to their customers. Others may have been induced to serve by the promise of the publicity. One organization, the Foreign Bondholders Protective Council, was influenced by motives of public service. However, the prevailing motive was the very high remuneration. Some of the committees looked like syndicates of joint adventurers organized to realize as large a profit as possible. John Henry Hayes, a member of and counsel to a committee, disclosed his conception in the following language:

[8] *Idem*, Part V, "Protective Committees and Agencies for Holders of Defaulted Foreign Governmental Bonds," pp. 105–106.

I told you that here are five men, as you can construe this thing, looking at it legally—there are five men, we will say, have gone into a joint venture, we will call it, and they have contributed capital to the joint venture with the hope, possibly, of making a profit. That is the possibility they take.[9]

Promotional services were thus recognized as legitimate charges against the depositing bondholders. For example, a member of a committee, on being questioned about compensation supposed to be due to a certain Mr. Rosenblatt, whose sole services had been to promote the committee, testified as follows:

Q. . . . Nevertheless, you thought he was entitled to a finder's fee or promotional compensation.
A. He was entitled to something.
Q. How would you describe it, for forming the committee?
A. Entitled to something for forming the committee.
Q. Bringing in the business?
A. Bringing the members of the committee together.
Q. That is, he was entitled to compensation for organizing the committee?
A. Yes.[10]

The report of the Securities and Exchange Commission adds this pertinent comment: "It does not appear that any disclosure was made to the bondholders of this agreement for the payment to William Rosenblatt of a finder's fee for originating the committee."[11]

Trading profits were also a motive, since membership on a committee gave information about the future of the nego-

[9] *Idem*, Part V, "Protective Committees and Agencies for Holders of Defaulted Foreign Governmental Bonds," p. 130.
[10] *Idem*, Part V, "Protective Committees and Agencies for Holders of Defaulted Foreign Governmental Bonds," p. 138.
[11] *Idem*, Part V, "Protective Committees and Agencies for Holders of Defaulted Foreign Governmental Bonds," p. 139.

tiations with the foreign country to which no individual bondholder had access. This was condemned but there was no effective means to prevent it.

Thus a situation of anarchy was created in which the helpless bondholder often had to choose among a number of committees, with no assurance as to the kind of treatment he was to receive and little remedy for any abuse of the committee's power. The success of the committee depended on its power to lure in the bondholders to deposit their bonds. Here all sorts of advertising devices were resorted to. First there was the use of prominent names. University professors served, thus lending to the enterprise the prestige of their institutions. We quote from the testimony of the counsel for the committee for the Republic of Colombia External Dollar Bonds:

Q. Why did you want a public figure?
A. Someone who—
Q. Who would attract depositors?
A. Occupy the dual function of being able to secure the deposit of bonds and to be of sufficient importance as the head of the committee to secure the respect of the Colombian government.
Q. Largely, then, prestige, here and abroad?
A. That is correct.
Q. Do you recall discussing the desirability of obtaining a college professor with Mr. Rosenblatt?
A. We had a number of discussions concerning the desirability of securing people who would be qualified to examine into the debt problem of Colombia, and I believe that it was a matter of discussion that some well-known economist would be a proper member of the committee. I don't recall the specific mention of these gentlemen.[12]

[12] *Idem*, Part V, "Protective Committees and Agencies for Holders of Defaulted Foreign Governmental Bonds," p. 172.

Referring to the protective-committee situation in general, the Securities and Exchange Commission report reaches the following conclusion: "The foreign field (like the domestic) abounds with examples of greed, overreaching and excessive practices."[13] The report recommended the formation of a central authoritative agency, along the lines of an organization which had been functioning in the field for some time, known as the Foreign Bondholders Protective Council.

It is not the purpose of this book to discuss the remedies in this tangled situation, but only to make two comparisons. The first is a comparison between so-called "waste" of government and the so-called "efficiency" of private organization, which is not supposed to "cost" anything because it pays its own way out of profits. The second is the comparison of the patronage and political techniques of these private organizations, theoretically removed from politics, with those of the so-called corrupt political machines. It is easy to observe that both organizations use the same methods. The difference is only in the standards which were applied to them. Since political machines are necessary evils, they are held up to much higher standards. Operating under a philosophy that everything would work out all right if only it were left alone, and that inefficiency and waste would cure themselves because the investor had free will not to deal with organizations guilty of permitting them, business institutions could gather in vastly more money than political machines under the protective slogan that if they were interfered with Capitalism would disappear. Persons who attacked the waste of private organizations were thus made to appear as radicals opposed to our fundamental social structure. The reality of the free will choice which the investor was sup-

[13] *Idem,* Part V, "Protective Committees and Agencies for Holders of Defaulted Foreign Governmental Bonds," p. 739.

posed to have between efficient and inefficient organizations is illustrated by the testimony of Mr. George E. Roosevelt in a hearing before the Joint Legislative Committee of New York State which has been noted before:

Q. So when a bondholder finds himself in the predicament as the holder of a defaulted bond, what choice has he?
A. Practically none.
Q. He can go in, or stay out?
A. And if he stays out, they bring on foreclosure, bid as little as possible, and he gets a small distributive share.
Q. And if he goes in?
A. He takes just what the committee wants.
Q. And in many cases he cannot get out once he is in?
A. Exactly.
Q. And there is no supervision over this committee that you know of under the law?
A. No.[14]

Often the ritual by which these levies were made became very complicated indeed, due to the fact that the concentration of financial power in a few hands compelled the actors to double in so many conflicting rôles that it was difficult to tell them apart. Let us examine a levy made to build sugar factories in Cuba directly, instead of through the foreign government. Cuban Cane, a great sugar corporation, elected to its board of directors one Charles Hayden, an investment banker of New York. Charles Hayden, the director, conducted negotiations with Charles Hayden, the investment banker, in order to induce him to float a loan to finance the company in Cuba and to head a syndicate of bankers. He succeeded.

By this ritual bonds were issued and sold. Years after-

[14] *Idem,* Part III, "Committees for the Holders of Real Estate Bonds," p. 96.

wards, when the bonds were about to become due, it appeared that they could not be paid. Charles Hayden was then chairman of the board of directors of the sugar company and in that position represented the stockholders. He was also head of the investment house which sold the bonds and in that position owed an obligation to the bondholders. He was also a director of the Chase National Bank and the New York Trust Company, who were substantial creditors, and in that position owed an obligation to the creditors.

There came a time when financial disaster to the company seemed imminent. The question arose as to what these different personalities named Charles Hayden should do under the circumstances to protect the banks and those holding securities in the sugar company at the same time. Being a man of quick action, Mr. Hayden came to the following decision: He wrote a letter to the president of one of the principal bank creditors, the Guaranty Trust Company of New York, addressing him as "Dear Bill," and advising him to insist on getting security for the bank indebtedness of the bondholders.[15] In other words, at a meeting held with Mr. Charles Hayden's compound personalities, the banker won out over the chairman of the board. The reason for this victory puzzled Mr. Abe Fortas, who was conducting the examination. He asked:

Q. . . . Let me ask you this, Mr. Hayden, did you think that that loan for 1928 and 1929 should be secured because you felt that a receivership was or might be coming?
A. Not in the slightest.

· · · ·

Q. But you made the suggestion to the banks, and I am trying to get this fact perfectly clear on the record, you made the suggestion to the banks here that the line of credit which they ex-

[15] *Idem*, Part II, "Committees and Conflicts of Interest," p. 457.

tended to the company and which had theretofore been unsecured should now be secured?

A. Because of an approaching maturity of a bond issue January 1, 1930, or at the end of the year, the calendar year, and there would be three months after the end of the fiscal year.

. . . . .

Q. Let me interrupt you just a moment. Mr. Hayden, if the banks were given security, their claims would be prior to the claims of the debenture holders?

A. Correct, and should be.

Q. Now, Mr. Hayden, you have said here in this letter that the banks were looking to you for complete protection at all times on their loans?

A. Correct.

. . . . .

Q. Didn't you feel that the debenture holders were looking to you for the protection of their investment?

A. I did, and excuse me for smiling, but there is not the slightest difference or conflict there in any way, shape or form. . . .

. . . . .

Q. For some reason the claims of the banks in your opinion were entitled to more solicitude on your part than the claims of the debenture holders?

A. Not at all, but they were entitled to a different method of treatment, not more solicitude.

Q. A better class of treatment?

A. No more solicitude, not at all.

. . . . .

Q. Mr. Hayden, would you assume the banks would look at the report and would be generally familiar with the circumstances of the company before making the loan?

A. I would.

Q. Why did you feel it necessary that you suggest to the banks that they take security? Why didn't you just inform them of the facts? Why didn't you just let them read the facts for themselves?

A. Because of the fact that I am very proud of a record of 44 years as a banker, and that I did not ever try to put anything over on anybody.

Q. A person does not usually go to a bank and say, "You have been extending us unsecured credit for a long time, but I think in view of facts A and B that you ought not do that now; you ought to make us put up security for loans." That is highly unusual, isn't it?

A. Not at all. It is something I have done all my life, and shall always do as long as I remain a banker.

· · · · ·

Q. But the banks made those loans on an unsecured basis before you wrote that letter?

A. I can't answer that.[16]

This proposal to save the bank as a method of saving the creditors of the company is only valid in the dreamworld of fiscal thinking. In the real world banks tend to foreclose when there are about enough assets to pay off their loans, and to advance more money only when it is a requisite to saving the stake already in the venture. In 1934 the banks regretfully found it necessary to take over the company. The company was then deprived of credit and the ritual of reorganization commenced.

No one was more active in this reorganization than Charles Hayden. He felt it was his duty to the customers of Hayden and Stone, on whom the capital levy had been made. Therefore, we now see him in a new rôle, that of chairman of the reorganization committee of Cuban Cane. As chairman it was evident to him that more cash had to be raised to put the company on its feet. The question was: Who should pay it in? Obviously, not the bankers, because it was no longer a

---

[16] *Idem*, Part II, "Committees and Conflicts of Interest," pp. 459–462.

banker's loan. Therefore it was up to the investors. Therefore Charles Hayden sent out circulars to stockholders, talking of a reorganization plan and asking for more money in
order to save what they had already put in. The amount, had
it been subscribed, would have bailed out the banks, but the
plan failed.[17]

In the meantime, Charles Hayden appeared in a new and
even more fascinating rôle—that of a free-born American
citizen speculating in whatever securities he chose to speculate in. Deprivation of that right leads to tyranny, bureaucracy, regimentation, and what not—all of them dangerous to
the American way of living. Therefore, Charles Hayden
bought and sold the securities which he represented as chairman of the reorganization committee, with the idea of making a profit thereon.[18] However, he made it clear at a hearing

[17] *Idem*, Part II, "Committees and Conflicts of Interest," p. 486.
[18] "Q. The inducement for you to go on this protective committee was
the possibility of making a profit by buying and selling?
"A. Not at all, and I won't allow you to distort my remarks that way.
"Q. I am not trying to.
"A. You have, I am sorry. I say I would have the same rights as any
other free-born American citizen, and I should not be debarred from doing
that because I was willing to give my time, labor, and brain power to
serving on a committee. I would ask no more privilege than an outsider
but the same privilege, or I wouldn't serve on such a committee.
"Q. Well, that is, you want some return for your time, thought, and
ability.
"A. Not at all. I cannot permit you to distort my remarks that way. I
say I want the same rights as any other free-born American citizen who is
not on the committee, which is to use my own knowledge and buy and
sell as I want; and if I can't continue to buy and sell if I went on a committee I wouldn't serve on one. . . .
"Q. Do you think a committee member could be compensated for his
activity, brains, and initiative, and energy, by regular compensation? . . .

                    .   .   .   .   .   .

"A. . . . it is my opinion that there would be shyster lawyers and
small bondholders who would go to the Federal Court or State Court and
say, 'How is it possible that this person's brain is so valuable that he

conducted by the Securities and Exchange Commission that in no way did he take advantage of the superior sources of information to which he had access as chairman of the reorganization committee. He denied that a person with such information and knowledge of the pending announcement of a plan was in a strategic position to trade in bonds. Referring to certain sales made under such circumstances, he said:

Q. Those sales [in May, June and July] were before any announcement to the public of that proposal?

A. It may be a coincidence. . . . It is the most far fetched thing in the world to try to take these dates and figure that there was some occult mind that knew some concrete thing and was quick on the trigger. You can think it but there isn't an atom of truth in it.

Q. It is a fact that this plan had nothing to do with it?

A. Not in the slightest, directly or indirectly, as far as my transactions were concerned.

Q. Do you recall the occasion for the sales?

A. As I have explained to you many times, I might have woken up that morning, as many fellows did, and saw something else that I thought would go up a great deal faster. . . . I am sorry, but I am willing, if it gives you any pleasure, to have you make all the inferences you like regarding morals or character, but I can only tell you my transactions were those of a speculative investor on the New York Stock Exchange, not based on inside information but based on the way I happened to feel the particular day I made the transactions. . . .

Q. . . . You say yourself it is difficult to remember four or five years back and I appreciate that. But I was wondering how

should get a fee of $25,000 or $50,000,' or some other sum. And I do not believe that people would serve on those committees if the right that every other American citizen has who isn't on the committee were taken away from them." (*Idem*, Part II, "Committees and Conflicts of Interest," pp. 341–342.)

you could be so sure that it was not the advent or the prospect of a plan.

A. Because I think that is such a petty detail in the life of a speculative stock on the Stock Exchange. . . .

.   .   .   .   .

All my purchases and sales of these securities were based on either my opinion of political and economic conditions in Cuba, which I gathered from the daily newspapers and nothing else, or the general conditions of the New York Stock Exchange which made me feel that I could reinvest my money better.

Q. And the prospective plan that was in draft form in May and not announced until August had nothing to do with it?

A. It had no more effect on it than whether some fellow threw a cigarette stub out that window. . . .

Q. You can be sure that that was not the cause and you can't be sure of what was the cause?

A. That is absolutely correct.

Q. How can your memory be so clear on one thing and not on the other?

A. No difficulty whatever. I can tell you if there was an eclipse of the sun at seven minutes past eleven but I can't tell you the date although I knew there was going to be one.

.   .   .   .   .

Q. Doesn't it strike you as a strange coincidence that this large liquidation took place before July 1931, then the plan was announced, and then the large substantial purchases took place shortly after the announcement of the plan?

A. . . . There was no transaction made by me based on the likelihood or the unlikelihood of the plan going through. . . .

Q. . . . the only thing that sticks in my mind is the fact that while these sales were taking place from May to July, you were wholly aware of the prospective plan of the Eastern Cuba Corporation.

A. That may be your conclusion, but the thing that surprises me is I don't see why all these fellows ask me to be a director when I am such a terrible fellow as you like to bring out. . . . I am willing to cooperate with you but you are trying to make these coincidences.[19]

Under such guidance a great sugar industry had been created in Cuba. It had been paid for by contributions by American investors which originally amounted to about seventy-five million dollars, represented by twenty-five million in debentures and approximately fifty million in stock. In 1929, in the process of a former reorganization, these investors had contributed more money in order to save what they had put in. In 1934 they had been asked for another contribution, which only a few had been willing to make, under another reorganization plan. The final wind-up of this capital levy for the benefit of the sugar industry is shown by the following testimony:

Q. Mr. Hayden, from your own acquaintance and association with this industry and your knowledge of the sugar industry, would you say that today the five banks that for all practical purposes now own this sugar company—
A. Yes.
Q. Have represented in that sugar company an investment which is—
A. $7,000,000.
Q. $7,000,000?
A. Yes.

      .   .   .   .   .

Q. That is, the five banks are in—
A. They are. They own it.
Q. And the old investors—
A. Are out.
Q. And the old stockholders in the securities of this company—
A. Are out.[20]

---

[19] *Idem*, Part II, "Committees and Conflicts of Interest," pp. 322–323.
[20] *Idem*, Part II, "Committees and Conflicts of Interest," p. 486.

It was thus that private industrial government obtained its revenues to build and maintain its organization. This was not a malevolent process; it cannot be charged with positive dishonesty. It was an inevitable result of thinking of these great organizations as individuals trading in a free market with their customers and their investors, without public responsibility. The levies which these organizations made on their retainers were fantastic and arbitrary because no one recognized them as levies, not because Charles Hayden or the bankers desired to be unjust to anyone. Even in the great depression realization of just what the process was doing to investors and to consumers came very slowly. The first reaction of reformers was that those in control of such organizations were bad men who needed more moral guidance. The picture of a reorganization as a sale was so firmly fixed that the first efforts at reform attempted to create by legislative fiat fair trading in a situation where trading and efficient organization were incompatible. The idea of substituting a body publicly charged with responsibility toward its retainers involved the admission that here was a situation in which competition between traders did not work—which was contrary to our whole business philosophy. Therefore, reformers sought legislation which continued this free-for-all fight but tried to make it conform to the Marquis of Queensberry rules.

As a net result of these operations a huge sugar industry had been established by means of successive issues of paper currency called securities. Most of that currency had gone out of circulation and become valueless, but the factory remained. No one considered these transactions inflationary, or in any respect confiscatory. Most conservative people would have died in order to defend the right of private organization to issue its own currency and to make its own capital levies. They would have done so, however, firm in the belief that it was the right of individuals which they were protecting.

It should be noted that the process by which Cuban Cane built and operated its mills was almost identical in outline with inflation on a larger scale in Germany. Germany issued all sorts of pieces of paper, from marks to municipal and government bonds, which were eagerly bought in this country. The net result was that Germany, so far as its material wealth was concerned, was vastly enriched. Roads, apartments, parks, and all sorts of municipal improvements resulted from this process. The industrial plant of the country was enormously improved. When the smoke all cleared away Germany was found in a much stronger position so far as material wealth was concerned than before the inflation. In the same way the little principality of Cuban Cane was richer in material goods than before its inflation. Those who happened to hold the pieces of paper, whether issued by Germany or Cuban Cane, found themselves much worse off in comparison with others. Their sacrifices had gone to make these principalities richer in material wealth, but they were sacrifices just the same. The chief difference was that German inflation exacted contributions both at home and abroad, but Cuban Cane was almost exclusively confined to the United States in making its capital levy.

This process, both in the case of Germany and of Cuban Cane, was destructive of the previously existing *distribution* of power and wealth. Nevertheless, it greatly increased the actual material wealth. It is important to note that in the climate of opinion in which the process was carried on it would have been impossible to increase the material wealth to the same extent by direct planning or taxation as by means of the disorderly process above described. A direct and planned increase of capital wealth which deprived investors of their existing place in what Professor Laswell has called "the hierarchy of deference, income and safety" would have been impossible. The energies of both the German and the American people were so great that they could not be confined within a set of fiscal symbols. Yet, on the other hand, any planned or admitted organization of those energies was taboo. Development had to come through *sub rosa* channels.

Types of Private Taxation

ENDLESS examples of this type of levy by private organizations could be studied. The money sometimes went into useful, and sometimes into useless, public works. Many of these private public-works projects were self-liquidating. Others were not. There was no plan about it and no way of telling. However, by and large the small investor lost more than the large. The tax fell more heavily on those of moderate means than on the rich, because the latter were playing the game from the inside. They had influence with the taxing authorities.

Take the example of Paramount Publix. Here fifty thousand so-called investors contributed to the greatest public-works project ever known in the amusement field. In this project there was a maximum of what in government would be called graft, but which in finance is recognized as legitimate tribute. Thus the directors voted themselves and the higher executive officers huge bonuses in order to encourage each other. The president of this principality took a salary and stock bonuses of more than a million and a half in 1930. The company lawyer got $75,000 a year and his assistants from $35,000 to $45,000. Kuhn, Loeb & Company, the bankers, received a huge present of stock simply out of gratitude.[21]

[21] "Q. Could you state what the occasion for this offering was?

"A. Mr. Zukor and the other officers of the company had felt for some years prior to this and had so expressed themselves to Mr. Kahn and my-

A list of relatives received fanciful sums for services of doubtful value. The whole story reminds one of the Court of Versailles, distributing largess to its courtiers.

There was nothing remotely resembling the profit motive described by Adam Smith in the conduct of this enterprise. It was more like the conquests of Alexander the Great. Magnificence was the keynote. These men were builders and spenders in a royal way, not commonplace traders. Romance hung over everything they did.

self that they were indebted to Kuhn, Loeb & Company for many services outside of the selling of their securities. . . .

"Now, Mr. Zukor had often said to Mr. Kahn he was indebted to him for this and would like to find some way of compensating him." (*Idem*, Part II, "Committees and Conflicts of Interest," p. 105.)

Other typical expenses are shown by the following excerpts:

". . . we had an insurance department which had an executive committee of its own, with premiums costing $600,000 a year. I was told—I don't know whether it was correct or not—we had never asked for public bids. So we asked for public bids and reduced the premiums that year by, oh, anywhere from 25 to 35 percent on our properties."

". . . I found that our telephone and telegraph charges had cost $800,000 in '31 and that a great portion of that was for telephoning to Hollywood. I found that the wire was open two, three, four hours at a time. Well, that intrigued me very much. So I made a telephone search and I took 100 and some odd telephones out of the Broadway Building that weren't necessary. I took telephones out of every theatre in America that the company owned that weren't necessary. I instituted a system whereby everybody that used a long distance phone had to make out a voucher and state the purpose. I put a girl in charge of the telegraphs, both incoming and outgoing, to check the number of words, and I cut the $800,000 to $400,000 in 1932."

". . . I found that the head of the legal department was in Europe on vacation when I came there. The company was having a lot of difficulties and I thought it was a strange thing for head counsel to be gone three or four months. He was getting $75,000 a year salary and his assistants were getting around $35,000 to $45,000 a year. I discharged—he resigned, and one of his assistants took the position at I think $35,000 or $40,000 a year, and these other assistants went on for $10,000 or $12,000 a year. We cut the expenses of the legal department from $800,000 that year down to a very reasonable amount. I don't remember the amount any more." (*Idem*, Part II, "Committees and Conflicts of Interest," pp. 82–83.)

Came the depression. Protective committees struggled for supremacy. Members of protective committees profited and traded. Great law firms examined thousands of legal opinions and wrote endless documents. And when the smoke had all cleared away, practically the same group was in control. This, of course, was inevitable. You cannot buy and sell organizations like Paramount. They are the kind of activity in which people struggle for rank and power—not for "property." A great tax had been levied on the American people to build an organization, to build theaters in little towns, to give them amusement. Had the Government tried it, it would have been met with bitter hostility. Columnists like Dorothy Thompson would have spoken about it as they spoke about bringing music to the mountaineers or employing actors to give plays during the depression. The fact that there were only a few excellent pictures in comparison with the numerous worthless pictures would have been used as conclusive proof that the Government was hopelessly inefficient. It was, in actual effect, a lottery tax which financed such public works as the Paramount Publix, and lottery taxes are taboo in this country.

The taxes levied by public utilities were of a somewhat more respectable character. Public-utility rates, since public utilities were an admitted monopoly, actually *looked* more like taxes to the users. Hence, here, to a greater extent than in any other field, the Government took control. Railroads and light companies were limited in the amounts which they could levy by way of prices. Men who would not have thought of Paramount Publix as a sort of government within government boldly talked about public ownership where utilities were concerned. Hence the taxes to be levied by these companies were regulated. On the investment side, however, prior to the depression, these corporations were looked at as private individuals. Even after the Insull collapse had wrecked the financial structure of Chicago and impoverished thousands, it was possible to build a great sentimental defense against the regulation of holding companies on the ground that regulation was a blow to freedom. On the investment side public-utility taxation was still a "private" enterprise.

The kinds of taxes levied by great organizations were as varied as the ingenuity of men. They operated a private mint, known as a stock exchange, which printed business currency. Sometimes this currency had substantial backing in terms of assets which could be bought and sold. However this applied only to smaller organizations. That type of asset in the nature of things could not exist in the case of an industrial empire. Its currency was necessarily fiat money, and for such concerns, the stock exchange was actually a private mint.

The stock exchange was a convenience but not an essential. Certain companies made more direct levies by individual stock-selling campaigns. For example, the Federal Public Service Corporation, a holding company controlling a number of municipal public utilities, widely scattered, sold preferred stock directly to its customers. This had a double advantage as is shown by the following testimony of its president:

Q. What was the purpose of this attempt to sell preferred stock to customers of the company? . . . Was one of the purposes of that program to cultivate public relations?
A. Yes; that would be one object in it. It was common practice with other companies to do the same thing.
Q. Does that mean, Mr. Crawford, that, for instance, if a person has stock in a utility company he is unlikely to support an attack on its policies or an attack on its rates?
A. Well, it might mean something like that.[22]

[22] *Idem*, Part II, "Committees and Conflicts of Interest," p. 121.

Acquirement of good will in this way, of course, did not mean relinquishment of control.

Q. Why didn't you give them voting stock? Why give them preferred stock? Why didn't you put them into the voting stock?
A. Well, of course, there was never any voting stock sold.[23]

The personnel of the private tax gatherers used in this method of private levy was interesting:

Q. I now show you, Mr. Crawford, a document which shows on its cover the heading "Stock Bulletin: 520 Shares. Welcome Home." Then there is the picture of a cup. Can you identify this?
A. Yes, I can.
Q. Is this a bulletin that was sent around to the subsidiaries of the Federal Public Service Corporation?
A. Yes, it is.
Q. In connection with the preferred stock campaign?
A. Yes.
Q. I call your attention to the second page of text of this bulletin, which contains a table headed: "The following table gives team quotas, total number shares sold, and per cent of quota, during the campaign just finished for October-November-December, 1931." Then under the heading "Teams" is listed "Wire chief." Can you explain what that means? Was there a team composed of men who were wire chiefs?
A. The chances are that was the wire chief's department.
Q. What is a wire chief?
A. A wire chief is a person who is in charge of the wiring and reconnecting and all that sort of thing in a telephone office.
Q. And they were selling stock?
A. That is correct.
Q. The installation department? What are they hired to do?
A. That is a group hired to install telephones.
Q. They were selling stock?
A. That is correct.

[23] *Idem*, Part II, "Committees and Conflicts of Interest," p. 122.

Q. The traffic department?

A. They have charge of the traffic, study the traffic and the control of traffic.

Q. And they were selling stock?

A. Correct.

Q. Then, the team 7, accounting department. Those were men who were hired to do the accounting?

A. A group in the accounting department.

Q. And they were selling stock?

A. Well, that refers not to selling, but to getting prospects.

Q. I am not using the word technically.

A. Yes.

Q. The construction department?

A. The same thing—

Q. They were hired—

A. To do the construction work.

Q. Of what?

A. Pole lines.

Q. And they were selling stock, in the sense in which we have been using the phrase?

A. Yes.

Q. The commercial department. What were they hired to do?

A. Well, the commercial department of a telephone company has to do with the new business, and that sort of thing.

Q. And they were selling stock?

A. Yes.

Q. The equipment department?

A. They handle the equipment, control the equipment, warehouses, and that sort of thing.

Q. And they were also selling stock?

A. That is right.[24]

It was all arranged like a game with cash prizes and cups and dinners and appeals to loyalty. The following bulletin shows how much fun it must have been for everybody:

[24] *Idem*, Part II, "Committees and Conflicts of Interest," pp. 127–128.

POINTS IN THE BIG GAME HUNT WILL BE FIGURED AS FOLLOWS:

(It's to your advantage to shoot big game—don't be satisfied
with only rabbits)

[Look out for skunks! *Deducts* 5 points *more* than
originally scored]

A rabbit   is a sale of 1 share and scores   5 points.
A fox   is a sale of 2 shares and scores   10 points.
A giraffe   is a sale of 3 shares and scores   20 points.
A bear   is a sale of 4 shares and scores   30 points.
A tiger   is a sale of 5 shares and scores   40 points.
A lion   is a sale of 10 shares and scores 100 points.
An elephant is a sale of 20 shares and scores 250 points.[25]

[It should be explained that the skunks referred to above were
purchasers who turned back their shares.]

Such methods tapped a source not available through the
stock market, as is shown by a bulletin of the company explaining who were the best prospects, which reads as follows:

The following is an analysis of the shareholders of a Western
Utility which is comparable in size to Federal Public Service Corporation.

In looking this over one can be guided as to who are the best
prospects to call on and sell our Preferred Shares. You will note
that housewives and house-keepers, farmers, ranchers, retired,
widows, and students are among those that buy the greatest number of shares.[26]

Though not all direct-selling stock campaigns were so
amusing, they nevertheless constituted a very effective
method of collecting revenue. They had one disadvantage,
however. This is illustrated by a letter written after it became
apparent to the customers of Federal Public Service that their
money was lost:

When anyone mentions preferred stock to me I feel like dodg-

25 *Idem*, Part II, "Committees and Conflicts of Interest," p. 132.
26 *Idem*, Part II, "Committees and Conflicts of Interest," p. 128.

ing. This is a very serious subject. The thing that has kept us from having serious trouble with consumers who own stock in our company is that we have not told the people that own stock that their money is lost. You know that it just takes one person to do damage to either an employee or the system. This is a lawless place; the people do not think anything of a killing. We have something like 15 to 20 murder cases every court. Nothing is done with one for murder. I am serious when I tell you that for the good of the company the preferred stock holders must be taken care of.

When you go to collect a bill and the party brings out some stock to pay with it keeps one nervous. I have been in some tough places myself having been shot some (to be exact) eight times. The next might be the one that would take me away. I want to keep all the consumers friends of mine and the company's. This Preferred stock is dangerous.[27]

Numerous other letters appeared in the Securities and Exchange Commission report. However, we are law-abiding people and apparently nothing came of such threats.

Of course, the taxation by great industrial organizations was not confined to the general public. Within their organizations they taxed their own retainers. Some corporations had a social-security program by which they sold their own stock to employees, deducting the price from their wages, so that these employees would have claims against the corporate government in their old age. It is astonishing how similar the first social-security act was to this. The notes which the Government owed to itself were the "security" behind the first social-security act. In other words, those who paid for social security in effect bought bonds of the Government, which had promised to support them in their old age, after the pattern of the employees' stock-benefit plan, because all the proceeds of social-security taxes were supposed to be put in government bonds.

[27] *Idem*, Part II, "Committees and Conflicts of Interest," p. 156.

One of the most interesting types of taxation levied is illustrated by the Ford Motor Company financing. This type of taxation has become familiar in European dictatorships. Ford simply shipped cars to all his dealers with the demand that they pay for them or else their business would be confiscated. With the aid of local banks they paid. There was nothing else for them to do. Many of the Ford dealers worked all their lives to contribute to Ford. However, the similarity of these payments to a tax escaped the attention of men living in the dreamworld of fiscal thinking. They were considered a free and voluntary trade between a big man called the Ford Motor Company and a lot of little men called dealers.

These same pressures were found in the distribution of securities. Great issuing houses had a number of good things to distribute and a number of sour issues. If a dealer wanted the patronage of the great house, he took the sour with the good, and got the money back from the public if he could. The investor was supposed to protect himself by diversification, so that he would get a reasonable number of winning tickets in this lottery scheme of taxation. It was taken for granted that a substantial number of tickets would lose.

The type of taxation involved in price combinations which charge all the traffic will bear is familiar enough not to require development. Other types of levying tribute by private organizations are so numerous as to defy classification. We are not here sitting in judgment on the way great industrial organizations grew. A world of trade between independent individuals gradually became an industrial feudalism. It was an active, vital, picturesque culture, producing, as all cultures do, the peculiar types of saints and sinners we have been describing. It should be remembered by the critical reader that saints must always be in the minority or they would not be saints.

CHAPTER XII

The Malevolence of Taxation by the Government

In which is discussed the curious myth that permanent public improvements, conservation of resources, utilization of idle labor, and distribution of available goods are a burden on posterity if accomplished by an organization called "government" which assumes public responsibility.

THE net result of a folklore which gave business all these agreeable and painless ways of levying tribute was to give business enterprise complete freedom. To this may be attributed our industrial development. As we have seen, successful organization requires a folklore which, instead of hampering it in meeting its practical problems, allows it freedom to experiment. Nevertheless, the same folklore which justified freedom to experiment on the part of industrial organizations offered the greatest handicap to similar activity on the part of the Government, even in fields where governmental activity was most imperatively needed. It set up standards by which the Government was judged by its failures, while an industrial organization was judged by its successes and its failures were excused.

This belief in the inherent malevolence of government resulted in a fiscal fairyland in which the following propositions, absurd though they were from an organizational point of view, appeared to be fundamental truths.

1. If government conserves our soil from floods and erosion in order to bequeath to posterity a more productive country, our children will be impoverished thereby and have to pay for it through the nose.

2. If government builds a large number of productive public works which can be used by posterity, posterity will be worse off.

3. We cannot afford to put available labor to work because that would burden posterity.

4. We cannot distribute consumer's goods now on hand, because that would burden posterity.

5. The less government does about controlling money and credit, the more orderly in their operation they become.

6. Credit inflation and depressions would be even worse than they are if government attempted to control them.

7. When a problem arises which concerns the production of goods, the question "Where is the money coming from?" is more important than "Where are the goods coming from?"

Therefore, we do not improve our country, or conserve its resources, or utilize its labor, or run its productive plant to its maximum capacity—out of consideration for our grandchildren.

What is the reason for the common feeling that we cannot afford to make such admitted improvements if they involve government spending, in the face of the fact that, from a common-sense point of view, they are both necessary and capable of producing income? The answer to that question is found in the fact that the Government possesses no acceptable bookkeeping to convey to the public the idea that such expenditures are a source of future wealth.

Private organization is protected from criticism of its expenditures by two important myths. The first is that any money which is wasted is "private" money and therefore of no concern to anyone. This is accomplished through the personification of the great industrial organization and has already been described at length in the preceding chapters.

The second important underlying myth which aids private organizations and hampers government activity along practical lines is the notion that the government has no "assets." When a private corporation spends money incalculably in excess of its current income for years to come, it nevertheless is able to "balance its budget" on the theory that it is acquiring "assets" in return for that expenditure. Therefore, it is not "spending" but "investing" in income-producing capital goods. These goods include assets without any tangible existence. The organization itself becomes its own greatest asset and its expectations and hopes are given money value. Even such current expenditures as advertising are considered an asset, because they are "income" producing. Advertising good will becomes a thing in itself and one of our national assets when the sum total of corporate assets are listed in terms of their money value. The fact that often (as in the case of many drug and food products) this advertising is in reality a social liability, which taxes the income of persons of moderate means by inducing them to pay tribute for useless things, does not prevent it from being protected as valuable private property is protected.

So fixed is this asset mythology in our current folklore that insolvent organizations like railroads can make themselves solvent by spending. The process is as follows: An insolvent railroad spends vast sums for luxurious equipment. Its increased activity increases its morale. The public observing that activity gains confidence in it. Wealth, as we have shown, is nothing more than a present-day guess as to what goods and services an individual or an organization can control in the future. The organization spending on a large scale raises hopes; men begin to believe in it; its stock goes up in value; its hopes are reflected in its bookkeeping; thus it becomes solvent. All it needs is enough money to pay its interest, and that in turn can be obtained through the increasing confidence of the public in the value of its "capital." Our mythology regards this "capital" as something which is permanent, having an existence apart from the organization and capable of being sold for the benefit of creditors if the organization fails.

Because private industrial organizations have assets, posterity does not need to pay if they raise money by borrowing. The money will be repaid from these "assets." If it is not paid, the banks making the loans will suffer, but they will deserve it since they were free to withhold the loans. The public may suffer incidentally, but that is not the fault of the system, since it produces the very best kind of bankers possible by eliminating those who are foolish and lose money. In the hands of good bankers the national wealth is increased by the creation of assets which are liquid and have a money value based on their prospect of producing income.

The Government is not permitted to use the techniques of bankers in order to make its property liquid and to give it a money value. It is not supposed to "own" any property which can be capitalized in that way, and if it does, it must turn it over to private financial organizations. For example, a police department renders services as necessary to the community as a news-gathering agency. Our mythology does not allow such an activity to be "capitalized" and operated under corporate bookkeeping. Everything which the police department does is written down as a necessary expense. It can never balance its budget without a subsidy from the taxpayers because we are unable to conceive of the Government as selling police protection. Private schools may capitalize their organizations and make money; public schools cannot.

So deep-seated is this notion, that the Government can only with the greatest difficulty raise money on assets which everyone admits it owns. For example, the Government owned the oil under the Salt Creek field in Wyoming. It was compelled, however, in following the ideology of the time, to "lease" the right to extract oil to private companies, reserving a small royalty. This was in effect a present of untold millions of dollars to private oil companies. The leases acquired from the Government became worth fabulous sums. The oil was wasted in fantastic ways. Nevertheless, the Government was not permitted to operate its own properties because of the certainty men felt that government is wasteful. (Incidentally, states could not tax these highly valuable oil leases within their boundaries because that would have been in effect "taxing" the Federal Government.)

The same thing was again illustrated when the Government attempted to use the water power in the Tennessee Valley to produce electricity. Sound conservative lawyers thought it unconstitutional. Sound conservative economists were sure it violated economic principles. The matter finally reached the Supreme Court. In fear and trembling as to the possible consequences of its decision on posterity, that learned tribunal, confining its decision to the narrowest possible limits, determined that the manufacture of electricity on the particular dam in question was justified under the war power.[1] Fantasy can go no further than this. Yet few saw anything ludicrous in the decision, in spite of the fact that it left the other dams built by the Government in connection with the T.V.A. still subject to continued and protracted litigation.

Of course there are instances where the Government has operated on an asset system of bookkeeping, for example, when it used the symbol "government corporation." Such disguise of government activity, however, was hampered in every direction by current ideals, because a "government corporation" involved so many ideological contradictions. Everybody "saw through" the device of a government corporation and said that it was just a method of concealed "taxation." This was when the governmental corporation

[1] *Ashwander* v. *Tennessee Valley Authority*, 297 *U.S.* 288 (1936).

did not "make money." When it did "make money" it was "governmental interference in business." Government was by theory so inefficient that it could never make money in business. If it did, it made money at the expense of private business, because it caused private businessmen to lose "confidence" so that they could not make any money. This loss of confidence, according to these myths, prevented private bankers from loaning businessmen the necessary "private funds." If the Government instead of a bank "loaned" them the funds, that led to "inflation." Uncontrolled private credit was not thought to be the cause of the inflation of 1929, or if it was, government credit would have led to more inflation. If anyone argued that properly controlled government credit might not lead to inflation, the answer was that credit could not be so controlled without changing our system of government. This the Constitution forbade, either because of its letter or spirit. Any new thing, even though not forbidden by the Constitution, acquired a character of unconstitutionality because new government activity was thought to lead to a "change in the system of government." The reason for this was that the "spirit of the Constitution" was more important than the letter.

Not only was the Government prevented from raising money pleasantly by the device of capitalizing its "assets," but in levying taxes public opinion demanded that it act as disagreeably as possible. Concealed taxes were regarded by liberals and conservatives alike as dangerous. They were the kind of things which "politicians" were trying to put over in order to spend money and get votes. The "thinking man" was not supposed to be fooled by this sort of thing. Direct taxation was the best, because people "felt" it and this made them think twice before voting for a government which indulged in "waste." All this was simply a subconscious reaction to the notion that private organization was the only right and proper instrument to distribute goods. Of course, it had nothing to do with waste. No one suggested that a method of advertising and pricing be recommended which would make people think twice before permitting slums to be built, or useless skyscrapers, or duplications of competitive equipment, or gadgets. The principles of "waste" did not apply to business at all, because of the theory that "waste" was automatically eliminated by competition. No one had the faintest idea what social "waste" was anyway. What was one man's "waste" was another's efficiency. These words simply reflected the social organization's instinctive attack on anything which disturbed the existing order.

The effects of this way of thinking on the "science" of taxation were most amusing. The rich wanted to broaden the income-tax base so that the poor would vote against public improvements. Liberals were against any form of taxation which the public would not "feel," because they shared the mythology that in this way they would impede useless government spending on projects favored by the rich. For example, the sales tax was condemned because it fell on the poor. In a world where prices were established by great private organizations on the basis of getting all possible profit, the cost of living in various states could never be charted by finding out whether there was a sales tax. Nevertheless, the sales tax was opposed often by those who advocated greater public spending for the poor. They wanted the funds raised in the most disagreeable way. This belief restricted the Government's activities.

There were some odd quirks to this tax philosophy. Tobacco, for example, was not supposed to be a necessity for the poor. Neither were movies, nor gasoline, nor liquor. These were "luxuries" and if a man was so depraved (as is the writer) to be dependent on a moderate amount of all of them, this did not make them necessities even for him. Hence those who were opposed to sales taxes as a burden on the poor did not suggest removing them from cigarettes. Nearly all the poor smoked cigarettes, and to a confirmed smoker tobacco is more important than a proper diet. However, there was just enough taint of immorality about the habit to enable liberals to advocate a sales tax on liquor and tobacco and at the same time to be against a sales tax on food because it was a burden on the poor.

Taxation morality, while it permitted collections from liquor and tobacco, refused to permit the Government to take anything by way of lotteries and gambling. There was nothing more obvious than the psychological need of the American people to gamble. Even churches recognized this method of raising revenue by conducting raffles. However, the Government was not permitted to tap that source, because we were going gradually to eliminate the desire for this kind of speculation. The result, naturally, was to turn the filling of this need over to a *sub rosa* organization, which not only levied enormous tribute from the poor but did not even provide honest gambling.

For example, no one can accurately estimate the annual "take" of the numbers racket and other gambling devices from the poor of New York City. Some people put it in the hundred millions. These games are dishonestly conducted and yet all efforts to suppress them fail. Not only does the Government refuse to utilize this pleasant and necessary activity as a means of raising revenue, but it spends huge sums on its prosecution. This drives the business down to lower and lower levels, because it becomes increasingly difficult for people of decent values to engage in it. The whole complicated process is a product of the ideology which keeps government in its place by not permitting it to raise money in pleasant ways.

According to current ideas, government should not tax

to subsidize needed industrial activities (except in "emergencies"), because this is an expenditure that will have to be borne by the taxpayer. However, if the tax can be correlated with a familiar symbol, it escapes this taboo. For example, the state has always built roads. Hence, government can spend billions of dollars in subsidizing the automobile industry by making concrete roads to every hamlet for automobiles to run on. Without this subsidy, the present development of the automobile industry would have been impossible. Compare this with the building industry. It is probable that today houses could be produced like Fords, by standardized production on a large scale. Yet building is slow in getting started, and, in spite of pressing demand, nonstandardized building material is the rule in the industry, and a bathroom costs more than a complicated machine like a Ford. It is probable that if the Government could subsidize a place to put these new houses, as it subsidized a place to put the automobile, the industry might rebuild our slums and create not only a building boom but a pleasanter, more attractive country with a higher standard of living. It is certain that the country would not be "poorer" if a few million more houses of good construction were built. Nevertheless, the subsidy to this industry by purchasing and preparing land cannot be given, as the road subsidy was given, since the myths of the time do not sanction it. We need slum clearance more than roads. It would pay for itself, as roads did. However, it is infinitely more difficult to start than the road construction was because the myths and portents of our folklore stand in the way. When we examine the entrails of our economic geese, such activities are attended by dire portents, unspecific as such portents always are, but nevertheless sounding in gloom.

Of course the above will be considered by the economic scholar as too simple an explanation of the complicated set of social pressures which handicaps housing in this country. The criticism will be valid in the sense that in the present tangled situation a subsidy for land on which houses could be erected might not be an effective way of encouraging the development of cheap housing. Such a proposal might be twisted and distorted by strongly entrenched organizations and might result only in the further increase of land value. We are using it as an illustration, not as a legislative proposal. The practical objections to the present adoption of such a subsidy to advance better housing arise because of other fixed ideals which might prevent the subsidy from becoming as effective for housing as it was for automobiles. An examination of all the psychological factors which complicate sensible real-estate improvement cannot be made here.

What may be called "selfish vested interests" are important factors preventing change. However, such interests, unsupported by ideals and folklore, are not so difficult to defeat. Selfish interests cannot form powerful organizations if they frankly recognize that they are selfish and fail to tie themselves up with some respectable social myth. For example, the selfish interests of hundreds of owners of office buildings were opposed to the construction of Rockefeller Center in New York, which drained them of their tenants. They even went so far as to commence a suit. However, their efforts were ineffective, because Rockefeller Center did not violate any current taboos. This fact prevented the opposition from uniting with any enthusiasm. They could not find a magic inscription with which to fight Rockefeller Center and therefore could not give their selfish interests the color of a campaign for right, truth, and justice—even to themselves. People who fight for selfish interests, realizing that it is selfish interests they are fighting for, are always ineffective. They fail to get the support of loyal crusaders. They fail to be loyal crusaders themselves. Had it been the Government which was erecting Rockefeller Center, it could have been hampered with real effectiveness at every turn, by the same group, which would have had the backing of all right-thinking men and women who desired to preserve their ancient liberties. The Government may build roads, but not buildings.

Under such circumstances building through governmental agencies had to follow the traditional lines which confine it to the popular conception of public monuments and memorials. As this is being written, a controversy is going on in Washington on the advisability of cutting down the cherry trees in order to build a costly and useless memorial to Thomas Jefferson. The writer does not predict how this fight is going to come out. There seems, however, little possibility that the memorial will take the form of a housing project. Housing projects, which are fitted to our conception of what the poor can "afford," are not considered sufficiently ornamental to perpetuate the names of great men.

To be sure there are exceptions. The town of Coral Gables in Florida, with under 6,000 inhabitants, managed to acquire about $50,000,000 worth of improvements from speculators all over the country, part of which tribute was collected by municipal bond issues, and part by issuing the notes of a private corporation. In other words, Coral Gables got itself into the position of a sort of foreign government. It enlisted bankers on its side, paid them heavy tribute and built a very lovely city at the expense of people who lived far away. It then proceeded to default and went through the protective-committee process in the orthodox way. The houses and hotels and swimming pools, however, remained in Coral Gables. The extravagance of Coral Gables met with universal condemnation, but that did not take away the buildings.

This was the process by which some of our most important public developments were built. Chicago became one of the most beautiful cities in the world because it was fortunate

enough to have *sub rosa* political machines and politicians
with an eye for municipal beauty and convenience. For a
time Chicago was supposed to have been bankrupt, but this
phase passed away, as it always does, leaving the magnificent
boulevards, lake front, and other great public improvements
for the enjoyment of its citizens. A thrifty city, living up to
the standard principles of government, would have had to
remain ugly and uncomfortable, because it followed sound
principles of taxation and public expenditure. In other words,
here again, in a climate of opinion in which mythology prevented government from doing obviously necessary things,
they could only be accomplished by the creation of a *sub rosa*
political machine.

The general belief that taxes were a necessary evil, to be
resisted so far as possible, turned the learning of taxation into
an amazing and complicated metaphysics. There was no
order, nor rhyme, nor reason. There was a mass of over-
lapping taxing bodies, each representing some facet of the
confused religion. There were conflicts between state and
Federal governments, municipal governments, county governments, and corporate governments. The Supreme Court
of the United States created huge reservoirs of tax-exempt
securities by intimating that state bonds could not be taxed
by the Federal Government. It created a great class of municipal employees who were exempt from income tax. By treating corporations as individuals, courts produced the fantastic
metaphysics known as nonrecognition of gain or loss in reorganizations. Corporate taxation became the most complicated metaphysics the world has ever known. Tax attorneys
made great incomes because they became skilled in using this
peculiar terminology.

The collection of the income tax from powerful individuals
and organizations became a combat, rather than a business
transaction, in which forty-five thousand registered lawyers

and tax accountants were pitted against some twenty-eight hundred persons employed by the Government.[2] So strong was the belief in the essential malevolence of government that methods to avoid taxes became respectable which would not have been tolerated by the same group of people to avoid their private indebtedness. The Supreme Court of the United States, representing as it did protection of the great organization against the predatory Government, provided the slogans for this contest. It held that tax avoidance was a perfectly proper motive and attempted to distinguish it from tax evasion. It refused to condemn artificial and finespun technicalities as methods of avoiding taxes, except in language so vague as to be useless in preventing ingenious lawyers from concocting such schemes.

The net result was that new loopholes in the income-tax laws developed as fast as old loopholes were closed. The principal method of tax avoidance in 1937 was for a rich individual to split himself up into a large number of artificial personalities, none of which had sufficient income to come within the higher bracket. After these artificial personalities had been created, they proceeded to trade with each other for the purpose of establishing losses, rather than for making money, so that their taxes would be reduced. The courts were sympathetic and created a literature so vast that almost any scheme could be plausibly supported with learned authority. It was almost impossible to obtain a penalty for fraud in evasion of the income tax provided outright perjury was not resorted to.

In 1937 the President called attention to these methods of tax avoidance and was met with a storm of protest on the ground that he was persecuting the rich. The tax investiga-

[2] Statement of Secretary of the Treasury Morgenthau at the Hearings before the Joint Committee on Tax Evasion and Tax Avoidance, 75th Congress, 1st Session, June 17–24, 1937.

tion which followed aroused little public interest and overwhelming editorial condemnation. It disclosed the fact that
the very rich man was in the habit of making each recurring
expense a separate taxable entity. He would incorporate a
residence or his yacht. He would establish trusts for the education of his children. He would create personal holding companies to do his investing for him. The line between the
proper and improper use of such a license was almost impossible to draw. Cecil B. De Mille, a noted moving-picture
director, incorporated himself and worked for the corporation at far less money than was actually paid for his services.
The balance was put into a corporate surplus to avoid sur-
taxes and the whole scheme was upheld by the court.[3] This is
a typical case and is given here only because the method used
was so naïve. Rich men incorporated in the Bahama Islands
and in Newfoundland and in Panama in order to give their
income a situs in a foreign country.

When interviewed on the ethics of such transactions, Mr.
J. P. Morgan said: "If the government cannot collect its
taxes, a man is a fool to pay them." His remark represented
current business ethics toward the Government. No respectable person could make the statement that if a *bank* was unable to collect its notes, the debtor would be a fool to meet
his obligations. In effect a sort of legalized bankruptcy proceeding has grown up almost exclusively devoted to tax
avoidance and made respectable by the current belief in the
inherent wastefulness and malevolence of the Government.
The right to fight long and expensive legal battles has become identified with human freedom, and on the banner of
every great tax avoider is inscribed the motto "Taxation without litigation is tyranny."

Of course, one of the most important functions of the tax-

[3] *Commissioner* v. *Cecil B. De Mille Productions*, 90 F. (2d) 12 (1937).

ing power is regulation. Businesses and other activities can be encouraged or discouraged by this device. But since government regulation was looked at with suspicion, taxes for regulatory purposes also became subjects of bitter controversy. The Supreme Court of the United States in the case declaring the Agricultural Adjustment Act[4] unconstitutional developed the doctrine that the taxing power could not be used to control agriculture, because agriculture was something which the Federal Government was not supposed to control; this sort of control interfered with states rights, the home, freedom, and our system of government. Other regulatory taxes, such as one which prevented oleomargarine from competing with butter, were sustained.[5] One never knew just when a tax ceased to be a tax and became a penalty, but the net result was to add to the ominous cloud which hung over activity by the central government. The phrase "due process" further complicated the tax situation in unpredictable ways.

There were, of course, other notions which exemplified the malevolence of government when it entered the field of temporal affairs. For example, all right-thinking people considered it dangerous for a government department to select its own personnel. Civil service boards were thought to improve morality and increase efficiency in this regard. A supervisory court called the Comptroller of the Currency watched over all expenditure and constituted a separate little Supreme Court with power to stop all government activity in what he considered unauthorized paths. This officer also served to harass governmental employees in all sorts of minor ways by questioning their travel expenditures. The law did not permit government employees to live as well while traveling as

[4] *United States* v. *Butler, 297 U.S.* 1 (1936).
[5] *McCray* v. *United States, 195 U.S.* 27 (1904).

the employees of great corporations. Government employees were limited to five dollars a day, on the theory that if they stopped at a good hotel the taxpayers would pay. If an employee for a public utility stopped at a good hotel, this was none of the business of the rate payers. A poll taken by the Institute of Public Opinion showed that an overwhelming percentage of voters opposed the organization of governmental employees into a labor union. People generally were in favor of the humiliating provision of civil service boards and budget bureaus for government servants. They were against giving them the dignity of an independent union through which they could assert themselves as private labor could.

The list of such things could be indefinitely extended. However, the central idea was that "government" does not spend its "own" money. It can have no assets. It cannot use corporate methods of balancing its budget. These were all incidents of the prevalent belief in the essential benevolence of private government.

These attitudes became marked during the depression because of the great pressures which compelled government to extend its activities in areas where private industrial organization had failed. Such activity, colliding with the folklore we have been describing, created more spiritual discomfort than had been known since Darwinism collided with the Christian religion. Every priestly organization threw itself into the breach. The campaign of 1936 was a regular revival meeting in which supposedly intelligent men talked and acted with the kind of idiocy usually exhibited by scholars and intellectuals when they become excited. The Supreme Court of the United States courageously deserted all known forms of legal logic to throw itself into the economic breach and set the nation back on the proper social course. When in 1937 the Supreme Court of the United States was attacked by Roosevelt, the din began all over again. Federal Judges got down from the bench and made speeches of which the following from Judge Otis is an example: "I shall not argue with one who says when the sun is burning in its zenith in an unclouded sky, 'there is no sun.' . . . I cannot argue with one who thinks it right to pack a court, or stuff a ballot box or bribe a jury."[6]

Senator Wheeler in the heat of his passion to save the Government from the formulation of a creed which would permit it to act effectively in practical affairs discovered that God himself was opposed to the judiciary reform bill or President Roosevelt. We quote from the *New York Herald Tribune* (July 15, 1937): "The Senator from Montana, Burton K. Wheeler, took the last word on that today when, amid the chorus of tributes and praises, he called upon the President to drop his fight for the court bill, 'lest he appear to fight against God.' "

Such emotional outbursts have attended every issue which threatened to extend government activity into the area supposed to be reserved to private organization. The same sort of oratory was used successively against the Securities and Exchange Act, the legislation on the gold standard, the N.R.A., the A.A.A., as in the debate on Roosevelt's judiciary reform bill. For example, in speaking in the famous gold clause case[7] Mr. Justice McReynolds pronounced the following priestly curse from the bench of the Supreme Court of the United States: "Nero undertook to exercise that power. Six centuries ago in France it was regarded as a prerogative of the sovereign. . . . It seems impossible to overestimate what has been done here today. The Constitution is gone. . . . The people's fundamental rights have been preempted by Congress. Some day the truth will be seen."

[6] From an address delivered by Judge Otis, February 12, 1937.
[7] *Perry* v. *United States*, 294 *U.S.* 330, 1935.

All of the above sounds like an attack on individuals and attitudes, but it is not intended to be such. It is idle to attack the human race for being what it is. Heated and extreme expressions are inevitable whenever men are going through a spiritual conflict between actual needs and an inherited folklore. Indeed this language may be considered as an encouraging sign, because it clears the way for the resolution of the conflict. It offers the same kind of release as profanity does in minor situations. It is one of the symptoms which always accompany the death of a taboo.

For example, the struggle for procedural reform in England during the last century, and the present conflict in the American Medical Association caused by proposals for sensible public-health administration, though their subject matter is entirely different, are accompanied by the same type of argument. Such arguments represent the catharsis by which a people are slowly abandoning an old religion. The process by which that catharsis is accomplished is this: Respectable, learned, and conservative people keep on shouting, gradually getting more and more extreme until their words have no meaning whatever. As the emotion gradually exhausts itself, the realization that their statements are nonsense gradually dawns on the debaters. Then the struggle is over. The typical excerpts which we have just cited indicate that in 1937 this stage may have been reached in the United States. If not it is certainly on the way.

In the confusion created by the last-ditch defenders of the faith in the essential malevolence of government, a clear note of common sense is beginning to be heard. The National Resources Board, which in 1935 published a report that was practically unnoticed, produced in 1937 a study on the effect of new inventions and new industrial techniques which was startling in its implications. It was typical of a fact-minded literature which was growing in extent and compelling men to face practical problems with a view to solving them by new organizations.

To be sure, in creating new organizations to solve these problems the old attitude refused to recognize that such organizations are the product of growth. Organizations, like any army, are necessarily inefficient when they are formed. Yet the standards of the day require that a *governmental* organization should be mature when it is born. Standards for private organization are more practical. They recognize that the United States Steel Corporation today is a gradual development from complete anarchy. They realize that a large number of automobile companies had to rise and fall before the present highly effective combinations appeared. This thinking is possible through the symbolism of private property. The notion is that nobody "pays" for the mistakes of private organizations, except the investors, the laborers, and the purchasers, and that their loss is not a tax but is something due to their own fault for investing in, working for, and purchasing from, the particular organizations. In the case of governmental organization, every mistake is a tax on posterity.

Actually, the progress of any organization necessarily begins with a vague idea of the sort of enterprise which is to be undertaken. Then follows a constant change in the details by which the objective is accomplished. Legislation which grants a charter to a new activity cannot be a blueprint of the future. Its only function is that of a sort of political platform. Had Henry Ford, when he started, tried to follow a blueprint of what he thought organization would be today, he would have failed within a year. This simple fact is, naturally, not observable to those caught in current folklore about government waste. For example, as this is written a wages and hours bill is pending in Congress. What the exact terms of that bill are is probably just as unimportant as the picture which Henry Ford had of his future organiza-

The Folklore of Capitalism

tion. The important thing is to get the idea accepted and an organization started. Amendments to the bill will follow as a matter of course. The first function of such legislation can be only to give an organization a respectable place in which to begin the necessary fumbling which all growing institutions have to go through with.

As an example of the first stage of that process, we quote an editorial from the *New York Times* which shows a growing acceptance of the rôle of governmental organization.

THE DOCTOR AND THE POOR

With hospitals facing a crisis because heavy taxation has curbed philanthropy and with doctors called upon to treat the needy at least partly at their own expense, some form of State medicine is inevitable. But if the indigent are to be treated at public expense organized medicine runs the risk of falling under official control. Hence the search of the American Medical Association for a policy which will enable it to maintain its present position, yet participate in Federal and State plans (June 9, 1937).

You will note, however, the typical reaction to the old myths. What does the *New York Times* think is the cause of our present health situation? The effect of heavy taxation on private philanthropy! Nevertheless, the editorial shows that the practical nature of the problem has invaded the sanctuary and is troubling the priests. This is the first step in the acceptance of a public-health administration by an organization with public, instead of private, responsibility.

The importance of such first steps often goes unrecognized by liberals who do not realize the handicaps which attend the beginning of a new activity by an institution which has never considered that activity as part of its function. Institutions, like individuals, acquire the characters given to them by the public. When they embark on a new field in which they are supposed to be incapable of acting efficiently, this attitude robs them of confidence and morale. They try to conform to old forms; they are afraid of common-sense, practical measures. A period of self-justification and fumbling is inevitable, and during that period the acceptance of the idea is much more important than the details of its attempted execution.

Conservatives on the other hand see in the acceptance of the idea the acceptance of every possible logical implication which their imaginations can conceive of. Thus child-labor regulation leads to unlawful searches and seizures, and public-utility regulation leads to tyranny. Those who are working in such political situations must expect, therefore, not only attacks from their enemies, but also from their friends. Practical action in a new field always alienates both the conservatives and the radical groups, who stand side by side attacking it. During the last campaign, when Republicans were distributing notes against the Social Security Act in pay envelopes, the *Nation* brought forth a leading article on the act entitled "Social Security Betrayed." It was all part of the struggle which had to attend the beginning of practical action in this field.

When a notion is finally accepted as a commonplace thing for the government to do, management becomes more important than logic, and the inherent organizing ability of a people gradually gets under way while intellectual conservatives and radicals battle over something else.

CHAPTER XIII

The Social Philosophy of Tomorrow

IN which the author plays safe and refuses to be specific.

SINCE I am writing in an age where Reason is still king, it is not sufficient to describe social institutions as one describes the organization of an anthill. Ants have no souls and we are writing this book for men who do have souls. Therefore something must be said to point out what men *should* believe in order to make them better, more coöperative, more just, and more comfortable. No one writing on social organization can escape the demand that he formulate a social philosophy. Not only does the demand come from others, but the writer himself is so much a part of the culture of his own time that he feels uncomfortable if he fails to produce a platform of principles on which he can stand in order to repel attacks.

And yet, if we look backward over history, we can see how impossible it is to stand in one age and predict the social philosophy of the next. On what basis could anyone in the Roman Empire predict the peculiar philosophy of feudalism? How could the wisest man in the twilight of the Middle Ages have predicted the philosophy which glorified the trader and made human greed the fountain of justice and morals? How would it have been possible to have foretold the development of the great modern corporate organization out of a philosophy of rugged individualism? Even Adam Smith, who described his own time so accurately, stated with complete conviction that the development of the great corporation was economically impossible because men would not work for corporations as they worked for themselves. Unless the profit motive is to disappear, he argued, such organizations will be absolutely impossible, because of the underlying factors which make up "human nature."

So today, in the most highly organized and specialized society the world has ever known, men are convinced that, except in time of war (and we are going eventually to abolish war) centralized control by organizations which do not operate on the "profit motive" will lead to inefficiency, bureaucracy, tyranny, and worse.

And the curious thing is that so long as men think that way, the development of the new organizations always proves that they are right. Great corporations *were* actually inefficient in Adam Smith's day and the best work was done by individual craftsmen. Centralized governments today actually *are* tyrannical, bureaucratic, cruel, and so on. Germany, Russia, and Italy do not present attractive pictures of the world which is supposed to be created when a nation follows a consistent ideal.

However, one of the reasons that we are always able to prove our point, as Adam Smith did, is that our philosophy makes us judge the institutions which do not violate that philosophy by their successes and those which do violate it by their failures. Sweden is a much pleasanter country to live in today than Germany. Yet the nonprofit enterprises in Sweden, such as coöperatives and those subsidized by government, are the very things which we are sure would produce in this country conditions like those in Germany and Italy. A philosophy of government is a series of parables through which men see the world before them. Today the parable of the wild Russian, or the cruel German, has an emotional relevance which the parable of the bright Swede cannot have for us. Instinctively we explain away the success of Sweden on the ground that the Swedes are a homogeneous people or whatnot. (Some of the Balkan states are also homogeneous peoples.)

This selection of parables is part of the process of judging institutions which fit into our philosophy by their successes and those which do not by their more obnoxious aspects. This is the way we judge the comparative efficiency of government activities and the activities of great organizations. We escape from facts which contradict our theories by saying on the one hand, "One must not be fooled into condemning the good corporations by the bad," and on the other hand, "One must not be fooled into believing that a few instances of governmental efficiency are any excuse for its numerous failures."

In this climate of opinion the new nonprofit organizations which struggle to fill social needs against a background of myths which deny them a respectable place go through the confusion we have been describing in this book. While they are engaged in this battle for recognition they necessarily become very much like the little pictures which men have of them. This is true with the individual personality. It is also true of the institutional personality. If everyone says that any particular government department is a useless bureaucracy, those who work for it will be affected and it will begin to look like a bureaucracy of the kind it is supposed to be. All sorts of human elements will contribute to this result. The most efficient young men will use the bureau only as a stepping stone to more respectable pursuits. Then the government trains many of the lawyers who subsequently fight against it. Those who stay will become timid and avoid positive action by reciting principles which to their enemies will look like red tape.

In any combat situation each side will always look like villains to the other. And under these pressures each side will become like the villains they are pictured to be, because of the necessity of fighting fire with fire and villainy with villainy.

Any group of high-minded people which begins a righteous war against oppression will soon find itself compelled to use the cruel tactics of the oppressors. Thus atrocities on both sides will occur. The best fighters are never gentle people. If a situation is created where fighters are essential, they will use fighting tactics. The gentle righteous people for whom they are fighting will be compelled to justify these tactics on some grounds or other. There are only two ways of doing this. The first one is the great principle that the end justifies the means. The second is to deny that these tactics are being used at all. A choice between these two lines of defense will depend on the temperament of the individual and his audience, but the mutual atrocities will go on regardless of which defense is used. Peaceful combat has its atrocities not less renowned than war. In the country of the blind the man who can see is always classed as a radical or a cynic.

Thus a government institution which everyone insists is a bureaucracy bound by red tape will become like a bureaucracy bound by red tape. A political machine which does the practical work which those devoted to principle insist is no part of the business of statesmen will look like the kind of thing that respectable people think a political machine must be.

This is inevitable. It accompanies the struggle of every new organization to attain a respectable place. It is part of the confusion which accompanies growth. But before condemning it as a "bad thing" it should be remembered that in this world (which looks so queer and paradoxical when viewed through the eyes of that logical little man, called Reason, in the top of everyone's head) the struggle against a prevailing folklore is the very thing which makes the new organization strong—which binds it together. No nation, no social institution, ever acquired coherence without some sort of a fight. Out of the fight come its myths and its heroes. Situations in which there is no conflict, and in which men do the practical obvious thing that makes them comfortable, do not create that hierarchy of divinities for which men stage reverent parades. The Civil War gave unity to this country, and today strong men sing songs and weep tears over the union which was cemented by the war between the blue and the gray; and they praise the gray as much as they do the blue. The experience with the N.R.A. is an illustration on a smaller scale that a labor movement does not obtain coherence when collective bargaining is granted by the government while labor rests on its oars. The C.I.O. has obtained its millions because of the romance of a great combat. Institutions seem curiously like individuals in this respect. The individual for whom all struggle and conflict has been carefully ironed out generally develops into a jellyfish.

Therefore, the social philosophy while institutions are growing is necessarily characterized by extreme, contradictory statements of principle used in the series of conflicts which accompany growth. Men do not fight and die except for extremes. It is for this reason that in times of social change, when new organizations are struggling for a respectable place, we find that social philosophy is made up of opposing Utopias. Men cannot fight over practical things. They do not march and parade and develop their heroes in a common-sense atmosphere. Every age has its social philosophy; otherwise it would not develop organizations. The social philosophy of the United States today is that of a great battle in which both sides are fighting each other to attain the same end. The sum total of law and economics which is the literature of our social philosophy today *must* represent the two sets of principles held by opposing camps, in order to justify the struggle. Even the Republicans fighting to save America in the last campaign did not regard the Democrats as traitors or rebels. Both parties regarded the other as unspeakably wrong, and yet they had to justify a system which gave the wrong, the illogical, and the immoral side a chance to win. Therefore, opposing beliefs lumped together composed the confused social philosophy of the age.

In times when the emotional conflict is not so keenly felt, social philosophy appears more consistent and less confused. Its inconsistencies are concealed by ceremony or literature, instead of emphasized and brought into the open by battle. This is what is meant by a "rule of law." Yet the term "rule of law" would have no meaning except for organizations which had previously developed a mythology and a hierarchy of divinities through a combat.

The social philosophy of today, as in all periods of combat between new institutions and old, is the philosophy of a war to end war. The sum total of its slogans offers an arsenal of weapons with which each side can attack the other. What of the social philosophy of tomorrow? To what set of formulas, since we all need formulas, should the readers of this book give their allegiance?

In the first place it is necessary that the philosophy of any social institution be positive and not negative. When legal and economic doctrines become purely negative, when they are designed solely to defend against fancied dangers, they are on their way out. Let us examine this formulation with reference to the familiar Supreme Court controversy.

That distinguished and revered priesthood (and we mean no criticism of the Supreme Court by this observation) had up to the time of the last election been devoting itself almost exclusively to protecting the American people from their unholy desires. The Constitution had become a hair shirt, through the wearing of which salvation could be attained. A bare majority of the Court appeared to regard any extension of government power as something fraught with grave danger. Three dissenting justices consistently opposed this policy of obstruction. They felt that the Constitution, if it were to survive, would have to become a sermon of hope rather than a ritual of gloom. They tried to express a faith in national government through their dissents. However, in the bitterness of the controversy, the very fact that these justices could survey the activities of new governmental organizations without either indignation or panic created alarm in the rest of the Court. Things went so far that the learned Justices actually began calling each other names in public in scholarly language from the bench. The Court lost its atmosphere of judicial calm. After the election of Roosevelt it ceased, in its majority opinions, to represent that reconciliation of conflicting ideals which had heretofore made it the greatest symbol of our national unity. Large groups of people in the United States began to regard the Court as their enemy rather than their impartial judge.

Of course, there were a lot of logical distinctions and nice reasonings back of the two opposing attitudes in the Court. However, the learned details were actually unimportant. Intelligible and plausible briefs could be written on both sides of the political questions which the Court was deciding, even in spite of the fact that the majority in writing each decision tried to settle the questions once for all. The Supreme Court of the United States, which was once the repository of a generally accepted social philosophy, reacted in a time of conflict as such bodies always react. When governmental philosophies became a source of controversy, they provided a set of opposing slogans for each warring group. This always happens in all theologies. Perhaps it was chance that the majority of the Court was fighting for the old world that had disappeared and only the minority recognized the new one. Yet if one observes the history of similar institutions, one finds that this is the rule, not the exception. The conflict in the outside world produced the conflict in the Court. And always in such conflicts respectable institutions hang back, frightened by the exuberance, the lack of respect for old landmarks, and the surge forward of heretofore unrecognized groups which accompany change.

However, it should not be forgotten that the Court furnished slogans for both sides. The great opinion of Mr. Justice Stone in the A.A.A. case gave positive philosophical authority to government participation in the production and distribution of goods. The opinion had fire and enthusiasm. It was an offensive weapon of great potential force against the complete denial of national power by the majority of the Court. The footnotes which accompanied the opinion were like the engraving on the handle of a revolver: they make the gun a prettier instrument, without interfering with its utility as a weapon. That opinion, though of course not intentionally designed for such a purpose, became the bible of those who enlisted in President Roosevelt's attack on the Court. It owed its power not to its learning but to its moving rhetoric.

In this situation it was inevitable that the purely negative philosophy of the majority finally became untenable. There were only two possible outcomes to the proposal of the President. Either the Court would change or there would be a new Court. Observers generally credit Mr. Chief Justice Hughes with the political skill which accomplished the change. It is represented in two opinions, one sustaining the minimum-wage law for women and the other permitting the Wagner Labor Relations Act to be applied to the Jones and Laughlin Steel Company.

These opinions represent a transition from a negative to a positive philosophy of federal power. They are technical and uninspired. However, they did clear away the underbrush. They showed that the Court was capable of change.

Finally, there appeared Mr. Justice Cardozo's opinion in the social-security case. Here was a note of hope and positive affirmation. It was again more a matter of rhetoric than anything else, because the ideas were commonplace enough. However, in the Jones and Laughlin case the Court seemed to be saying that it was sorry but it could not find anything in the Constitution which prevented the Wagner Labor Relations Act from applying to the Jones and Laughlin Steel Company. In Mr. Justice Cardozo's opinion the Court seemed to be saying "Hurrah! This is the kind of thing the fathers positively intended Congress to do under the Constitution."

Here we have, on a small scale, a way in which new social philosophies appear. There is first the battle, with the fighting speeches on both sides. Then there is the reconciliation with the past. And finally there is the inspirational synthesis of a new point of view. The social-security decision did much to restore the prestige of the Court because of its note of positive affirmation. Without it the writer has little doubt but that Roosevelt's Court plan would have been quickly passed. The Constitution appeared for the first time in years to be leading, instead of obstructing us, in our use of national power. All these decisions were, to be sure, written in the heavy language of the law. The social-security decision and the dissenting opinion of Mr. Justice Stone, however, used that language in such a way as to create a new atmosphere around old words. These decisions are not significant apart from the combat which created them. The ideas which they propound will appear very commonplace when the decisions are read twenty years from now. But their significance will not be affected by that fact.

Of course, social philosophies have no significance at all except with reference to the conflicts out of which they arise, or to the institutions which they support. We have already shown that the logical structure is unimportant. Hitler subscribed to Socialism, but he could have done the same things under the Mormon Bible if the words in that Bible had had emotional relevance to the German people.

Therefore, if one wishes to guess the social philosophy of the future, he must guess first what class will come into control of the organizations which make and distribute the goods and, second, whether the change will be violent or slow. If it is violent, a whole new set of terms will dramatize the sudden rise of the new organization to power. The old terms will flow back gradually during a period of confusion, while the new organizations fumble and fail as organizations always must fail to live up to the promises of their creed. And finally a note of positive affirmation will be heard which, like Lincoln's "Gettysburg Address," seems to link the new organizations to some heroic event in the past, to express the contradictory notions and ideals of the people, and to fill them with the pride and morale necessary for expansion.

If the rise of the new organization is slow, the terms will change their meaning, rather than be supplanted by new terms. Capitalism will become "socialistic" in a slow revolution. In a more violent one, "Capitalism" will be supplanted by "Socialism" and then in the period of stabilization "Socialism" will gradually become "capitalistic." This is what is happening in Russia. We can note today the charge being constantly made by those who were most idealistic about Socialism in Russia that the Communists are abandoning their ideals and "reverting" to Capitalism. In contrast to this we heard speeches *ad nauseam* in the last campaign that the New Deal was in devious and hidden ways making our capitalistic system socialistic. The observer who watches this process should never be alarmed about the "stupidity" of the so-called intelligent people who make speeches of this kind. It is part of the process of change in a rational world. All he needs to worry about is the character of the people who are gradually coming into power. Does he think that they are good organizers and at the same time tolerant and humanitarian? If he reaches this conclusion, he need not worry about "failure to balance the budget." All "balancing the budget" ever can mean is that an institution has achieved public acceptance of its objectives. If it has, there will never be any difficulty about balancing its budget.

If the observer wants to guess whether we will balance our budget by "taxation" or by the Government's adopting the techniques of bankers and creating "assets" to which it can give money values, he must first realize that anything he predicts is only a guess. There are no economic "laws" on this point. Then he should study the culture of the people, remembering that unpleasant methods of collecting revenue will never be permanently adopted as the principal techniques of successful organization. People in this country dread taxes and love financing. Unless this attitude changes, new government activities will be financed in all probability by asset bookkeeping. If, on the other hand, the attitude toward taxation does change, it may become the means of budget balancing as it has in England. The writer's guess at present is that the Government will continue to tax and gradually increase its participation in finance. It is already moving in both these directions today. There are signs of acceptance of taxes somewhat heavier than we have had in the past. There are also many signs of the Government's becoming the greatest credit agency in the country—in other words, learning and using the techniques of bankers.

This much only about the social bookkeeping of the future the writer can say with confidence. In the first place, it will personify whatever organizations achieve a stable place in the distribution of our goods. In the second place, it will not be descriptive of actual conduct because practical situations will always require deviations from doctrine. Therefore, liberals will again rise to importance, as they do in times when a settled governmental philosophy is accepted with unquestioning faith. Liberal movements always die in a time when the folklore is questioned. They rise again when men think they know what the eternal verities are, and therefore can find a firm platform from which to attack the continual backsliding from those verities.

In the third place, the social bookkeeping of tomorrow will be supported by that same attitude which we call today *"laissez faire"* economics. All this means is that those who defend institutions against logical attacks which cannot easily be answered in logical terms necessarily have to develop an argumentative technique which protects them against continual reform. The best and easiest method is to develop a philosophy which justifies letting existing institutions alone, even when they are violating principle. Of course, *laissez faire* is just as Utopian as Socialism. Human beings in power cannot let things alone, no matter how much they believe in that philosophy. But just as some form of creed based on abstract social justice will always be the battle cry of the reformer, so some sort of creed based on letting things alone will always be the answer to a demand that an institution be compelled to practice what it preaches. Injustice obviously must always exist because without it the conception of justice has no meaning; and without the ideal of justice human activity loses all appearance of dignity.

It is a hopeful sign that there is beginning to appear a philosophy about social philosophies. I will attempt no list of writers with this point of view because there are so many today who are looking at social philosophies from the outside, recognizing the part they play and at the same time using them. Men are coming to realize that political government is necessarily a dramatic spectacle, that games are really important in the growth and development of institutions, and that these games can be controlled. Even at the height of the last campaign the bitterness was softened by the realization that a play was being staged. This is a new thing in our political thinking. It holds the promise of giving us greater control over our ceremonies and creeds, without losing any of their emotional drive. It is, of course, hard from the point of view of the rational man, to regard law and economics as folklore and at the same time play seriously a game which depends on the use of the formulas of these sciences. Yet we have already accomplished this feat in our treatment of emotional maladjustments of individuals.

This point of view toward governmental institutions is easier for the unscrupulous to take than for respectable people. It is an essential to success in building a political organization in America. In Russia, Germany, and Italy, where old ideals were suddenly swept away, a certain necessary realism has compelled these governments to recognize that the political party is always the real government. They therefore dragged political machinery out into the open and made the political leader the nominal as well as the actual governor. This enabled them to use political techniques more frankly and openly. Trials became an admitted method of political propaganda. In this country the trial of political issues by the Supreme Court of the United States, while it was actually political propaganda, was supposed to be something else. The failure of the unfortunate conservative bloc of the Supreme Court of the United States to realize that they were actually deciding political issues came near to wrecking the Court. The Court was finally compelled to make a public reversal of its former attitude which would have been unnecessary had the majority known, as Mr. Justice Stone knew, the limitation on the judicial function. A most useful social philosophy for the future is one which recognizes the functions

which dramatic contests of all sorts perform in giving unity
and stability in government. The most primitive type of such
contests is war. The most civilized types are games and judicial trial. The frank recognition of this fact is the beginning
of knowledge of social institutions. It gives us an understanding of the part that football teams play in the growth and
traditions of a college, and the similar part that such an institution as the Supreme Court of the United States plays in
the growth, tradition, and unity of a nation.

For an illustration of all this, we close with a quotation
from Walter Duranty:

Joseph Stalin, you must understand, is building Russia—making
men out of mice and putting courage, backbone and unity into a
people that have been slaves for centuries. That is Stalin's job
which Lenin set for him and while Leon Trotsky talks about
world revolution Stalin is trying to do his job.

The job has two essential factors—to bind together this vast
country with its multifarious and multilingual races and to give
them a common cause, aims and hopes. America, in a sense, has
the same problem—what is called the melting pot—of assimilat-
ing former Europeans into the integrated life of the United
States.

That is comparatively easy, but in the U.S.S.R. there are
seventy-nine major languages and hundreds of dialects and to
make a soup of this mixture requires a skilled cook.

Today we saw how Stalin brews his broth. Five young girls
from Buriat, Mongolia, on the edge of China, came into the sport
stadium Dynamo, which is the headquarters of the Soviet Physical Culture League. In 137 days they had covered 4,000 miles and
their plump, cheerful faces today adorn the front pages of Mos-
cow newspapers.

Two are quite pretty and one, who is only 17 years old, has the
most attractive and serious small face. With them in the photo-
graphs there is a tall Russian man, who "ran the trip." And that
is the answer to Stalin's soup. The Russians and the Russian Com-

munist party are training, driving, badgering and bustling these backward 170,000,000 people to make them men, not mice or slaves.

Thirty thousand people at the stadium cheered uproariously when the Mongol girls came in. They felt a vicarious pride in the girls' achievement, because it was done for Russia and as a tribute to "Women's Day" on Monday.

You can say this sounds like nonsense, but when Charles A. Lindbergh flew the Atlantic weren't you thrilled? That is how the Russians feel and how Stalin is solving the national problem here. These Mongolian kids and the welcome they received in the Soviet capital are symbolic and tremendously important because it means a new Russia which is one and undivided.

And there are new games of skill and courage, like ice hockey, for a people that were slaves and knew no games. After the arrival of the Mongolian girls the final men's and women's championship hockey matches were played. The rules allow no body checking, which makes the game slow to any one who has seen American hockey. But it is a hot struggle and the crowd went mad. That is the way they are building this new Russia. (*New York Times,* March 7, 1937.)

When Stalin recently abandoned this technique for a great purge, the morale and prestige of Russia fell. International opinion realized that Russia, for some inexplicable reason, was failing in organizational methods, in spite of the evidence of the internal power which such a purge represented.

Games of this inspirational character may be played by dignified old men reciting the parables of the law, as well as by young girls. It is the essential of a properly dramatized civilization that there be dramas to suit all moods and tastes. The Supreme Court of the United States, Memorial Day, and Charles Augustus Lindbergh are the stuff out of which vital and expanding social organizations are made.

CHAPTER XIV

Some Principles of Political Dynamics

IN which a science *about* law and economics is distinguished from a science *of* law and economics.

THE last six chapters have been devoted to an analysis of various myths connected with the personification of our great industrial enterprises. These particular ceremonies are fundamental to our present disunited industrial feudalism. They are the most important psychological factors which are now hampering the growth of organizations with a definite public responsibility. The use of the individualistic ideal to justify dictatorial business institutions is also one of the greatest obstacles to considering the real problems of freedom of the individual.

We believe that this folklore is on the way out. Its artificiality is becoming more and more apparent, and the need for new types of organization justified by a different folklore is growing more pressing each year. We are today in the midst of the confusion which inevitably accompanies the growth of these new organizations. No one can say how long it will last. Yet there are certain general observations which may be made, and which are applicable to all types of organization. They will not serve as the basis for any infallible predictions. They will only give us the kind of understanding of social institutions which makes it possible to discard irrelevant factors in making predictions or diagnoses. These generalizations will be the subject of our final chapter.

In making these generalizations we are handicapped by the lack of a terminology. There are no adequate terms to describe the study of modern social institutions, either from the point of view of an anthropologist studying a primitive tribe, or from the point of view of a psychologist observing a psychopathic personality. Our general literature of law and economics is forced to leave out what it calls "politics." This pressure on these sciences necessarily creates a theological terminology which is difficult to use for the purpose of making observations.

One might think that anthropology might be a descriptive term for a study of modern religion and political forms. It will not serve, however, because the anthropologist stops at the solemn threshold of law and economics, convinced of his unworthiness to proceed. He says in excuse, "I am no economist or lawyer." The Supreme Court of the United States has for years offered a more fascinating study in primitive ritualism than anything that the Malaysian tribes had to offer. The American Law Institute, composed of a group of men sitting around and doing responsive readings of the law, financed by the Carnegie Foundation, has never been adequately described. The American economic scholars meeting in Chicago every year have never been visited by observant men asking themselves the pertinent question: "Why should such apparently intelligent men, when gathered in a group, attempt authoritatively to conceal the facts about political institutions?" The study of the reaction of social organizations to the formulas produced by such bodies, and the effect of the general folklore on those formulas, have not been given a classification or a name. There are of course novels and biographies which have attempted the job of describing the moving force of economic and legal folklore, but they have done this at odd times and not in an orderly scientific study, since they were written for a public rather than for a laboratory. The serious anthropologist and the serious psychologist, seeking information rather than literary effect, have left their own culture severely alone. There are, of course, exceptions, but they are few enough so that they prove the rule. They have passed by law, economics, political machinery, depressions, inflation, business confidence, Fascism, Communism, and all the various principles and systems of government as if they were the business of someone else. Neither the "anthropology of social institutions" nor the "psychology of social institutions" serves as a descriptive term, in view of what men in these fields have been doing in the past to describe the generalized observations which we wish to make in this chapter. They *ought logically* to describe such a study, but the connotations which have now clustered around these terms prevent them from *actually* describing it.

Therefore, I choose the term "Political Dynamics" to refer to a science *about* society which treats its ideals, its literature, its principles of religion, law, economics, political systems, creeds, and mythologies as part of a single whole and not as separate subjects, each with its own independent universe of principles. The term is not original and is already becoming familiar. I select it because it represents the easiest transition I can think of from the term "political economy" which described an individualistic era. We have reached a time when men are beginning to realize their complete interdependence, when the personality of the individual is submerged in the personality of the organization. What I have in mind is a science of the diagnosis of maladjusted organizations in an age where organizations have replaced individuals as units.

The following somewhat sketchy principles are set out only to show the kind of observations which can be made from the platform of such a science. Most of them are of course "half truths," because any classification of the tumbling stream of events which is not actually separable into classified elements represents only an emphasis on some particular phase of the scene and ignores other phases. Nevertheless, we must classify if we are to talk at all, and I therefore submit the generalizations which follow.

1. When men are engaged in any continuous coöperative activity, they develop organizations which acquire habits, disciplines, and morale; these give the organizations unity and cause them to develop something which it is convenient to describe as personality or character.

Illustrations: Yale University has a personality distinct from that of Harvard. Tammany Hall in New York has a personality which can easily be distinguished from that of the old Thompson machine in Chicago. The American Telephone and Telegraph Company has a very different personality from Paramount Pictures.

2. The personality which organizations acquire is the result both of accident and environment. The accidental features depend mostly on the types of individuals who first assume control. The environment puts great pressure on those individuals to conform to what is expected of them in terms both of practical results and the representation of sentimental ideals.

Illustration: It is apparent that the so-called "ten cent stores" have contributed tremendously to a lower cost of living in making commonplace articles such as hardware, glass, and all the various things they sell, in such quantities that useful and artistic objects have become widely distributed. It is equally apparent that the chain grocery stores have not created a similar situation in food stuffs. There is not the same vertical control of the manufacturing process from the raw materials to the finished product. There is a tendency in the chain stores to suppress competition and then to raise prices after that competition has been suppressed. They have done far less to create a wider and cheaper distribution of food stuffs than the ten cent store has done in hardware.

This difference is probably the result of accident in the rise to power of a different type of men in each of these different mercantile organizations. It is, of course, difficult to say whether standardization in the chaotic hardware industry was harder or easier than in the chaotic food industry. The accident of the type of individuals in competition with the growing chain stores probably had much to do with the final result. The local grocery stores were more numerous and may have had a firmer place in community life than the local hardware stores. Nevertheless, one has a feeling that Henry Ford, starting in the grocery business, would have accomplished the same kind of results as he did in the automobile business.

3. Once the personality of an organization is fixed, it is as difficult to change as the habits of an individual. The same type of men succeed each other, moved by the same attitudes as their predecessors.

Illustration: Paramount Publix grew to be a colossus in the amusement industry by virtue of the most wasteful and extravagant habits imaginable. It was a combination of the personalities of Lorenzo the Magnificent and Jean Jacques Casanova in the motley crowd of business enterprises, many of which affected the dour attitudes of our Puritan fathers. Came the reorganization. A distinguished businessman named Hertz was given power over the budget to effect economies. From a puritanical standpoint, this was an easy task. Waste was everywhere. Hertz cut down expenditures about twenty-five million dollars in one year. He was promptly forced to resign. Every economy that he instituted was entirely defensible. Yet the institution, instead of improving, appeared to be going to pieces under the strain. The

persons whom he discharged were, no doubt, parasites. Yet
fear and anxiety spread to the most useful members of the
organization. Mr. Swaine, the hard-boiled and able attorney
for the bankers, had difficulty in explaining before the Securities and Exchange Commission why the activities of
Hertz were stopped, because he was talking in the highly
moral atmosphere of a public investigation, in which it is
difficult to get a practical point across.[1] Yet what he said
seemed inescapably true. It was as if a father was trying to
reform a drunken and profligate son by putting him in a
strait jacket. Dogs cannot be trained that way, neither can
persons, neither can organizations. Changes in institutional
habits are made only by the gradual substitution of new
habits. Failure to realize this factor of institutional personality brings the efforts of most reformers to futility.

In this principle of political dynamics is found the basic
reason which impels a new revolutionary government to kill
the leaders of the older institutions. They are filled with rage
at the complete impossibility of changing old institutional
attitudes by what they consider unanswerable arguments.

*4. Not only do organizations acquire personalities, but
they also acquire three-dimensional substance. Thus habits
and disciplines and hopes of a great organization are given a
money value. Capitalized earning power is called "property"*

[1] Securities and Exchange Commission, *Report on . . . Protective and
Reorganization Committees,* Part II, p. 87.

"Mr. Hertz has been more than modest in his description of his accomplishments in Paramount. He did a magnificent job. . . .

"However, as the year went on the burdens upon Mr. Hertz, worries,
quite understandably, were such that Mr. Hertz became toward the end of
the year increasingly nervous and I personally, by reason of my professional relationship with the situation, Sir William and Mr. Kahn became
very much worried about the personnel situation which was developing.
Mr. Lasky dropped out. And the atmosphere at Paramount was charged at
all times with high excitement. Everybody was afraid of his job."

*and is then treated as if it could be moved from place to place
and sold. Then people dealing with these imaginary personalities deal with them as if they owned this sort of property.
Without this alternate reification and personification of the
same things a corporate structure could not exist and do business under a money economy.*

Illustration: A whole system of theoretical economics has
been built up on the unconscious assumption that organizations, which from one point of view are considered individuals, from another are storehouses of tangible property. To
say that the Baltimore and Ohio Railroad Company owns
the Baltimore and Ohio Railroad is like saying that the
United States Marine Corps owns the United States Marines.
Yet in an age where the ownership of "property" is an essential quality of a great individual, the personification of the
organization compels us to think of it in these terms.

*5. Organizations which are personified in the mind of the
public have the effect of making their members unconsciously submerge their own personalities and adopt the personality of the organization while they are acting as a part
of it.*

Illustration: A friend of mine, the head of a moderately
large law firm, at great personal loss kept all of his law clerks
during the depression. He was also a director of a public
utility. As a director he voted to fire employees and cut wages
and at the same time actually increased the salaries of certain executive officials. While acting for the company he was
unconsciously compelled to assume the mythology of the
hard-boiled public-utility magnate. As a person he was a different individual. Rosenwald, as head of Sears, Roebuck and
Company, paid low wages and was uninterested in better
working conditions for his employees. As an individual he

was one of our greatest philanthropists. He had a complicated explanation for these two different rôles and seemed to
believe that he had thought the whole thing out logically.
Instances of this kind among our knights errant of business
are too commonplace to develop further. Liberals, observing
this phenomenon through the spectacles of their theories,
are unable to understand it. They therefore assume that businessmen are hypocrites, not realizing that they are observing
a fundamental principle of human organization.

Another illustration: Employees of organizations which
have high morale and discipline take as much satisfaction
and pride in the size of the buildings, the luxury of the executive offices, and the various other exploits of the organization as though they were their own accomplishments.

A third illustration is taken from an account by Douglas
Churchill in the *New York Times* of June 13, 1937:

A few weeks before Jean Harlow's death she said, in discussing a
tragedy in her life: "When I left the church after Paul's funeral
[Paul Bern, her former husband] people broke through the
police lines and surged about me. There were words of sympathy
and ghastly words and demands for autographs. I was shocked.
They seemed too heartless. Later, as I thought about it, a realization came. They meant no disrespect. They were kindly and
gracious and thoughtful in their own lives, and had I been an
individual they would have treated me as one of their own. But
to them I was not a person, I was an institution. I had no more
personality than a corporation."

This amazing phenomenon of a mechanical age, this succession of light and sound vibrations, has created a new world as
much apart from normal life as metaphysics. Nothing like it has
ever been known. Today, through the motion picture, the public
idolizes shadows that vanish with the turn of a switch. It is not
strange, then, that so weird a result should stem from an equally
unbelievable source. To make it even more fantastic, the result
is responsible for the cause.

6. *Institutional personalities acquire the characters given them by the folklore of the times. Since every character is necessarily a whole bundle of contradictory rôles, institutions have to appear in all these contradictory rôles.*

Illustrations: Thus a business corporation is supposed to make money for its stockholders by hard bargaining and efficiency. It is also supposed to be a successful business leader with all the trappings of leadership. It is also supposed to represent the best in morals and ethics. Our industrial feudalism has produced a combination of magnificent buildings, hard trading, low wages, high executive salaries, philanthropies, and all the alternating extravagances and economies that go with these.

For similar reasons a government organization which the public insists is "bureaucratic" tends to become "bureaucratic."

7. *Institutions once formed have the persistency of all living things. They tend to grow and expand. Even when their utility both to the public and their own members has disappeared, they still survive. The economic theory that marginal business concerns will be eliminated by competition has just about as much truth in it as a theory that marginal churches which do not actually increase the comfort and happiness of their members tend to eliminate themselves. Sometimes they do; sometimes they do not. The answer depends on factors which determine organizational strength, not comfort and peace to the members of the organization. That last is only one of a number of elements and perhaps one of the least importance.*

Illustrations: Struggling churches and colleges are often supported by people who haven't the slightest belief in their utility because they feel that it is not consistent or logical to change their attitudes. The psychology which makes possible the survival of such institutions is similar to the psychology which compels parents or relatives to keep an idiot child at great expense for medical care and nurse's services, long after all possible affection for the child has disappeared. This accounts for the support of thousands of absurd organizations long after they are no more than a burden. Keeping them going seems the only decent thing to do.

For example, as this is being written, the writer has just sent a small check to an institution which he regards as peculiarly useless. The process was as follows: The first demand was ignored. The second demand came in the form of a letter asking whether I was going to go back on my old friends and desert the cause, or whether I was still with them in spirit. I sent the check with the depressing realization that this struggling institution will be a burden on me and others as long as we live. It will always be in trouble, but it will probably, somehow or other, manage to survive.

Habit, as well as sentiment, is a powerful factor. In the anarchy of the soft-coal industry in West Virginia the writer has seen a coal-mining company go bankrupt only to be taken over by its creditors, who go bankrupt, only to be taken over by *their* creditors, who go *bankrupt,* and so on.

The economic law which is supposed to cause marginal businesses to be eliminated does not work at all when it deals with organizations whose members prevent each other from expressing the doubts which all of them feel. No one likes to change his former position before his fellows. There is nothing so inelastic as a great organization of any kind because of men's passion for appearing consistent in public.

8. Institutional creeds, such as law, economics, or theology, must be false in order to function effectively. This paradoxical statement means that they must express contradictory ideals, and must authoritatively suppress any facts which interfere with those ideals.

Love of consistency and devotion to realism will wreck any institutional creed. When consistency is emphasized, conflicting ideals which may be very important in retaining loyalties have to be abandoned. When realism is stressed, it immediately becomes apparent that the institution is not living up to its ideals. Therefore, attempts to make creeds consistent, or to make preachers practice what they preach, are effective as destructive, but not as constructive, forces. What radicals are constantly calling hypocrisy in legal, economic, or ecclesiastical bishops is in reality their ability to act well on the institutional stage which has been set for them by a complex of forces for which they are not responsible.

Because of this principle expert technicians seldom make good senators, and business organizers, when thrown into the political arena, are always disappointing. The difficulties of the engineer in government were illustrated by the career of Mr. Hoover, who was always in a state of confusion because he could not look at legal and economic principles objectively. It was his sincerity that wrecked his administration. In the same way, a technical training in the psychology of sex is not particularly good preparation for a romantic lover.

All this is just another way of stating the obvious truth that the rôles of the actor on the stage and the technician who directs the play are entirely different. Ability in one of these lines has little relation to ability in the other. The creed of any institution is public presentation of a drama in which the institution is the hero. The play is spoiled unless the machinery behind the scenes is carefully concealed. In this lies the explanation of the paradox that legal and economic principles must be false in order to be effective.

9. The contradictory ideals of an institutional creed and the variance between these ideals and the actual conduct of the institution must be reconciled. If no emotional conflict is felt the reconciliation may be accomplished by a very simple ceremony.

Illustration: The equality and democracy of the army are represented by the fact that the officers salute the privates. The complete superiority of the officers is represented by requiring the privates to salute first. There is no argument nor literature on the subject because a disciplined army has fewer spiritual conflicts than any other type of institution.

Equality and democracy in industrial organization are represented by employer-employee banquets, by our great "success" literature, by our businessmen's clubs and so on. The *Saturday Evening Post* seldom goes to press without a story celebrating this idea. So generally accepted is this myth that persons in the United States who are not successful usually blame themselves. The Lynds in their second book on Middletown attempt to state objectively the creed, generally accepted even by unsuccessful Americans. This creed which is too long to insert here illustrates the commonly held belief that a business autocracy is real democracy.

Observations which deny this myth of equal business opportunity are branded as communistic.

10. The ceremonies which an institution adopts to reconcile its conflicting ideals are addressed to its own members, not to outsiders. Therefore they are seldom convincing to the critics of the institution.

Illustration: The persecution of Jews in Germany as a means of building morale is almost incomprehensible to an outsider. An outsider who judges this kind of ceremony by his own standards is therefore very easily misled into thinking that an institution which does such queer or such immoral things cannot endure. Most of the predictions of the early downfall of the Russian, German, or Italian dictatorships were made on the theory that since they were adopting the wrong "principles" they were bound to fail.

The only realistic way to judge the effectiveness of any ceremony is to observe its effect on the institution itself, not on those outside of it. If the ceremony increases confidence and quiets doubters, the fact that it is illogical and absurd is immaterial. Of course the institution may develop ceremonies which bring it into conflict with other institutions, but this is an aspect which we are not considering here.

Political arguments in a campaign are actually addressed only to the side for which they are made. They never convince the other side. Indeed arguments so framed that they would convince radicals of the desirability of any given activity would turn conservatives against it. Of course the members of the institution, when they have found a satisfactory ceremony, always believe that it represents the "truth," and are anxious to parade it before their enemies. The usual result is that the enemies are outraged at the lack of clear thinking on the part of their opponents. Thus political debate is in reality a series of cheers in which each side strives to build up its own morale. The extreme and violent statements are the stuff of which battle cries are made, and hence in a heated campaign those are the only effective material for debate. This accounts for the fact that supposedly sensible businessmen like Colonel Knox go to such fantastic extremes during a campaign. What they are actually doing by such a process is cheering themselves up, and creating enthusiasm in their own organization. In no struggle between organizations, under any form of government, has logic triumphed because it was on the one side or the other. Logical persons usually succeed in alienating all their followers sooner or later because they are always pointing out contradictions in ideals which are emotionally necessary.

11. Where the conflict between the ideals and the practical needs of an institution becomes so acute that it cannot be reconciled by a ceremony, we find the institution splitting itself into two separate parts. The one represents the ideal, and the other the practical activity which contradicts that ideal.

a. The simplest form of resolution of such a conflict is to segregate the ideal into some sort of church where it need only be brought out on ceremonial occasions and therefore will not conflict with practical activities.

This was illustrated time after time in the testimony of large employers before the Senate committee on the wages and hours bill. These employers were vaguely conscious of the cruelty of low wages. The more learned resolve that conflict by subscribing to learned institutions which are supposed to figure it out for them and thus enable them to forget it. The more naïve simply join the Church and let their religion take care of the matter for them. As an example of the latter process we quote from the *Washington Post* of June 12, 1937.

John E. Edgerton, former president of the National Association of Manufacturers and now president of the Southern States Industrial Council, was the witness at hearings on the Black-Connery wages-hours bill.

Baldish and grim-faced, his sandy eyebrows knitted in a scowl, Edgerton had told the committee that he had "allowed" a number of grandmothers to work for $6 a week during the depression "as a humane thing."

Apparently shocked by his testimony, both Republicans and Democrats joined in close examination of the aggressive witness.

Representative Clyde Smith (Republican), of Maine, and

Representative Reuben T. Wood (Democrat), of Missouri, asked him how a family could live on less than $16 a week. Edgerton, obviously irritated at the questioning and at the repeated laughter of spectators at his answers, snapped:

"I've never studied those social problems *except in my church connections.*"[2]

Smith asked: "Should all other employes in other plants suffer just because you pay less wages and work your plant 24 hours a day?"

"No," mumbled Edgerton.

Wood took up the questioning. It went like this:

Q. Sixteen dollars a week, with about 42 working weeks, amounts to $620 a year. Do you think $620 a year is sufficient to allow a family to live decently, with schooling for the children?

A. It all depends. *Some people can't think of a living standard unless they have four glasses of beer a day, or some wine.*[3] [Note the unconscious resort to a moral code to justify cruelty. No one, including the writer, can escape this on occasion.]

Q. Of course, some of your men might drink champagne on that fabulous wage you pay them. Answer the question, do you think $620 a year is enough?

A. Enough for what? Oh, I won't answer that question. The amount of money I pay out—whether that's enough for ordinary comforts—that's not relevant to this bill. It's a different question.

Representative Richard J. Welch (Republican), California, then asked about Edgerton's statement that "There are 1,000 things a man could do on $16 a week." Welch said: "What are some of these 1,000 things a man can do on $16 a week?"

Edgerton burst out: "Why, I've never thought of paying men on a basis of what they need. I don't inquire into what they want. I pay men for efficiency.

"Personally I attend to all those other things, social welfare stuff, in my church work." (Here the crowd in the hearing room roared with laughter.)

Edgerton, glaring at the spectators, sneered:

"Of course, some people don't know about that sort of thing,

[2] The italics are mine.   [3] The italics are mine.

church work and so. . . . *But that's the feeling side of life, church contributions and church work. That's not business."*[4]

As an example of referring a conflict between ideals and the practical situation in labor relationships to learning rather than to simple faith, we quote a column of Dorothy Thompson, writing on the wages and hours bill.

BLINDNESS IN CRISIS
U.S. Unknowingly Faces Change in Government Through Four Bills.

.   .   .   .

The wages and hours bill is presented as a measure of social justice. It creates a labor standards board, to be appointed by the President, of five men at salaries of $10,000 a year each, and these five men are to hold the power of life and death over American industry, both interstate and intrastate.

Congress will do no more than fix a general objective. It will be up to these five men to decide hours, rates of minimum pay and labor standards of all kinds, for all parts of the country, setting one standard here and another there, their edicts having the force of law, and disobedience entailing fine and imprisonment.

The conclusion of the column reads as follows:

Crisis before U.S.

"We face an even greater crisis than in 1932," said the President in a speech exhorting support for the plan for reorganizing the judiciary.

We do indeed. And the question before us, as Americans, is whether we are going to face it, or go grinning dumbly toward an uncertain fate, trusting the laws of chance and the President.

For it is possible to take steps which never again can be retraced. The processes of history are not always reversible. We can start a program which then will go on, under its own impetus, invested with police powers which the people cannot con-

[4] The italics are mine.

trol. I cannot recall a case in history where a popular body, having yielded its powers, ever was able to recapture them. (*New York Tribune,* June 11, 1937.)

Here Dorothy Thompson comes to exactly the same conclusion as Mr. Edgerton. However, her church is a sort of composite of the lessons of history and the principles of economics and the guaranties of the Constitution. She gives a general impression that she has made a deep study of these mysteries and that these voices inform her that nothing should be done by actual *concrete individuals* to control the situation. The heading "Blindness in Crisis" means that the administration is blind to the complicated reasons which prove that control of labor anarchy by the Government leads to disaster.

b. Where a separate institution has arisen in order to represent an ideal by separating it from the practical situation, it is never able to reach any conclusion leading to practical action. Its failure to reach such a conclusion is part of its function because the debate convinces everyone that nothing should be done about the practical situation without further study and prayer.

Illustration: The National Policy Committee was formed so that learned men could throw light on the problems of the day. Its special committee on labor was composed of a distinguished group of professors, lawyers, and businessmen. Their conclusion on a practical method of making labor unions responsible was as follows:

Interest of Committee members in the question of the incorporation of labor unions seemed to wane after it was pointed out that, if we did not have Federal incorporation, incorporation in individual states might result in certain states making available to labor unions all sorts of wide powers that they do not now possess, and, if we did have Federal incorporation, that would probably lead to the Federal incorporation of business corporations.[5]

The rest of the report of the committee's discussion shows that it fulfilled its function of representing conflicting ideals, and leaving practical action up in the air.[6]

The most important institutions to represent ideals in government uncontaminated with the complicating political and psychological factors which actually mold institutional conduct are our universities. Any meeting of a political science or legal association of professors furnishes a perfect illustration of the inability of institutions which perform that purpose ever to commit themselves on definite action.

12. Conflicts which create such elaborate systems of learning are symptoms that old institutions are no longer meeting practical needs in an acceptable way. The learning serves both of the opposing sides. For the conservative it justifies old institutions. For the radical it proves the necessity for the new institutions which are struggling to gain recognition. The debate becomes a substitute for practical action.

Illustration: Thus, theological learning increased when the medieval church became confused in its practical objective, just as economic learning increased when the great industrial organization ceased to expand and became faced with new

[5] The National Policy Committee, Washington, D. C., *Special Committee Memoranda*, No. II (1937).

[6] "The Committee believes that an immediate and vital need is the establishment by the Federal Government, of Commissions of Inquiry, to study disinterestedly and carefully the working of specific economic experiments such as the Railroad Labor Act and the Guffey Coal Act, for the purpose of periodically reporting to Congress and the public on the workings of these experiments, and of attempting to appraise from time to time their results as these affect not only labor but managerial efficiency, capital investment, and the general welfare."

problems. Again, when we felt no conflict about our punishment of the criminal, there was no literature of criminology. Our present vast literature on crime is a product of a new attitude toward the criminal, coupled with a refusal to give up the old attitude.

13. When one of the two contradictory ideals which give rise to elaborate systems of learning concerning institutional creeds disappears, the learning disappears with it.

Illustration: At the beginning of the century, when the Protestant church clung to an old theology and also insisted on doing practical social work, the struggle between modernism and fundamentalism produced huge tomes and treatises. When the church decided its main function was social utility, its entire theological learning became unimportant and the modernist-fundamentalist controversy disappeared. Again, when men desired liquor and also the ideal of prohibition, books poured from the presses. Today the philosophical literature on the liquor question is practically nonexistent.

With respect to relief, wages, and budget balancing, we are struggling today with two contradictory ideals: (1) that rugged individualism will be impaired by feeding the poor; and (2) that humanitarianism compels us to feed them. The spiritual struggle revolves about the words "budget balancing," "bureaucracy," "paternalism," and the like. When we recognize the obligation to distribute food to those who need it, there will be no more literature on this subject than there is on the subject of whether a man should take care of his mother-in-law. There may be jokes and complaints, but no learned philosophy. However, the institutions which finally solve that problem will be faced with new conflicts, which will be reconciled in exactly the same way.

14. A conflict often arises between an ideal and a social need not accepted as legitimate or moral. This creates a situation in which an immoral and undercover organization will arise. The ideal will be represented by a moral organization which proves that the social need is not a real need at all, but a form of sin. The need will be represented by an immoral organization, which will be accepted and tolerated as a necessary evil, in the same way that the Church accepted the existence of the Devil.

Illustration: During prohibition we saw a great enforcement organization and a great bootlegging organization, each functioning at full speed. Today our ideals of government create a situation in which the political machine is a necessity and at the same time an evil in the minds of all righteous and right-thinking people. For example, we quote from Westbrook Pegler:

A political machine has no more right to dish out the customers' money to Joe Dokes and George Spelvin just because they turned out the vote, than a grassroot royalist has to incorporate his suburban south 40 as a commercial parsley ranch and claim losses on that account. The trouble is that the custom of planting bums in appointive jobs in reward for political service has prevailed so long that your hard-shelled politician thinks you are being naïve when you exclaim, "My God, can such things be!" (*Washington Post*, June 11, 1937.)

Of course, Mr. Pegler is naïve, as all preachers must be. The political machine exists because people like Mr. Pegler do not wish government to be practical. They insist on its conforming to contradictory standards, of which contradictions they are completely unaware. Scrupulous people therefore find it difficult to work in political organizations while preachers like Mr. Pegler are screaming at them. As a result only unscrupulous people can do the practical work required of political organizations. This isn't Mr. Pegler's fault, or the politician's fault. It simply represents the inevitable working of the law of political dynamics.

Of course, it is true that political machines contain a greater proportion of nonrespectable people than private industry. But it is not true that they contain a greater proportion of ineffective and useless people than more respectable organizations. Indeed, the "graft" in respectable organizations is actually much larger, because it is cloaked with the mantle of piety. But even if Mr. Pegler should ever read the investigations of the Securities and Exchange Commission into corporation reorganizations, he would still regard "politics" as the more dangerous phenomenon, because politicians are not dealing with "their own money" as corporate executives are. The born preacher must attack "sin." Sin is always determined not by the facts but by the mythology of the time. It is the writer's guess that there are as many bums among reporters as among politicians. However, Mr. Pegler does not feel the same spiritual conflict about American newspapers that he does about government.

15. Where a conflict between an ideal and a practical need not recognized as legitimate has created a respectable institution to represent the ideal and a nonrespectable one to do the job, the need will be filled by the two organizations conducting a public battle with each other. The respectable organization will satisfy the ideal by trying to abolish the nonrespectable one. The nonrespectable institution will survive because the struggle will compel it to maintain an efficient disciplined organization. A curious paradox will result. The reform organization will owe its existence to the vice which it attacks, while the vice which it attacks will be tolerated because of the belief that it is the fault of no one, since all respectable people are in favor of reform.

a. It is difficult to define the term "organization" with reference to this principle. Sometimes it is more accurate to say that the same organization engages in respectable and *sub rosa* activities at the same time, as in the case of great corporations which maintain labor relations committees and spy systems at the same time. In other cases there may exist two entirely separate organizations closely linked together, as in prostitution where the police are driving prostitutes out of town publicly and tolerating them privately.

Illustrations of this principle are: The great bootlegging organizations during prohibition, organized prostitution, the political machine, organized gambling, undercover organizations in international politics, the divorce mill at Reno, Nevada, organizations to hire athletes at respectable colleges, wars against crime, and so on. We will outline this process in more detail with respect to the political machine.

The social needs which are filled by the political machine are so many and varied that they are almost impossible to catalogue. Whatever the government has to do but cannot do in public must be accomplished by this undercover organization. On its lowest plane it operates the relationships between government and organized vice. Here the political machine itself splits up into two organizations, because prostitution is subject to such heavy taboos that even corrupt political machines handle the problem with much more difficulty than such functions as giving patronage to deserving politicians. The most despicable and cruel elements of society assume the task of filling this need. Whenever this age-old profession is regulated in a more orderly and less cruel manner, the taboos of the time demand a crusade, which forces it back into the hands of the more reckless criminals. These investigations are as much a part of the institution of prostitution as the two opponents in a tennis game are part of the game. Because of our climate of opinion this sort of game between reformers and criminals is a necessary part of the sex life of a great city. So also is the great literature on the subject, composed for the purpose of making right-thinking people more comfortable about the situation. Women's clubs conduct their wars on crime and achieve a sense of unity and virtue thereby. The whole community is fascinated and repelled at the same time and finds an outlet in speeches and crusades. These crusades are not remedies for the evil, but a part of the total complex which creates it.

Municipal governments may rise and fall through this conflict between organized vice and social ideals. The battle never has ended, and, in the nature of things, never will end so long as our present myths are worshiped. The writer is not here taking sides as to whether the preservation of the myths about sexual conduct is worth more than prophylaxis. What would happen in New York if illicit sex relations were made safe, and would this be a "good" thing? Such questions are for the preacher. We are using prostitution only as an illustration of what inevitably happens when a social ideal and a social need conflict.

Other tasks of the political machine are more easily tolerated. In a country which demands paupers' oaths and the utmost humiliation before relief is granted to the unemployed, the greatest political machines have owed their real strength to the fact that they took care of underprivileged people without humiliating them.

The writer recalls a conversation with a member of a corrupt political machine in a large city. The local papers had been filled with horror over the recent election of a prosecuting attorney alleged to be in alliance with gangsters. Editorial writers were in despair over the ignorance of the voters and wanted to know what a human race was coming to which followed demagogues and refused to learn by experience. The political worker said: "I am naturally a humanitarian. Under the present political set-up I have thirty families to take care of. I do all that is humanly possible for them, not on the cruel basis of relief agencies, but in a way that permits them to hold up their heads and remain human beings. What I do is against the moral reactions of people who know how help should be administered to the helpless, but it works. I have five hundred votes as the result of my work, which I absolutely control. These people do not want to vote for gangsters. But they know that if I am out of power they will be turned over to a cruel system of charity. Can you blame them if they feel that they would be disloyal to their own group to vote for an administration which would make their lives miserable by preaching to them that they should willingly suffer indignity for the sake of decreasing the burden on large taxpayers?"

Here again the writer is not taking sides. He is only explaining why reform administrations backed by the best people seem to have short-lived existences in great cities. They do not, and because of the nature of their moral preconceptions cannot, build up political machines of the character required to fill the need.

Of course, many readers will doubt the humanitarian work of the successful political machines of our great cities. Current folklore compels us to believe that corrupt politicians are rapacious and cruel. The writer believes that the exact contrary is true, that theirs is a technique which requires generosity and kindliness. Few political leaders become immensely wealthy. Many of them are poor. They are unable to operate on principles of petty thrift and hard dealings with individuals characteristic of the successful trader. There is, however, no statistical way of proving this observation and it will generally be denied because it is a necessary part of the intellectual atmosphere which surrounds the political machine that the machine appears to be wicked and unworthy. Any time that the tasks which present political machines perform become recognized as proper objectives of government, they will no longer be delegated to *sub rosa* machines. The *sub rosa* organization arises not because of bad people but because certain social needs must be made to appear to be bad, and there is no other way of giving those needs that appearance and filling them at the same time.

To illustrate the charitable function of the political machine, we quote from a penetrating sketch of a noted Tammany district leader which appeared in the *New Yorker* of July 25, 1936, by Jack Alexander.

Nowhere else has the great parasitical business of American ward politics reached the level of development to which Tammany Hall has raised it. Largely responsible for the abiding success of Tammany is its general staff of thirty-five district leaders, a varied band consisting of lawyers, ex-bartenders, ex-judges, college graduates, ex-teamsters, ex-longshoremen, and similar fry. Their basic function, each in his own district, is to amass and preserve a strong voting majority. Clothed with a quasi-official status accorded by loose political organization and public apathy, they use their control of public funds and political expedients for exacting private contributions, to garner the votes of the poor, and to swell their own power and that of Tammany Hall. Against the harsh criticism of civic reformers, the district leader fortifies his feelings with the consoling thought that while he takes from the rich, or at least those able to pay taxes, he gives to the impoverished. Broadly viewed, he is indeed a redistributor of wealth, but with an unfailing knack for bettering his own fortunes in the process. . . .

     .   .   .   .   .

In the districts, vote control is built up largely by what the leaders call their charities. This means that in exchange for a beneficence, the voter becomes a sworn follower of the district baron. Leaders have learned that human favor is fickle unless mortgaged in some way. A man may vote your ticket one year because he likes you and turn against you the next year because of political convictions. But if you put him under personal obligation, he is your voter for life, and so are his adult kin. Poverty and misfortune, so widespread in congested Manhattan, give the leader his main chance, and the darker the squalor the more resplendently he shines. Because the poor are grateful, the leader makes his district clubhouse a disbursing place for coal in winter, fresh milk for ailing babies in summer, turkeys at Christmas and Thanksgiving, and lunch money and clothing at all times. Governmental charity has proved to be no competition, for Tammany relief is free of red tape and questionnaires, and it goes on forever.

16. Where there is a conflict between an ideal and a social need recognized as legitimate, it tends to create two organizations, both of which are respectable. However, the one representing the ideal will have the higher place in the hierarchy than the one ministering to the practical need.

The operation of this principle may be observed in practically every organization which pretends to lofty ideals. Perhaps the best illustration is the separation of administrative tribunals from courts. Courts represent a rule of law above men. This compels the denial of personal power built on the exercise of human judgment or benevolence. To introduce this personal element into a logical set of abstract principles is to confuse the symmetry of the judicial system. Therefore, administrative tribunals appear to apply practical considerations to court decisions. So long as the ideal of the rule of law is paramount, the administrative tribunals will have a lower place. They will be kept in that place by a literature which keeps emphasizing the dangers of personal power.

The effect of this literature is usually to introduce great confusion in administration because courts representing the ideals are out of touch with practical problems. A typical instance is found in judicial interference with tax administration. Here the courts are representing the ideal that taxation by government is a necessary evil, requiring constant judicial supervision. We cite as an example the judicial treatment of a simple problem which would have been easily solved had there existed no spiritual conflict about the collection of taxes.

Prior to 1925 the Bureau of Internal Revenue was confronted with the following very simple situation: A widow was given the income of the trust during her life in lieu of her statutory rights in the estate of her husband. The question was whether the income from that trust should be taxed to the widow or to the trustee. The method that had been used was a common one of protecting beneficiaries and a large number of taxpayers were affected.

The Bureau first ruled that the widow should pay the tax. Litigation immediately followed. In 1925 in the case of *Drexel* v. *United States*[7] the Court invalidated the Commissioner's ruling. The Commissioner asked for an immediate final determination by the Supreme Court of the United States. That Court, however, denied certiorari. Shortly thereafter three separate Circuit Courts of Appeals followed the opinion in the Drexel case.[8]

Since the Commissioner had been denied access to the Supreme Court of the United States, which alone could settle the matter finally, he had no choice but to change his ruling in conformity with these decisions. He therefore ruled that the taxes in such cases should be paid by the trustees instead of the widow. Immediately the trustees took up the fight. Finally, in 1933, eight years after the Drexel case and ten years after the original ruling, the Supreme Court in the

[7] 61 *Ct. Cl.* 216.

[8] *Warner* v. *Walsh*, 15 F. (2d) 367 (1926); *United States* v. *Bolster*, 26 F. (2d) 760 (1928); *Allen* v. *Brandeis*, 29 F. (2d) 363 (1928).

Butterworth case[9] held that taxes upon the income from such trusts should be paid by the beneficiary, sustaining the first ruling by the Commissioner.

As a result of that decision the Commissioner had to reverse himself again and for a second time attempt collection from the beneficiary. A new judicial obstacle was immediately thrown in his way. In the decision of *Davis* v. *Mays*[10] in 1934 the Court refused to order the trust companies to discover the names of the beneficiaries so that the Government could reach them.

This handicap was not the only one, because in the meantime the statute of limitations had been running—first, on the returns of the trustees for the period in which the income was thought taxable to the beneficiary, then on the returns of the widow when it was found that the income was taxable to the trust. The statute of limitations had not, however, run upon the refunds which could be claimed by the trustees who had been taxed under the second ruling of the Commissioner. Therefore the Government was forced to defend suits for refunds. The matter was again on its slow and tedious way to the Supreme Court. Finally, in the recent case of *Stone* v. *White*,[11] it has been decided that the United States in such cases is entitled to set off what is due from widows before making a refund to the trustee.

Thus the supremacy of "law" over "bureaucracy" was vindicated, but in the process tax collection was thrown into confusion for ten years. The Commissioner was compelled to reverse his ruling twice; hundreds and perhaps thousands escaped the payment of tax because of the discretionary denial of certiorari by the Supreme Court of the United States, which was completely out of touch with the administrative problems facing the Commissioner.

[9] 290 *U.S.* 365.   [10] 7 *Fed. Sup.* 596.
[11] 301 *U.S.* 532 (1937).

Judicial history is full of similar developments. In the last century, indictments and pleadings in criminal cases were tangled in a maze of technicalities comparable to tax administration today. One of the invariable symptoms of this condition in the administration of law is the rapid accumulation of precedents. Today this particular symptom is strikingly in evidence in tax law. The judicial tax opinions are collected in seventeen volumes of *American Federal Tax Reports* which average about 1,200 pages each, making a total judicial literature of about 19,000 pages. Added to that, the Board of Tax Appeals has published between 8,000 and 9,000 opinions respecting income, estate, and gift taxes. On top of that about a thousand new opinions are being printed each year. Tax administration is being overwhelmed by too much law. Administrative rulings are swamped by these precedents. They can no longer be relied upon because no one is learned enough to foretell all the judicial hazards which such a mass of conflicting opinions creates.

17. The confusion accompanying most liberal reform movements is due to the fact that they are generally attempts to make the institution practice what it preaches in a situation where, if the ideal were followed, the function of the institution could not be performed.

Illustration: This principle is responsible for the sad fate of reform movements in politics. It is further illustrated by the long struggle for the procedural reform of the law.

Our modern method of trial by combat is not, and cannot be, an investigation, and yet it must pretend to be one. Therefore, a long succession of procedural reforms is aimed against the so-called "sporting" theory of justice, in spite of the fact that the entire dramatic effect of the judicial institution depends on the fact that it decides contests. When the procedure is "reformed" so that the trial is more of an investigation, the

institution no longer looks like a "court," but like an administrative tribunal. To save its peculiar character the institution unconsciously resists such reforms, while admitting their theory. This conflict creates the vast metaphysical learning which surrounds legal procedure. The reformer seldom realizes, however, that this is not the fault of the courts. It is the inevitable result of the existence of conflicting ideals which the courts are compelled to dramatize. Procedural reform can only be effective where the reformer realizes that the judicial process is necessarily a dramatic contest.

18. Where the ideal and the practical needs are not in conflict, an institution arises which attains the maximum practical efficiency of which the organizing ability of the people is capable.

In such an atmosphere the government can run the army, with no complaints about bureaucracy and with the general support of everyone. In such an atmosphere grew the great industrial corporation in the United States, which on the whole has been an extraordinary, efficient machine for the production of goods. Where it has failed is in its inability to change its objective, not in its inability to achieve it. Therefore, the great business corporation can play its politics openly, with a minimum of hypocrisy. It can admit its failures and move on to other things. Better than any other set of ideals up to the depression, the corporate personification fitted into the folklore of the times as a method for the production of goods.

19. Neither the ceremony nor the literature which surrounds social institutions can be consistent, logical, or rational because of the inherent nature of the psychological forces which bind men together in groups.

This fact causes little confusion or conflict in the case of a few ancient institutions whose acceptance is traditional and whose prestige is based largely on what may be called senti-mental reasons. For example, in church ritual today people generally do not feel it important to believe that the sacra-ment is the actual blood of the Savior. Again, people in England are not bothered because the ceremonial pretensions of the king are neither logical nor in conformity with fact. Old institutions, supported by long-standing tradition whose function is admittedly sentimental, need not go through the struggle of pretending to practice what they preach. Most going social concerns are faced with the necessity of appear-ing to be actually consistent with their ceremony and litera-ture and here arises constant spiritual and mental confusion.

Today business ceremonies among great corporations are taken with such seriousness that they often get in the way of the actual efficiency of the organization. The great corporate offices housed in medieval splendor in New York City are an example of this. One is confronted with the spectacle of thousands of employees hauled to New York offices in crowded subways, living in the most expensive and uncom-fortable manner, although none of them are required to be in New York for any other reason than to surround the great corporate executive with something that looks like a court and to give a princely atmosphere to his office. So far as fur-thering the avowed purpose of the corporation is concerned, the services of these workers could be employed more cheaply and efficiently in smaller towns near the actual producing unit of the corporation. The prominent persons in such or-ganizations who have a real reason for being near the finan-cial center are few. The doctrine of the business corporation is efficiency. Its actual need today is public acceptance and ceremony. Hence, it cannot be consistent. Neither can it admit its inconsistency. Therefore, its ceremonies and literature are necessarily much more cumbersome and wasteful than those which support an institution like the kingship of England, because no one is permitted to admit they are only ceremonies. If the prestige of financial corporate executives could only be kept alive by an annual parade or a weekly service, fewer people would have to live uncomfortably because of the need for such ceremonies. That, however, is impossible in our present climate of opinion.

To sum up, institutional doctrine is never a frank description of the practice and the purpose of the institution. Therefore, we who try to make institutions live up to their pretensions are the worst of executives. The history of human organization is strewn with the wreckage caused by people who tried honestly and sincerely to follow the logical implications of accepted doctrine.

20. A social need which runs counter to an abstract ideal will always be incompetently met until it gets a philosophy of its own. The process of building up new abstractions to justify filling new needs is always troublesome in any society, and may be violent.

This principle does not apply in situations toward which men can take a fairly objective attitude. No change of theology is necessary to introduce new methods into the manufacture of goods, because no taboos are involved. The attitudes which once prevented mechanical improvement are relics of the distant past. The operation of taboos against mechanical improvements among uncomplicated and primitive people seems to us one of the strange chapters of history. Yet it occurs in the highly sophisticated Chinese culture of today, which cannot, by any stretch of the imagination, be called primitive. It was a civilized and not a primitive culture which once forbade the use of Arabic numerals. In the Roman Empire it took learned men with years of training to make the simple numerical computations which a boy of fourteen can make today. They used an accounting machine called an abacus. There was, of course, a vested interest in the continued use of the Roman system of numerals by a small class who operated abacuses. Yet it was not this class but the public opinion of people who had no interest whatever in preserving abacuses which made it possible to forbid the use of Arabic numbers. In the same way, people with no conceivable interest at stake are fighting the distribution of cheap electrical power by governmental corporations. The same vague fear of some sort of spiritual ruin which preserved the Roman numerals perpetuates today the taboos against sensible governmental control over soil erosion.

In social organization today our taboos and our need of propitiatory magic to support any change are as compelling as they used to be in the acceptance of new medical or mechanical devices by ancient peoples when such devices went contrary to some ancient accepted principle. In the area of social control we are now going through a world-shaking struggle, which threatens to be long, complicated, and pathetically ludicrous, to build up a set of abstractions or a social philosophy which will permit us to satisfy the practical needs of our society.

21. Public debate is necessarily only a method of giving unity and morale to organizations. It is ceremonial and designed to create enthusiasm, to increase faith and quiet doubt. It can have nothing to do with the actual practical analysis of facts.

Illustration: An individual cannot live effectively without a code of ethics and a set of ideals. He must put these into words and at least a part of his conduct must be devoted to a ritual designed to celebrate these ethics and ideals. The same thing is true of an organization.

Therefore the function of all political arguments, either used in campaigns, on the floor of legislative assemblies, or before courts is to reconcile the spiritual conflicts within an organization and to attract followers to that organization by appealing to their prejudices. In other words, every person seeking power over groups of people, without the use of physical force, must create enthusiasms which will make them follow him. There is no difference between the demagogue and the statesman, except on the basis of a judgment as to the desirability of the social ends and social values which move the one or the other. The man with the social values which you do not like, you will call the demagogue. You will say that he appeals to emotion and not to reason. This, however, is only because "reason" is the respectable end of the two polar terms, "reason" versus "emotion," and you instinctively want it to point toward your own organization.

a. The notion that legislation becomes more expert because of prolonged public discussions of proposed measures is an illusion which follows the notion that public debate is addressed to a thinking man through whose decisions organizations have group free will. All prolonged public discussions of any measure can do is to reconcile conflicts and get people used to the general ideal which the measure represents.

Illustration: The prolonged discussion of the social-security bill produced an act which represented all the conflicting little pictures appearing in the atmosphere of the time. The bill was like a pension; it was like insurance; it recognized the doctrine of states rights; it recognized the notion that a government should not interfere in business, or be the owner of "assets," together with the notion that in social-security legislation the Government should be like an insurance company, with assets to back its obligations to the insured. From the point of view of social values the really great contribution of the first social-security bill was that it made the public recognize that the state owed a positive obligation toward the needy and that charity was not the solution of the problem. The social-security act will become more practical after the continued acceptance of this ideal removes it from the necessity of public debate.

b. Public argument never convinces the other side, any more than in a war the enemy can ever be convinced. Its effectiveness consists in binding together the side on which the arguments are used.

Illustration: Liberals go about in a constant state of amazement that great corporate executives do not agree with the theories which they advance in such convincing terms. Conservatives are constantly shocked at the logical atrocities committed by the liberals. The cruelties and outrages on the logical process committed by the other side become part of the combat propaganda in peaceful as well as bloody combat. There are about as many atrocities committed on the one side as on the other, but the partisans can see only those of their enemies. This should be accepted as a political fact by the observer. There is no possible way of avoiding it. Intellectuals are caught in this inevitable process as much as the ignorant.

c. Victories in political government depend upon the ability of a party to build a unified organization which has sufficient attracting power to cause the majority to desire to be attached to it. The attracting power depends on the ability of the organization to understand and put into slogans the unexpressed aspirations of the people, and to reconcile needed organizations with these.

Illustration: The present failure of the Republican party is due to the fact that the central organization has lost touch with the ideals of the newer generation. For this reason they are unable to select an appealing hero and when they attempt to be purely political and appeal to the emotions of the mob, they have the lack of skill characteristic of those who do not understand the culture in which they are operating. In other words, they have lost organizing ability.

d. It is important that political debate be positive and affirmative and not negative. When slogans appeal only to fears they hinder organization. The side with the positive slogans will therefore have the advantage.

Illustration: This is characteristic of all arguments, great and small. In a lawsuit, where the record does not disclose issues which predispose the judge to one side or the other, the affirmative argument will be most effective. For example, if the plaintiff claims judgment on the ground that the transaction constitutes a trust and the defendant denies that it is a trust, plaintiff has the advantage. If on the other hand defendant admits that it is a trust, but claims he should win on the broad affirmative principles of "estoppel," he will have the advantage. It is a failure to understand this simple psychological phenomenon which makes brilliant dialecticians such poor advocates. They take comfort, however, in blaming the ignorance of judges and spend their time in research trying to find a better way of selecting judges than the one we have. Needless to say, the schemes the dialecticians advocate are seldom adopted. If they ever are adopted, the same situations arise again, whereupon the brilliant dialecticians prove that the scheme would have been all right if it had not been ruined by the misinterpretation of the judges. Law schools are erected as a refuge for this type of thinking.

In the same way a study of political campaigns will show that an affirmative argument, however fantastic, is better than a negative one. The career of William Hale Thompson, who maintained himself in power by a series of affirmative absurdities, which included a call to arms against the King of England, illustrates this. His opponents spent their time showing how wrong he was. Just as soon as they had exposed the falsity of one slogan, Thompson was off on another. He always maintained the aggressive. His opponents were always on the defense. His success was amazing.

e. Liberals and intellectuals usually fail as political organizers because they desire their slogans to be accurate and logical rather than political. When they try to become politicians, a feeling that they are betraying the great truth of intellectual integrity makes them confused and ineffective. They are the very worst kind of combat troops because they are constantly siding with the enemy.

Illustration: Thus we find Oswald Garrison Villard, the great liberal, joining with the Liberty League to defeat the court plan of President Roosevelt, on perfectly logical grounds but unmindful that political battles are wars between opposing groups. Recently Heywood Broun criticized violently the editorial policy of the *Nation* because that publication refused to realize that the objectives to which it was committed could only be accomplished by building up new organizations. The *Nation,* he claimed, was spending half its time undermining the emotional position of its own side.

f. A political party which attracts only learned men and thinkers, instead of organizers, will always fail in reach-

ing its political objective, because its campaign will be
based on the illusion that correct logic will win in the
long run over political techniques, or else that if it
doesn't win it is the duty of intellectuals to keep on trying to create an atmosphere where it will win.

Illustration: Norman Thomas and his Socialist party.

22. *The failure of respectable people with humanitarian
values to be effective in this country may be traced to their
complete misunderstanding of the functions of public controversy. Unaware of the fact that it is not logic but organizations which rule an organized society they select logical
principles as objects of their loyalties instead of organizations.*

Illustration: The disappearance of intellectuals in every
government which operates in a logical frame of reference is
inevitable. It has been marked in Russia, Germany, and
Italy. Governments which are trying to stabilize themselves
in precarious situations and which are, because of this very
fact, operated by violent and bold men, usually kill or deport
the intellectuals of the country. First they liquidate the intellectuals on the opposing side. Then they liquidate their
own intellectuals, who inevitably become nuisances because
they insist that the new organization live up to its conflicting
ideals regardless of political consequences. We suspect that
this latter process has much to do with what is going on in
Russia today in the persecution of the intellectual followers
of Trotsky.

England seems to have a better understanding of the necessary inconsistencies of public ideals. It therefore on the
whole is able to keep more humanitarian people in power because of its realization that government has two functions:
(1) to put on a public show; (2) to be exceedingly practical
behind the scenes. To this ability—to believe in principles and

at the same time make them work for organizations, rather than compel organizations to work for principles—may be attributed a large part of the success of that small country in dominating a continent composed of nations far stronger in physical power.

23. The fact that rigorous dialectic and the so-called intellectual skills are not effective in organization is not a condemnation of intellectuals. The intellectuals symbolize the dreams of mankind of an ordered world. They help to create intellectual order out of the tangled folklore of the time. They are the makers of policy and the formulators of principles in situations where the public demands slogans.

Illustration: We choose our illustration from a narrow field. Its relevance to the function of all the larger policy-making bodies—legislative, religious, or judicial—should be apparent.

Testifying before the Securities and Exchange Commission as to the organization of Foreign Bondholders Protective Council, a practical body which also had to have ethical and philosophical concepts to give it unity, the President, J. Reuben Clark, Jr., said:

Q. Mr. Clark, I believe you stated yesterday that the meetings of the members of the Council were held annually except for special meetings that might be called.

A. That is, the meetings of the directors.

Q. The full members?

A. Yes, sir.

Q. And I believe you stated that there had been one special meeting called?

A. One special meeting.

Q. Then it would be fair to say that the directors, the full members, do not actively participate in the work of the Council? Is that true?

386 386The Folklore of Capitalism

A. Yes, sir. But I should like to make something of an explanation there, if I may. We are not conducting a business in the sense of investing money or incurring monetary obligations, or anything of that sort. There is only the work of the detail of negotiations after broad, general principles are settled, and these principles have from time to time been reported to the directors; so that unless you were to ask the directors to come to New York to participate in any kind of negotiation there would be very little that the directors could do.

Q. May I ask you this question? Do the directors serve a real function, from your point of view? Are they useful?

A. Yes; they are useful.

Q. In what way are they useful?

A. Well, they are useful because they are able to explain in their various areas the functions and purpose of the Council. They are useful in giving us the advantage of their views and wisdom on broad principles of policy.

Q. Do you get their views?

A. Yes; when they come to meetings. They have settled some of these questions of policy; and they have been reported to them and discussed by them.

Q. The discussions are largely on matters of policy, general policy, not specific situations? Is that true?

A. Yes, sir; that is true.

Q. Have they been useful in bringing in members and getting contributions or advances?

A. Yes, sir; they have been useful in that respect

Q. Your executive committee is the group that does the work?

A. Yes, sir; that is correct. We hold an executive committee meeting once a week, and at that meeting everything which the Council is doing or contemplating doing is reported to the executive committee and passed upon by the committee, including the details of all negotiations.

Q. Mr. Clark, are the negotiations carried on by the president and the vice-president?

A. Primarily; subject, of course, to this consultation with the executive committee.

.   .   .   .   .

Q. That is, the president or the vice-president of the Council?
A. Yes, sir; the executive vice-president.
Q. The executive vice-president?
A. Yes, sir; the executive vice-president.
Q. Would you feel that the Council would operate and function as well without a board of directors of the size that it has?
A. Not at the present time. If the Council were more firmly established or were in the position, let us say, of the British Bondholders Council, it might be that the actual service of the directors could be performed by a fewer number of persons.
Q. May I ask you this question, Mr. Clark? Are the directors useful primarily from the point of view of public relations of the Council?
A. I should hardly like to say that. . . . That is certainly one of their principal uses and values. But we have had some very valuable suggestions from them in the matter of our policies.[12]

It is apparent that the Council referred to above is performing a function similar to that of the Supreme Court of the United States. The activities of this particular group do not need an elaborately formulated body of doctrine, or a highly specialized priesthood, but all the essentials of a typically ceremonial and authoritarian institution are present. So far as practical activity is concerned a smaller committee which argued less about policies would get more done. Yet it is hard to imagine any group of men engaged in any organized activity, whether it be athletics or business, which can get along without some ceremonial body devoted to giving it what the Chinese call "face."

24. The gradual decline and fall of social institutions are not the result of revolutionary ideas held by their opponents, but rather are the product of the phobias against practical common-sense action produced by their own ideas.

[12] *Supra*, Note 1, Part V, "Protective Committees and Agencies for Holders of Defaulted Foreign Governmental Bonds," pp. 82–83.

Whenever the slogans of any organization cease to be a source of inspiration and positive action, and instead become a source of fear, the power of the organization declines. This is particularly true of economic and legal philosophies. Revolutionary ideas are ordinarily described as the cause of revolutionary movements. A better way of putting it is that the failure of older social organizations to act leaves a vacuum into which some new organization is bound to flow. The slogans of the new organization will certainly be contrary to the slogans of its enemies. The growth of the new organization, however, will be due to the opportunity created when the older one was unable to act. The notion that a new organization must reason its way into power or else lose the support of all thinking men is a common superstition among the commentators of our own day. For example, we see it expressed in editorials and articles about the labor movement. John L. Lewis, if he would only think straight, could form a much more effective labor organization, in the opinion of the *Tribune* and the *Times*. Such an attitude prevents any understanding of a new political movement on the part of most of our current writers on current events. Lewis is taking advantage of a social need which his opponents are unable to meet. He is building the tradition and morale of his organization through combat tactics. The strategy of his opponents consists largely of the expression of fears and lamentations. It offers no positive program. Until this psychological situation is changed one may predict a continued increase in the power of the C.I.O.

An objective study of government is necessarily troubling to the intellectuals of our time because the prevailing mental pictures of our folklore compel us to deny the facts before us. Since those pictures represent current ideas of order and dignity in human affairs, objective observation of the facts of social organization appears to those who believe in its current myths to present government as meaningless, amoral, and uncontrollable except by methods condemned by our folklore as unscrupulous. Men cannot face the world without some sort of religion; they cannot feel comfortable about their government without a set of ideals which cannot be supplied merely by scientific observation. Scientific observation, therefore, cannot be used in government affairs unless it can be fitted into some governmental creed which is anything but scientific.

For example, we cite two scientific studies which, taken in conjunction, could contribute the background for a program of practical action, the utility of which would not be denied by anyone. The first is the report of the National Resources Board, which gives us an idea of the vast possibilities available for our comfort if they could be used. Second, is the work of Robert and Helen Lynd on Middletown, which presents a picture of the psychological hazards which make it difficult for existing organizations to use those resources to the fullest extent. Yet the use of these two scientific studies in conjunction as part of the training necessary to understand government has as yet little recognition. An advertising enterprise designed to sell goods to Middletown could quite frankly base its campaign on such data. A governmental program, however, must proceed on the assumptions of current mythology. In other words, we lack a religion of government which permits us to face frankly the psychological factors inherent in the development of organizations with public responsibility. Governmental effort based on such factors is considered Machiavellian, and contrary to proper principles. We tolerate such an attitude on the part of politicians as a necessary evil.

A governmental creed which enables men to face the facts about social organization without disillusionment and with positive enthusiasm for the opportunity presented is a prerequisite to the use of scientific method in government. This is something more than the traditional "realistic" approach. There is plenty of "realism" in this country today, but it is the realism that leads to cynicism. In other words, modern realists are still so emotionally bound by the mythology that the facts which their honesty compels them to admit only make them sad because the human race is not different.

Yet all the signs today point to the fact that a new creed, which can reconcile itself to the facts of human organization, is about to be born. It as yet has no formulas. It is represented vaguely by the personality of Roosevelt who has become a symbol for a political attitude which cannot yet be put into words. The fact that Roosevelt has become the symbol of a new attitude is shown by the fact that so many of those who support him are hostile or else indifferent to the particular measures he advocates.

Many commentators express surprise at this. How can specific measures advocated by Roosevelt be so unpopular with groups of people who still keep faith in him? Hostile editors, observing the failure of some Roosevelt policy, are puzzled over the continuing Roosevelt support. They attribute it to his charming smile, his radio voice, and whatnot. The answer to the problem of Roosevelt's popular support in spite of the defeat of so many of his plans has little to do with his personal characteristics. Institutions which express in concrete form the vague aspirations of any group always arouse that kind of allegiance. Never has this been expressed in a more striking way than by the parade of intellectuals who testified against the Roosevelt Supreme Court plan before the Senate Committee. These individuals stated that they disapproved of the majority decisions of the Court on national affairs, yet they considered it essential to the nation that the Court continue in power over national affairs. For these persons, composed of radicals and conservatives alike, the Court represented the supremacy of intellect and reason. Hence they were for it, no matter what it did. To attribute this to Hughes's charming manner or Sutherland's public personality is to make the same mistake about the influence of the Supreme Court which is being made about the present Roosevelt influence.

What Roosevelt represents to the great majority of the electorate cannot be so easily formulated because no authoritarian literature has developed (as it has with respect to the Court) to explain him as a symbol. Yet he expresses for a majority of the public the current distrust of old myths and the belief that the Government has a new rôle to play in providing for security of individuals in their jobs and in the distribution of goods. The position of a living man as such a symbol has always been precarious, because dead men are much safer in such niches than the living. Nevertheless, the writer believes that Roosevelt will continue to fill this symbolic need until something else is substituted. If he is beaten it will be by a philosophy of strong affirmation and not by attack.

In Europe the rise of personalities to express national aspirations which older institutions could not fulfil has taken the same course. These social phenomena are inevitable. The type of personality that will take the place of a philosophy of government depends on the culture of the time; and the results, particularly in conditions which border on anarchy and where defeat and discouragement have created a national psychosis, are not always happy. But we are here not sitting in judgment on such phenomena, we are only observing them.

When national aspirations are expressed in an individual who is also in command of practical affairs, a nation does not have the stability which comes from a Church which is removed from the marketplace. Individuals can become symbols only in unstable times. Lincoln would never have been the great myth of national unity had it not been for the Civil War. He came to represent a new conception of the State. Roosevelt has a less secure place because the aspirations which he represents are less concrete. Nevertheless, the mental pictures of a society which are first—in times of confusion —represented by an individual, inevitably become part of the folklore later. And in that process comes stability.

Roosevelt will lose his present symbolic importance when the attitude toward government which he represents has become expressed in an inspirational literature which is generally accepted as a sort of backlog of fundamental principles. In this highly organized age, attitudes toward the function of government must be redefined, and until that process is complete a personality will take the place of a philosophy.

The redefinition of attitudes which must take place has nothing to do with the advocacy of particular measures. Legislation will be in the future, as it has been in the past, the result of pressures of various sorts. Political principles must always be infinitely elastic. It is only important that they represent public attitudes and do not strangle public needs.

Here lies the opportunity of those spinners of national dreams whom we call our intellectuals, and who are composed of our lawyers, our economists, and our editors. Today an individual personality is more important than any governmental principles because those principles represent fears and inhibitions instead of inspiring action. The Constitution has ceased to be a charter of positive government. It is only a protection against unholy desires. Editorial economics, which are the only kind that ever reach the people, are simply a list of impending disasters. Those who most desire to substitute the ideal of a rule of law for the worship of a single personality are doing everything to defeat their own ends by refusing to advocate an attitude toward the function of government which will make that personality less important.

This usually happens in times of social change. And yet I have a feeling that it need not happen if the functions of governmental creeds and mythologies are understood by our priesthood. Understanding can at least tend in the direction of preventing anger and excitement in government which destroy practical judgment. It can prevent the application of impossible standards to new organizations fumbling about to fill some social need. It can tolerate experiment as something essential in meeting changed conditions. It can modify the bitter clash of extreme positions. And best of all, it can divert the minds of intelligent people from the futile task of trying to dictate the culture of the next generation, while neglecting the problems of their own day.

I have no doubt as to the practical desirability of a society where principles and ideals are more important than individuals. It is an observable fact that such a society is more secure spiritually and hence more tolerant. Yet the belief that there is something peculiarly sacred about the logical content of these principles, that organizations must be molded to them, instead of the principles being molded to organizational needs, is often the very thing which prevents these principles from functioning. The greatest destroyer of ideals is he who believes in them so strongly that he cannot fit them to practical needs.

Index